TURNAROUND

TURNAROUND

A MEMOIR

MILOŠ FORMAN

AND JAN NOVAK

faber and faber

LONDON BOSTON

To my parents,
all of them

First published in Great Britain in 1994
by Faber and Faber Ltd
3 Queen Square London WC1N 3AU

Printed in England by Clays Ltd, St Ives plc

© Miloš Forman, 1993

Miloš Forman and Jan Novak are hereby identified
as authors of this work in accordance with Section 77
of the Copyright, Designs and Patents Act 1988

A CIP record for this book is available
from the British Library

ISBN 0-571-17289-X

2 4 6 8 10 9 7 5 3 1

CONTENTS

PROLOGUE: WHATEVER DOESN'T KILL YOU   3

I.   ČÁSLAV   7

II.   BOHEMIA   29

III.   PRAGUE   67

IV.   APPRENTICESHIP   85

V.   CZECH FILMS   127

VI.   NEW YORK   167

VII.   AMERICAN MOVIES   201

LIST OF ILLUSTRATIONS

1　Riding my favorite Christmas gift (© Miloš Forman)

2　With Mother and my dog Rek (© Miloš Forman)

3　The last happy summer at Mácha's Lake (© Miloš Forman)

4　An instrument of fate – pension Rut (©Miloš Forman)

5　The family after Father's arrest (© Miloš Forman)

6　Playing a Paris alderman in *Ballad of Rags* in Prague (© Miloš Forman)

7　The mandatory May Day parade of 1953 (© Miloš Forman)

8　As the second assistant director on the set of *Grandpa Automobile*, 1956 (© Miloš Forman)

9　Alfred Radok on the set of his *Grandpa Automobile* (© Miloš Forman)

10　My wedding with Jana, 1958 (© Fotzavody, Prague)

11　Pavla Martínková, the female lead in *Black Peter* (© Jaromír Komarek)

12　Mrs. Matoušková offering her delicious *buchty* to Vladimír Pucholt (© Jaromír Komarek)

13　Playing a coin-tossing game with Ivan Passer and Vladimír Pucholt (© Jaromír Komarek)

14　Věra's and my wedding ceremony, 1964 (© Jaromír Komarek)

15　Věra pregnant with Petr and Matěj (© Jaromír Komarek)

16　Directing my ex-sister-in-law Hana Brejchová in *Loves of a Blonde*, 1965 (© Jaromír Komarek)

17　Working the clapper on the closed set of *Loves of a Blonde* (© Jaromír Komarek)

18　The "blonde," Hana Brejchová, and the "blonde killer" Vladimír Pucholt (© Jaromír Komarek)

19　Vrchlabi volunteer fireman Debleka runs the beauty pageant traffic in *Fireman's Ball*, 1966 (© Jaromír Komarek)

20　The cold gray morning after the dance in *Fireman's Ball* (© Jaromír Komarek)

21　With cinematographer Miroslav Ondříček and the writer Jaroslav Papoušek (© Jaromír Komarek)

22 Sidney Lumet, James Ivory, Jerzy Skolimowski, Jan Kadar and my-
    self, 1964 (©Miloš Forman)
23 Landing in New York with Ivan Passer and Maurice Ergas, 1967 (©
    Miloš Forman)
24 Linnea Heacock and David Gittler in *Taking Off*, 1970 (© Mary
    Ellen Mark)
25 With Vincent Schiavelli (© Mary Ellen Mark)
26 On the set of *Taking Off* (© Mary Ellen Mark)
27 With Nathan George and Jack Nicholson on the set of *One Flew Over
    the Cuckoo's Nest* (© Peter Sorel)
28 Will Sampson in *One Flew Over the Cuckoo's Nest* (© Peter Sorel)
29 With Danny De Vito, Jack Nicholson, Will Sampson, Vincent
    Schiavelli, and Louise Fletcher (© Peter Sorel)
30 Five Oscar winners for *Cuckoo's Nest*, 1976 (© Academy of Motion
    Picture Arts and Sciences)
31 With sons Petr and Matěj (© Academy of Motion Picture Arts and
    Sciences)
32 On the set of *Hair*, 1977 (© Mary Ellen Mark)
33 With Twyla Tharp on the set of *Hair* (© Mary Ellen Mark)
34 The cast of *Hair* (© Mary Ellen Mark)
35 With President Johnson in the "be-in" scene from *Hair* (© Mary
    Ellen Mark)
36 With James Cagney on *Ragtime*, 1980 (© Jaromír Komarek)
37 With Mandy Patinkin on the set of *Ragtime* (© Mary Ellen Mark)
38 With Elizabeth McGovern on the set of *Ragtime* (© Mary Ellen
    Mark)
39 With Uncle Boleslav and his daughter, Jana, in Náchod, 1979 (©
    Mary Ellen Mark)
40 With Boleslav's wife, Anna (© Mary Ellen Mark)
41 With my boys in Prague, 1979 (© Mary Ellen Mark)
42 Visiting Jan Werich with Jean-Claude Carrière and Cheryl Barnes
    (© Mary Ellen Mark)
43 With Debelka of *Fireman's Ball* (© Mary Ellen Mark)
44 With Jana and Věra (© Mary Ellen Mark)
45 With Hana Brejchová of *Loves of a Blonde* in Prague, 1979 (© Mary
    Ellen Mark)
46 On the shore of Mácha's Lake (© Mary Ellen Mark)
47 With F. Murray Abraham on the set of *Amadeus* (© Jaromír
    Komarek)
48 The castle in Kromeriz, Czech Republic (© Jaromír Komarek)
49 With Twyla Tharp in the Stavovske Theater (© Jaromír Komarek)

50 Tom Hulce as Mozart in *Amadeus* (© Phil Bray)

51 With Meg Tilly and Colin Firth, 1988 (© Jaromír Komarek)

52 Many a tough task rests on a director's shoulders (© Mary Ellen Mark)

TURNAROUND

PROLOGUE:
WHATEVER DOESN'T KILL YOU

On March 25, 1985, I sat near the front of the Dorothy Chandler Pavilion in Los Angeles. I was wearing one of the couple of thousand tuxedos in the place, and my shoes were perfectly shined. Around me glittered sequins on dresses that cost more than automobiles and the air was packed with swirls of sublime perfumes.

I'd been nominated for an Oscar for directing *Amadeus,* an adaptation of Peter Shaffer's play about the hate-in-awe relationship of a Hapsburg court composer named Salieri to Wolfgang Amadeus Mozart. *Amadeus* was my ninth film. Before it, I'd directed four films in Czechoslovakia, where I was born, and four films in America, but like myself *Amadeus* was a hybrid, an American film shot in Czechoslovakia. In fact, the production had been my ticket back to Prague after ten years of exile.

Czechoslovakia was still firmly a totalitarian country when we shot *Amadeus* and, as an émigré, I was considered a traitor by the government. The Communist rule had lasted for over forty years, and it had strongly shaped my life. Without it, I'd never have wound up in America. I had thought that I'd never live to see the end of it, though I knew that it couldn't last forever.

My parents had been strong Czech nationalists, and, in a way, they died for it. Some of that tribal feeling had seeped deep into my own identity, and even after I'd been separated from my country and culture, which happened by default and which left me with a family stranded in Prague, I was pulled strongly back. I am a sentimentalist who doesn't feel whole with all the roads to the landscape of childhood blocked, without a way to confront the memories that make you what you are. I felt incomplete when I was cut off from the places I'd scored my first goal, stolen my first kiss, perfected my goulash, had alcohol spin the world around me for the first time and yelled my first "Cut!"

I'd been trying to get back to Prague, for a few days at least, a visit, a quick embrace, a reality check, but it took ten years before I schemed my way in with *Amadeus*. I went in as an American citizen, with an American film, on which the Communist government made American money—these production dollars being the bottom-line reason why I'd been allowed back into the country at all. Though I was always under surveillance during the filming, I'd at least been able to visit home again, so even before the nominations, *Amadeus* had already given me a lot.

The film was also making me rich. It had been produced independently, under a highly unusual agreement between Peter Shaffer, producer Saul Zaentz, and myself. Shaffer gave the partnership his play and his screenplay, I threw in two years of my life, Zaentz put up all the money, and we split the ownership of the negative of *Amadeus* three ways. The deal had been conceived by my agent Robby Lantz, and it was spelled out in a simple, two-page memo that amounted to little more than a handshake.

Millions of dollars of profit ride on winning Oscars, and *Amadeus* had some tough competition. I was up against three fine directors—Robert Benton, Roland Joffe, and Woody Allen—and, as if that weren't enough, a true legend of the movie business. In 1984, David Lean made a wonderful version of the classic English novel by E. M. Forster, *A Passage to India,* and the old master was seventy-six years old, so he was bound to be the sentimental favorite of the academy.

I hoped to win anyway, but so secretly that I barely dared admit it even to myself. I'd already won the Directors Guild Award, which had foreshadowed the Oscar winner in all but two years in the history of these two awards, but the way I interpreted this historical statistic was that, in any given year, anything could happen. I kept wiping my palms into the soft fabric of the seat and running a speech I'd prepared through my mind every time there was a lull in the ceremony.

I had some experience with squirming in the seats of the Dorothy Chandler Pavilion. I'd lost there twice in the sixties when my Czech films *Loves of a Blonde* and *Fireman's Ball* failed to win Best Foreign Film. But I'd won, too, for Best Director and Best Picture for *One Flew Over the Cuckoo's Nest* in 1976.

That particular night remains a goulash of impressions and emotions in my memory. My twin sons, Petr and Matěj, had just flown in from Prague the night before and slept right through most of the evening. They were twelve years old and complete strangers to me. I hadn't seen them in six years, and I was just starting to get to know them again, so my first Oscar hovers somewhere in a blur of deeper feeling. When I received the nomination in 1984, I resolved to enjoy playing my part in the whole grand game of Academy Awards.

I've always done everything in my life to win. The will to win is one of my basic drives, so I keep an eye out for the signs of it in other people. When arguably the greatest athlete ever, Michael Jordan, through sheer excellence and force of will, led his team to the highest honors of his world, he cried with happiness. But the way I read his feelings, it was not the inflating emotion of unalloyed joy, the helium happiness that makes you float, it was the happiness of a man who is finally claiming what should have been his a long time ago, the happiness of a relief from the quest, the happiness grounded in the knowledge that this victory will only make the next one a bigger job. It was the hard happiness of an overachiever, the happiness of a man who had been too tough on himself for too long and who was finally seeing it pay off, though perhaps I am projecting my own ambitions and emotions onto another life: I found in my own life that winning can be as hard as it is wonderful, but that there are no alternatives.

I've never been able to handle failure. By failure, I don't mean embarrassments, moments when you stand somewhere and hope that the earth will open up and swallow you. I've had my share of those, and they pass. The attention shifts from you, and life goes on. But to fail miserably, to be working on something for a long time, giving it everything you have, to be willing it to happen with every ounce of your personality, to charm and whip and trick other people into the project and make them believe in it and give it their best, only to see the whole enterprise die with a whimper, on someone's desk, with a guilty voice on the telephone, with a self-appointed censor lying to you, through a translator and through a smile—that sends me into hibernation. Suddenly, I can't summon the strength to heave myself out of bed in the morning. Daylight feels like shampoo in my eyes, and I can't keep them open. My knees are rubbery when I try to stand up, but if I collapse back into bed, an indescribable sweetness floods my body. And perversely, this elation is more wonderful than any ovations from your peers, any laurels, any payoff.

Amadeus was already doing very well that Oscar night. Peter Shaffer had won for Best Screenplay Adaptation, F. Murray Abraham had walked away with Best Actor honors, and we had also won for art direction, costume design, sound, and makeup. Finally, the man I'd been waiting for, Steven Spielberg, strolled up on the stage with an envelope in his hand.

My blood pressure shot up, and I very badly wanted the envelope to contain my name even while I stuck out my chin for a punch of disappointment. I felt the heat of the klieg lamps on me and got my good loser's smile ready while I concentrated on the piece of paper that Spielberg was ripping open on the stage.

"And the winner is . . ." He took a dramatic pause, and I decided that I didn't want to win this Oscar after all because suddenly I felt the stare of hundreds of millions of eyes on me, the whole scary planet eyeballing me. Suddenly I dreaded all the paparazzi, star-fuckers, academics, and there was a beat of panic and I froze. At last Spielberg looked up and called my name, and the current of emotion switched again. I felt a surge of warmth, a beautiful electric shock that bounced me out of the chair, and I ran up on the stage and the world was a smear of impressions, the auditorium unreal, Spielberg a shadow who shook my hand, the heavy Oscar the stuff of independence, of more of my kind of movies, of a bigger life.

I gave a speech, more or less running through the words that I'd prepared, but as I spoke, I was thinking again, why me? Why the hell me? Why had so much luck been bestowed on me? I'd had this sensation for many years, on and off, the feeling that I don't deserve all this extravagant fortune, all those breaks and rewards I'd copped, that I must be robbing somebody else in a zero-sum scheme of luck.

The only feeble answer that I've ever been able to come up with is that, as someone else observed, whatever doesn't kill you makes you stronger. Perhaps that insight applies in my case. Maybe that's why it was me.

And because I've always tried too hard to win, the other thing that went through my mind was: so I won, so great, so it's downhill from here.

But then, one minute before midnight on the depression clock, just in the nick of time, I remembered an old Czech joke: a husband comes home unexpectedly. The wife barely manages to hide her lover in her bedroom closet. For two hours, the lover sits there among the best perfumes, the most exquisite fragrances, the rose oils and orchid scents and passion musks, the jasmine soaps and baby powders and the talcs and ointments. The wife finally manages to shoo the husband out of the house again, and the lover rushes out of the closet screaming, "Quick! Get me a piece of shit!"

PART 1

ČÁSLAV

SILENT OPERA

All my life, I've had the notion that you could get badly hurt by looking back, so I rarely looked back to my childhood. It was just too distressing in a oddly remote way, and it nearly caused me to forget some wonderful memories of that distant time.

I was born in the town of Čáslav in central Bohemia, right on the sturdy oak bed of my parents. The year was 1932, and the bed stood in a two-story house that took up the corner of two dirt streets, not far from a train station. Its windows overlooked a small park of silver spruces and oaks and beige houses of mortared brick. The neighborhood had a lot of gardens with flower beds and fruit trees, enclosed by ornamental fences.

Čáslav was a town of about ten thousand people, whose history went back to the thirteenth century. Beside a large Gothic church that belonged to the Catholics and a smaller Protestant church where my family went to worship on Sundays, its most striking feature was the square. It was the size of a small airport. Medieval armies could group there before marching off to battle.

And in this small town with a large square, one Saturday night when I was four or five years old, my parents took me to a huge hall full of people. They wore ties and dresses, smoked cigarettes, talked and laughed. I was closer to their shining shoes than to their faces as we pushed our way through a long row of wooden benches. We sat down, the lights were switched off, and a strong beam of rays pierced the darkness. It shone from a hole in the back wall that you could plug up with a coin and quickly spread into a thick cone of light that threw astounding pictures on a white sheet of canvas up front.

Gray faces as big as houses opened their door-sized mouths and closed them again, but no sounds came out. The only thing you could hear was the whirr of a machine somewhere in the back. Suddenly, the flickering picture jerked away and you saw a crowd of farmers. They, too, kept opening their mouths noiselessly like fish, to be gone again in a wink, replaced by a page with some words floating through a sea of musical notes. A moment later, it, too, was gone and the giant faces returned, but now, slowly, the people around me began to sing along with the lips on the white sheet: "Why shouldn't we be merry, if God gives us our health?"

They started softly, but quickly got up their nerve and soon were belting out the chorus at the top of their lungs.

I happened to be watching a documentary of a performance of Bedřich Smetana's opera *The Bartered Bride,* but it was a *silent* documentary. This opera had long been regarded as the musical representation of the Czech nature, so the audience was simply supposed to know the music. At the time, I didn't even know what opera was. I'd seen people singing in church, but this was different, this was so strange because here and there around me ladies began to sob and everyone sang louder and pretty soon they were all crying and the whole building was shaking with the rousing tune.

In the democratic Czechoslovakia of the late thirties, people were getting choked up at the drop of a hat. Across the border in Germany, Adolf Hitler was demanding that our country hand over to him its German-populated territories. He was threatening to take the Sudetenland by force if the Czech government continued to reject his claim. On that Saturday night in 1937 or 1938, it didn't even occur to me that the behavior of the Čáslav moviegoers may be peculiar. I figured that these massive crying jags went on at the Cine Progress every night, and I didn't know *what* to think about it.

Soon after that my parents took me to the Cine Progress again, and this time the show was Walt Disney's *Snow White and the Seven Dwarfs,* a movie that put me in a trance. The colors were so beautiful, the music so unearthly, the familiar story so gripping that I didn't know what to do. I did whatever everyone else around me was doing. I roared with laughter, yelled in delight, bit my lips, cheered the dwarfs, fell in love with Snow White, and I never wanted it to end.

At the time, the first citizen of Čáslav was Mr. Pick. He owned a soap factory that produced colorful bars in the shapes of Disney's dwarfs, so I'd been washing my hands with Doc, Happy, Sneezy, Dopey, Grumpy, Bashful, or Sleepy every day, but this was going to stop. I marched home, and I forbade anyone in the house ever to use Pick's soap. I took the dwarfs out of the soap holder and put them into a nice box that I'd carry around with me everywhere. I'd open the box, look at them, and find that I couldn't bring myself to stop sniffing them.

FAMILY BIBLE

Many of the people with whom I had shared my youth are dead or live abroad, but our house in Čáslav remains in the family. My sister-in-law Boženka and her children have become the keepers of the battered suitcase of family mementos that comes with the place. Included in the cache is a leather-bound Bible. Its Gothic script is very hard to read, but it doesn't matter because you go straight to the pages of lined paper in the back of the book where our family has been sketching its tree. It reaches all the way back to the early 1800s.

The paper has yellowed, and the ink of the early entries has faded to gray shadow. The old-school handwriting swirls with curlicues as my ancestors write about themselves in the third person. They put down only the bare-boned facts of their lives. They note their names, birth dates, occupations, domiciles, and their children. They leave it to someone else to finish their biography with a brief description of where, when, and how they died. You can see an imprint of their personalities in the handwriting, and you are touched by the confidence with which they regard the future of the family as they cram their simple words between the lines to save space for many more generations.

Who were these people?

My great-grandfather was a prison guard. My grandfather whom I have never met was a railroad official. He had eight children of whom my father, Rudolf Forman, was the oldest. My grandmother died shortly after their youngest was born, so my father had a big hand in bringing up his brothers and sisters. He got stuck on kids for life, becoming a Boy Scout leader and later a teacher. When he earned his degree, he found a job at the Teachers' Institute in Čáslav, where he trained future grade-school teachers.

He met my mother, Anna, when he was in his late twenties. My oldest brother, Blahoslav, was born six months after their wedding in 1917, though somehow no one ever talked about its being a shotgun marriage. Another boy, Pavel, followed two years later. I arrived twelve years after Pavel, and for years I wondered whether I had been another accident, or an afterthought, or some tool of reconciliation or rejuvenation. The gap between me and my brothers always struck me as suspiciously big, and, in the end, I'd learn that there had indeed been a dramatic reason for it.

My mother was a beautiful and enterprising woman of dark looks, great energy, and a fine brain for business. She was nine years younger than my father, and she invested most of her vitality into a summer hotel my parents had built on the shores of a big lake in northern Bohemia. My father chose the scenic spot in a pine wood, some fifty yards above the waterline, a place he'd been camping and known intimately since his youth.

The body of water had for ages been known simply as the Large Lake, but the name must have seemed too prosaic to my father. He wrote an article for the local newspaper proposing that the lake be named after Karel Hynek Mácha, a romantic poet whose best work had been inspired by it. The area was just catching on as a vacation spot, so the proposal quickly took and the place has been known as Mácha's Lake ever since.

My parents started building the summer hotel in 1927, and it was easily the biggest project of their lives. They called it Rut, and it was one of the first such establishments in an area now choking with summer dachas and resorts. It had fourteen rooms that were rented out on a weekly and monthly basis. There was an office, a dining hall, and a pastry shop. The building was not winterized, so the season ran only from June to September.

Every May, my mother left the men of the family to their own wits in Čáslav and made the three-train, six-hour journey to Mácha's Lake. She unlocked the building, chased out the mice that had snuck in over the winter, swept out the cobwebs, brushed the dead flies off the windowsills, unpacked the stored sheets and plates, had the rooms repainted, hired a pastry chef. When the school year ended at the beginning of July, my father and the boys joined her. They cooked for the guests, sold sweets to the walk-in customers, did all the repairs around the property, hiked in the woods, swam and fished in the lake.

They had wonderful summers, and they made money, too.

THE ROAD NOT TAKEN

The first great divide of my life occurred when the Germans came, shortly after my dad had made his road-not-taken decision.

At the time, Hitler had been handed the Sudetenland at the Munich Conference in the fall of 1938, and everyone knew it was only a matter of time before he grabbed the rest of the newly truncated Czechoslovakia. Some old friends of the family, the Koukols, left for Sweden and England, where they had a lot of property. They soon sent word that they would help us follow them and get started abroad. They offered to give our family a new life. My mother was ready to go, but my father refused even to contemplate the idea. He was not going to betray his nation in its bleakest hour. Čáslav was where he lived, Čáslav was where he belonged, Čáslav was where he was going to die.

I'd just started school, so no one asked for my opinion, and it wasn't until after the war that I'd even learned of the offer. My parents had signed me up at the Teachers' Institute in town, where my father taught the teachers who taught me and where he could closely oversee my education.

When I try to picture Dad now, I always see him as a giant towering over me. I never got to see him from a vantage point higher than a kitchen table. At fifty years, he was old enough to be my grandfather and, as the superior of my teachers, he packed twice the authority of the other parents. He was a kind, somewhat distant presence in my life, but he took a lot of interest in my studies. He wanted to know about everything I had done in class. I didn't mind telling him, and he patiently listened to all my opinions. My teachers were his students, so maybe Dad was using me as his pocket inspector.

I don't remember the Germans arriving in Čáslav, though I know it happened shortly after my seventh birthday. Suddenly, they were there, and one spring day in 1940, the director of the school strolled into my classroom. He had never done this before, so you could hear a pin drop. He whispered something into the teacher's ear and then headed straight to my desk.

"Miloš, you're coming with me," he told me softly.

I followed him out the door, down a hallway to a staircase, and up the stairs, where I saw my dad, standing on a landing with a couple of men in leather coats. I'd see my father around the building all the time, so there was nothing peculiar about the situation. I climbed up the stairs, and Dad moved toward me and started stroking my hair. I sensed now that there was something odd about him, but I did not know what it was. He spoke to me the way he always spoke to me, yet there was something strange about his manner.

"So how's everything, Miloš?"

"Okay . . ."

"Tell your mother that everything is fine, all right?"

"Yes, Dad. I will."

"Do you have any homework today?"

"Yes, Dad."

"Make sure you do it."

"Yes, Dad."

"Did you read the entire assignment for Professor Jirásek's class?"

"Yes . . ."

"That's good. You're a good kid . . ."

We just stood there for a moment. I wondered why Dad had me pulled out of class to ask me things that we were going to discuss again over dinner. The pause stretched on. Suddenly, one of the men in leather coats said something in German. I didn't understand him, but the tone of his voice was polite. Dad patted my head again and handed me an envelope.

"Give this to Mom, and tell her that everything's fine and that I'll be back, all right?"

"Yes, Dad."

Dad and the two men started down the stairs. The director and I watched them as they descended the staircase, swung the heavy door open, and walked out. The door slowly closed and I waited for the director to say something, but he just stood there and stared at the closed door.

"Go get your things, Miloš," he finally said. "You have that letter to take to your mother."

My heart leaped: I was going home! Dad had said that everything was fine, so there was nothing to worry about, and now it was turning out I didn't have to sit in school all day! I was happy. I ran quickly down the stairs. I clowned for my schoolmates while I collected my books. I took the longest possible route home, dragging my feet, enjoying my freedom. I never got to see what went on in town at this time of day, so everything looked interesting and I stretched out the walk for as long as I could.

I remember the sudden change in my mother when she opened the letter I'd handed her. She stiffened and the color drained from her skin. Then she burst into tears. I was shocked; I didn't understand her reaction. Dad had said not to worry about anything. Why was she so upset? What did he write in that letter?

Mom didn't tell me that Dad had been arrested by the Gestapo. She told me that he would be away for a few days, but that he was coming back. Perhaps she believed it herself. Someone had told her that these things happened, that most Gestapo detainees were merely questioned and released, and that, one of these days, Dad was sure to be coming back from the Gestapo jail in Kolín. This person was merely trying to comfort her, but my frightened mother latched onto the flimsy hope with all her heart. What was the poor woman to do?

The next morning, Mother kept me home from school. She took me to the train station instead. Dad might be coming home on the train from Kolín, she explained. "We want to be there to welcome him, in case he comes," she said.

The Čáslav train station was not a very busy place. It amounted to a couple of platforms, spanned by a vaulting catwalk. Every day, there were three trains from Kolín, the nearest railroad knot. The trains ran on time under the Germans, so a gleaming black steam locomotive pulled in five khaki cars precisely as it was supposed to. My mother held my hand, squeezing it hard, and we watched the locomotive brake to a stop, watched the train manager throw down a sack of mail, watched most of the car doors open, and scanned the passengers' faces. The last person hopped off the train. We stood there while the doors closed, while the train jerked into motion with angry bursts of steam, while it pulled out of the station and headed east. And we stared at it, as if Dad might still be on board, as if he had merely dozed off and slept through his stop, as if he might still pull the emergency brake and jump off.

"Well, Miloš, there'll be another train in a couple of hours," said Mom, and we walked home again.

Dad did not come on the next train, however, and he did not step off the evening train either. We had a long night ahead of us, but then there would be three more trains coming tomorrow.

One by one, we watched them arrive, but they didn't bring Dad back.

I don't remember going to school in those days. It seems to me that I just walked my mother to the train station every day for weeks on end, which probably isn't how it was. Maybe I'd only go there after school, maybe the summer vacation had started, but, in any case, Dad never showed up and the uneventful trips to the station began to bore me.

I no longer waited at my mom's side till the train stopped and everyone got off. I ran up on the catwalk as soon as we got to the station and stood directly above the main track. I didn't even look at the passengers much anymore. I waited for the train to pass right under me, shaking the rusty rods of the catwalk as if all that straining, banging, screeching metal was somehow going straight through me. The billowing smoke of the chugging steam engine, which smelled of sulfur and coal, felt wet to the skin, and left a film of sooty moisture on the face, enveloped me. I was in the clouds, and if I stared straight down on the cars passing a couple of feet below me, it seemed as if the catwalk were sliding against their motion, as if the train were standing still and I was flying with the iron bridge over it. It always took a while for the heavy smoke to clear. In fact, the passengers usually dispersed faster than the sulfurous fog. And every time the smoke drifted off, there would be only my mother standing on the deserted platform.

Our daily walks to the train station went on for about three months. They had become Mother's private ritual. It all stopped abruptly when the word came that Dad had been transferred from Kolín to a prison in Česká Lípa. Our life had to go on, so I went back to school and my mother started waiting for the mailman. He came only once a day, but every now and then he brought a letter from Dad.

That Christmas, I wrote a fervent letter to Ježíšek, the Czech Santa Claus, asking to have my father back. My mother prayed a great deal for his return. Her prayers didn't seem to be working any better than my letter, so Mom and I put all our efforts into scrounging up food for the packages that we were allowed to send to Dad several times a year, though we were going hungry ourselves.

My life in the war was nothing like what you usually see in the movies or read about in books. It had a few pulses of sweaty dread, but these were only intermittent accords in the densely ticking rhythms of everyday life. For example, what remained of Czechoslovakia, now called the Protectorate of Bohemia and Moravia by the Germans, held its traditional championships in track and field and yielded a Čáslav celebrity. His name was Jaroslav Oliva, and he had clocked 11.1 seconds in the 100-meter dash. He came in dead last in the finals, but that made him the sixth fastest man in the country, so if I saw him walking through town, I crossed the street and said a shy hello to him.

I remember, too, that by then I badly wanted to live in a place that

had streetcars. I must have gotten this idea from some postcard of
Prague, but I daydreamed about jumping on and off the open platform
of a speeding red streetcar, so I kept asking the adults just how big a
town had to be to qualify for them. They either didn't know or they
talked like oracles. Finally, I ran into an uncle who gave me a straight-
forward answer. He told me that only cities longer than five kilometers
could lay streetcar tracks.

The first chance that I got I paced off the length of the main street
that ran through our town like a crooked spine. It started up on a
plateau on the West Side, dipped down, crossed a railroad track,
climbed up to the square, and ran on eastward. I measured it several
times, but no matter how small the steps I took, I could never stretch
it to more than four and a half kilometers. I knew then that I lived in
a puny town and that I'd have to leave it one day.

EGGS AND STONES

During the war, the Germans squeezed every last egg from the occu-
pied territories for their war effort. They kept books on every farm
animal you owned, and you had to turn over all the eggs your hens had
laid over a certain quota. This meant no end of problems because
undernourished hens sometimes did not lay enough eggs to cover their
quota in the first place, so then you had to go and explain this at some
bureau and get stamps and sign papers because this food tax was serious
business. You risked the death penalty by raising a pig off the books. Of
all the domestic animals, only Lilliputian hens did not have to be
accounted for. Their eggs were so tiny that even the bookkeeping-mad
Germans allowed you to keep all of them.

After Dad's arrest, our money got short, so my mother managed to
buy six Lilliputian hens and we ate their tiny eggs for breakfast. She also
sewed and took in lodgers, so we were able to send Dad the packages
that kept him from starvation.

Working all the angles of our financial situation with her customary
energy and imagination, Mother one day decided to go and save what
she could from our summer hotel. Rut had been boarded up, but we
still had some things of value there.

In late fall of 1941 we moved from Čáslav to Mácha's Lake. Mother sent me to school there, and she let me take my dog with us. He was a russet dachshund, a gift Ježíšek had brought me on the last Christmas we celebrated together as a family. I remember Dad sitting down to the piano to lead us in caroling after dinner, a tradition I hated with a passion because it put off the opening of the gifts, and I recall how he lifted the keyboard lid and struck the first chord and how the piano gave a long, high-pitched howl. It took me a beat to figure out that the immense racket was coming from a box that lay by his feet. The russet puppy was the best thing I ever got for Christmas. I named him Rek, and we became great buddies. He was following me everywhere by the time Mother took us back to Rut.

Mácha's Lake was a strange place during the war. There no longer existed any Czech schools in the Sudetenland, so I had to go to a German class where the teacher pointed me to a desk in the back of the room. I didn't speak any German and I didn't know any of the kids, so I just sat there and tried to make something out of what I heard. The class burst out laughing, and I had no idea why. I was only glad that no one paid any attention to me. I missed Čáslav. I wondered what Rek was doing. Finally, the last bell of the day rang.

I walked home down a road that twisted its way through tall pines. I sauntered along, kicking pine cones and staring at the ground when, suddenly, something struck me and a stab of sharp pain pierced my shoulder. As I spun around to look back, a rock bounced off a tree trunk beside me. There were six or seven German boys from my class, standing some fifteen yards away, staring at me in silence, clutching rocks in their fingers. The shortest of them swung his arm back and pitched a pebble at me. He missed, so another boy threw a bigger rock, which I ducked.

A gaggle of girls behind the boys looked on. No one jeered at me or yelled any taunts. In fact, no one uttered a sound. Their faces were all business. They threw their rocks hard, but without a shred of emotion, as if they had been ordered to stone me by someone else, as if they were conducting an experiment.

I was just stunned and confused; I didn't know what to do. I stood there ducking their rocks. No one made an attempt to rush me or beat me up, but they didn't stop stoning me either. I finally got hit in the stomach with a big rock, and I limped home and showed the bruise to Mom.

My mother was not someone who quit easily. The next morning, she kept me home while she went to have a talk with my German teacher.

She came back and told me that I didn't have anything to worry about anymore. Nothing of that sort was ever going to happen to me again. She had the teacher's assurances, and she trusted him, so she sent me back to school the following day.

I didn't know what to expect. No one looked at me in the classroom. Nothing happened. I could sense that I was under the teacher's protection and that everyone feared him. I sat there and did my math, which was the only lesson I could follow. I walked home down the same pine-shaded road. I moved quickly and looked back a lot, but nobody bothered me.

A few days went by. I had no problems in school, other than being bored and lost. The other kids looked right through me. My mom tried to teach me some German, but all I wanted to do when I got home from school was play with Rek. He was my only buddy in the world now, and I grew even more passionately attached to him.

One morning, the teacher took us out for a nature walk. We were crossing a slippery log bridge when someone shoved me from behind and I plunged into the icy creek below. The teacher was furious. He slapped the kids behind me and then sent me home to change my clothes. I hurried to the hotel with the clothes freezing to my body and the ice-cold water sloshing in my shoes. I never went back to the German school.

When I got to Rut, I found my mother furiously scolding Rek. He didn't like the Sudetenland any more than I did, and he had set upon the German mailman, tearing up his pants leg. We simply couldn't fit into this landscape anymore, so Mother hid away as much silverware and as many blankets as she could, and we got on the train and returned to Čáslav.

I was glad to be back with my old friends, but I was still spending a lot of my free time with Rek. He was getting to be more and more of a drain on our food budget, but I didn't mind going a little hungry to feed him, though Mom didn't like that at all. I was just glad that Rek was a dachshund and not a Saint Bernard.

One day, however, Rek's hunger got the better of him. He'd been left home alone, and he dug a hole under a fence in the garden to get to the henhouse. He didn't spare a single one of our Lilliputian hens. There was no atonement to be made for the killings as far as my mother was concerned. The next morning, some strange farmer with crooked teeth, an acquaintance of the family from a nearby village, showed up, and my mother tore Rek out of my arms and handed him to the man. I fought and screamed and cried and I hated everyone, but they were stronger, so my mother traded my dog for another bunch of Lilliputians.

I must confess that the loss of Rek was the most immediately traumatic moment of my childhood. When my father disappeared from my life, he remained a presence somewhere beyond the horizon. I had no idea of what he was going through; he was out there somewhere. We talked about him, we worked on putting his food packages together, we celebrated his birthdays, he spoke to me through his letters, so the emotional impact of that loss was oddly dissipated.

The brutal fact of life is that all the great losses of my childhood had a feeling of flatness about them, a sense of the anticlimax, while my separation from the dachshund was sheer pain. I fought for him physically, with all my strength, and I fought for him against my mother, whom I loved, and still he was wrestled away from me by a sinister stranger, shoved whimpering under his arm, and gone forever. What sort of a world was this?

It was the kind of a world where, a couple of mornings later, I took a slice of bread and wiped the last strands of yolk off my plate of scrambled Lilliputian eggs and wished I could have three more helpings.

DOWN, DOWN, DOWN

When I was a kid, I kept having the same dream. I dreamed it for years, in other people's rooms, on couches and sofas and in strange beds, not every night, but often, and I'd always wake up from it with a start, drenched in sweat and with my heart pounding.

The dream went like this: I am standing inside the back door of our house in Čáslav, peering at a witch. The old hag has claws for hands and cancerous warts on her face, and she is wearing rags that stink of piss. She looks very nasty, but she is slouching by the far wall of the garden, some thirty paces away, and I am not afraid of her. She is staring straight into my eyes, but I have one hand on the door handle and I can easily slam the door shut on her if I have to. I hear the voices of my father and my mother and my big brothers, talking and laughing lazily in the kitchen behind me, so I feel safe in the house, so safe that

I stick out my tongue at the witch and start making faces at her. I am careful to keep a firm grip on the door handle though, so there is no way she can get me.

Suddenly, the witch pounces, flying at me as if she were sucked into the door by some astronomical force, and she grabs me and the floor gives way and the bottom drops out of the world. I can't scream in the tight wrap of the witch's embrace because my heart has stopped beating and I can't breathe and my muscles are stiff with horror, and we go down, down, down.

FOOTSTEPS

I was ten years old and sick with fever. I lay in bed in my room on the second floor of our house. It was a bright summer day outside, but when Mom brought me the morning medicine, she had drawn the shutters, so the room was filled with pleasant twilight. I had some books to look at, but I was just resting with half-closed eyes, listening to the chirping of the birds in the park and to my mother shuffling around the house below me.

I heard a car stop by our gate, which, in 1942, was an unusual sound in our street.

Someone knocked resolutely on the door. The door clicked open. From my bed upstairs, I heard several muffled voices entering the hallway. After a while, footsteps began crossing the rooms below, doors banged, drawers and cabinets slammed, furniture was dragged around the floor. I lay there scared. I didn't know who the visitors were, and I didn't want to know because I already had a fair idea.

I tried not to look at the massive wooden cupboard that towered a couple of feet away from the far wall. It didn't fully screen the door of a small alcove that we used as a secret pantry, keeping a sack of potatoes there and maybe some lard, all the black-market contraband my mother had scrounged up in the surrounding villages which we weren't supposed to have, though everyone had a food stash just like it. We kept the door open to air out the pantry, and we would only lug the heavy cupboard back to the wall to hide it when we thought someone might come nosing around.

I finally heard footsteps coming up the stairs. There were too many, but they included a pair of light-stepping feet, so I prayed that it was Mom, and it was, but she was looking really grim as she cracked the door open.

"Here is your medicine, Mílo."

I'd just taken my medicine, but I said nothing. I dragged myself to the door, and Mom handed me a pill and a glass of water. Her face was white and drawn, and she looked at me intently, warning me with her eyes. Without looking at him, I took in the tall man standing at her side and eyeing her, stern and remote, already holding her in his power. I swallowed the pill like a good boy and washed it down with a sip of water, and Mom gave me a long, long look and then turned and closed the door. I listened to her footsteps retreat down the stairs.

So it was all true. The Gestapo was searching the house, and there was no more hoping that what was happening wasn't really happening, so it was up to me now to block the door of the alcove. I tiptoed to the cupboard so that the floorboards wouldn't creak. It stood on little ram-horn legs, and I bent down and grabbed one of them and tried to lift it. It didn't move. I pulled on it with all my strength. It didn't budge. I strained as hard as I could, but I couldn't even get it up high enough off the floor to slip a sheet of paper under it. I let go of the leg and tried to push the cupboard to the wall with my back. I put all my weight and everything I had into it, but my feet just slid away from me on the smooth floor.

I crawled back into bed, the sweaty pajamas sticking to my body, feeling smaller than the tiny leg of the cupboard. I was failing my family just when they needed me most, and it was only a question of time before the Gestapo found our stash. I covered myself with the blanket up to my neck and waited.

Sometime later, in the afternoon, came the footsteps I'd been dreading. Heavy, pounding the stairs, overlapping. Two men in short sleeves came into the room without knocking. They smiled at me. They took one glance at the cupboard standing away from the wall, strolled around it, and disappeared in the alcove. I could hear them rummaging inside. Now they knew everything, but when they came back out, they just flashed more smiles at me; maybe they hadn't seen our potatoes, which was impossible, so maybe they didn't care, so maybe there was some hope. The door closed behind them. They hadn't said a word, so maybe they were nice, maybe they felt sorry for us, maybe they had kids of their own, and maybe everything was still going to be okay.

There was some more muffled talking and walking around and

banging of doors downstairs. Then I heard people stepping out of the hallway, and the main door slammed shut. The gate screeched, the car started and drove off.

The house was silent.

I lay there under the blanket, stiff with dread and apprehension, sweating, feverish, trying not to know what I knew only too well, hoping that if I didn't investigate the situation it would not be happening, praying that those lightest of all footsteps would come back, praying that the door would fly open and Mom would rush in and grab me in her arms.

Nothing. A long time nothing. Silence.

Finally, the doorbell rang. I lay still and didn't even breathe. I listened to the bell buzzing, and, with all my heart, I wanted Mom to go and open the door. The bell kept buzzing and stopping and starting again, as if it were talking to me, as if it knew I was in the house.

Yes, yes, I'm coming.

I peeled the blanket back and climbed down the stairway. And no. Mom was gone. The house was empty. Things lay strewn around the hallway. The bell kept ringing, so I opened the door and there was a man standing there who looked to be at least a hundred years old. I was stuck in a fairy tale from the Brothers Grimm.

Our neighbors had watched the Gestapo take away my mother, peeking through drawn curtains. They knew that most likely I'd been left alone in the house, but they were afraid to be seen around our door, so they sent their ancient grandpa over. They figured he was too old to matter even to the Gestapo. They were scared, but they found a way to take care of me that day. They sent a telegram to my mother's brother in Náchod, and the grandpa slept with me in the house so I wouldn't be alone. He chose a bed in the other bedroom upstairs.

I don't think I slept a wink that night, which was endless and straight out of Goya. I was sick and sweaty and I missed Mom and didn't know if the morning would ever come. Suddenly, I heard sounds in the hallway outside my room. Something big was groping around there, bumping into things. I curled up under the sheets and stopped breathing. My only hope was that this new intruder wouldn't find me, but I didn't dare to hope anymore; I knew now that the worst possible thing that could happen always happened and that I didn't stand a chance. I was right. The thing pushed the door open and I braced myself to die, and then I heard a strange whizzing sound. It sounded as if water were splashing on the floor, and it smelled of piss.

The neighbor's grandpa had weak kidneys, and he got confused in the unfamiliar house. He couldn't find the light switch, couldn't find the bathroom, and he couldn't wait anymore, so he opened some door and he relieved himself, and then he stumbled back to bed. When I finally realized that it was the old man I didn't understand why he was pissing into my room. I didn't know what else he might do. I lay there terrified until the dawn, in the stink of piss. Glistening in the first pink light of the day, which rose after all, the big puddle of urine reached from the door to the wardrobe.

That morning, Uncle Boleslav came and helped me pack up the suitcase, which I was going to live out of for the next thirty-five years. We locked the house, got on a train, and headed to Náchod, a small town in northern Bohemia.

MOM

On August 7, 1942, my mother was one of twelve women arrested in Čáslav by the Gestapo. All the ladies were good customers of Mr. Havránek, the grocer. Earlier that week someone had stuck some anti-Reich fliers behind the shutters of Havránek's shop. Havránek did not run to the police with them as the Germans had decreed. He was one of the most garrulous characters in the neighborhood, so he told anyone who set a foot in his shop all about the fliers.

Soon the Gestapo showed up and wanted to hear the story, too. It's not clear what the Gestapo did to Havránek to make him name twelve of his lady customers. He never came back from the interrogation. He was probably tortured. He hung himself in his cell in Kolín. Havránek's suicide demolished the case. The Gestapo never established who had printed the fliers. They released eleven of the twelve ladies after perfunctory interrogations.

The only person never to return from the Kolín jail was my mother, even though Havránek may have given her name in error. My family had purposely been avoiding his store because loudmouths were dangerous in a country where an informer could use any bit of gossip to get rid of anyone he or she didn't like.

After the war, it turned out that the Gestapo man who made the decision to keep my mother had known our family before the war. He came from the Sudetenland and had, in fact, been employed by my parents during the construction of our summer hotel. They had hired him as a night watchman on the site. There didn't seem to be anything remarkable about the man. He passed through their lives doing his job and disappeared, but he was a firm believer in the superiority of the German race and my parents had been strong Czech patriots in the Sudetenland, so he probably nurtured a grudge toward our family. Later he joined the Gestapo and made an unspectacular career in it. During the war he wound up being stationed at the district headquarters in Kolín, and Čáslav fell under his jurisdiction.

One day he came across the name Anna Formanova again. The woman who had once employed him, a member of the superior race, in a lowly job was now in his hands. He took the stamp that read RETURN NONDESIRABLE and slapped it on her file.

I saw Mom one last time after that.

Early one morning in the fall of 1942, Uncle Boleslav and I got on a train in Náchod. We were going to try to visit Mom in prison, which didn't mean that we'd necessarily get to see her. We had all the papers and all the stamps, but you never knew.

This was my first trip to Prague, but I don't have any recollection of the city. I was overwhelmed by other emotions. In the huge hall of the main train station, my brother Pavel was waiting for us. Pavel was a budding painter then, and, as a young talent, he'd already had his first exhibit in Čáslav. It had cost him dearly because the local Gestapo informers found swastikas in the background of some of his grotesque oils, so the Germans were looking for him. The Gestapo was right about my brother's swastikas, but he was tipped off and managed to disappear in a hurry. The Germans opened an investigation, but then they filed it away. They had more important things to worry about. Nevertheless, Pavel had to spend the rest of the war on the move. That year, his papers happened to be relatively in order, so he took a calculated gamble and came to see Mom with us.

The three of us headed to a place more fearsome and depressing than any I've ever been to. It's called Pečkárna, and it's still notorious in Prague. The building had housed a bank before the war, and it has several money vaults under it, which the Gestapo used as soundproof torture chambers. And later, after the war and after the revolution, the Communist State Security set up its own confession factory there.

I recall a Gestapo man leading us down underground stairways. There were heavy doors and bars, and the place just reeked of suffering. The German showed us into a stuffy vault. He didn't say anything. He shut the door and locked us inside.

In the corner of the barren room stood a desolate wooden bench. We sat down. There was only the weak light of a naked bulb, hanging off a wire, but right away I saw a burst of big drops of dried blood spattered on the wall. You couldn't miss it, but no one said a word. The vault was not particularly small, but it gave me the feeling of having been shut into an iron chest and dropped down a mine shaft. Anything could have happened up on the surface, a storm, a great fire, a bombing raid, and we never would have known about it.

We sat there for two hours and no one spoke, or at least that's how I remember it. Finally, the door opened again and another plainclothesman brought in Mom. She wore a dress I knew. She looked dead tired. They clearly hadn't told her where she was being taken because she froze in shock for just a second, then threw herself at me, grabbed me, and held me with all her might for as long as we had together. Some ten, fifteen minutes maybe. With the Gestapo man standing by the door; sitting on the rough bench, talking, no one knowing what to say.

"So, Miloš, are you doing your schoolwork?"

"And what about Čáslav?"

"And did we have a lot of apricots this year, Pavel? You have to can them! If there's sugar . . ."

"So what about Mrs. Procházková?"

The conversation was a string of banalities, but it was my last fifteen minutes on Mom's lap.

"That's enough," said the Gestapo man suddenly. He opened the door and turned to Mom: *"Bitte."*

Mom kissed everyone, stroked our hands. She backed out of the room. She was staring back at us when he slammed the door behind them.

We sat there for another ten minutes of silence and trepidation. The door opened and another agent walked us up the stairs and out of the building. The world was still there. The same street lamps that hadn't been on in years, the same streetcars, the same trucks on the cobblestones, the same hurried crowds on the sidewalks.

In the spring, the mailman brought a small bundle in brown packing paper. It contained a beret the color of ripening raspberries and a rag doll my mother had made in prison. Later came a printed form with the name and the date typed in. Mother died in Auschwitz on the first of March 1943.

DAD

At that time, my father was still alive. We were still getting his letters and sending packages to him. And I still didn't know why those two polite men in leather coats had marched him out of my life. What did they want with him? No one would tell me.

I was too young to be trusted with the truth, which is that my father had belonged to an underground resistance group. It was called Pribina, and it had been set up by the reservists of the Czech army before the Germans came. Father had the job of a communications officer, so I suppose he was a sort of sleeping agent. It didn't take the Gestapo long to bust the organization. Soon after the war began, two of Pribina's officers in Prague spilled everything they knew. They were probably tortured and hoped to save their lives, but they only managed to implicate themselves further by the sheer scope of their knowledge. They both wound up on the gallows. They gave the Gestapo thirty-four names, one or two for every small town between Prague and Čáslav. Clearly the last name they could recall was that of my father because the arrests stopped in Čáslav.

My father knew of other people in the chain that stretched eastward, which speaks poorly of the conspiratorial methods of the group, but he denied everything, so we had grateful visitors after the war whose lives he had saved. He was dragged through the prisons of Kolín, Česká Lípa, Budištín, Zhořelec, Ulm, and Prague, but when the Gestapo could not crack him, he was finally handed over to the civil court machinery, so he had come close to saving himself.

By then, the whole family had been dispersed. Only brother Pavel got to attend our father's court session in Prague, though he had to go there incognito. In court, Dad looked very gaunt and sallow, but he was clearly himself. He smiled at Pavel, and Pavel beamed back from the spectator gallery. He hardly took his eyes off the old man and wished only that he could get closer to him. He was overjoyed to hear the verdict. The court sentenced father to the time he had already served in the investigative detention, which, in those days, amounted to the finding of not guilty. Pavel went away thinking Dad would soon be freed, that it was only a matter of days before we had him back. But we never saw him again. He was never released, the court order was never carried out.

After the war, no one understood why Father hadn't been released as the court in Prague had decreed, so my brothers dug up what had happened, which took a fair amount of detective work. From the court in Prague, Father's file went back to the Gestapo in Kolín, where the same Gestapo man who was responsible for my mother's arrest, the same night watchman from Rut, had stamped it, too, RETURN NONDESIR-ABLE, so Dad was sent on into the hell of concentration camps. He went through Theresienstadt, Auschwitz, and Buchenwald. The people who came back from there spoke fondly of him. They said he had a strong faith in God and he never gave in to the bestiality around him. He helped and comforted people, and he behaved with grace until the end.

By then the tide of the war turned on the Nazi night watchman, and he wound up being sent to the Eastern Front. He was shot, and he died there. If he was lucky, his body was bulldozed into the pit of a mass grave, but maybe he wasn't lucky, maybe he was still alive when the black birds of the Ukraine were plucking his eyes out.

My father died of scarlet fever when all the time left in the war was one day short of a year. He didn't die in Čáslav as he had once vowed he would.

PART 2

BOHEMIA

UNCLE BOLESLAV AND AUNT ANNA

In the summer of 1942, the Germans were still advancing in Russia and in North Africa, the Japanese were landing their troops on Guadalcanal, and I was "a child of the enemies of the Third Reich," so Uncle Boleslav ran a considerable risk by taking me into his house. I was another mouth to feed, too, and another body to clothe and keep warm, but Boleslav and his family always treated me like a son. They lived above a grocery store they owned, and they made me feel right at home in their small apartment.

I slept on a sofa in the kitchen and, whenever I had some free time, I hung around the shop downstairs. I liked to help Boleslav, so he'd let me wash the returned bottles, restock the shelves, or weigh various goods on the large balancing scale.

When I was not doing anything, I'd perch on the half lid of a keg of sauerkraut. I'd watch the shoppers and I'd listen to the conversations, and now and then I'd reach behind me, grab a whisk of sauerkraut with my fingertips, dip it in the bag of powdered sugar that lay beside the keg, and munch on it. It was my favorite treat.

My favorite time was when the coffee beans got roasted. They came in raw and they were rare and expensive in wartime, so my uncle wouldn't let anyone else near the job. He'd set up a metal drum with a crank on the stove and heated it to a very particular and scientific temperature. He then poured the green coffee beans inside and proceeded slowly and very steadily to turn the crank that rotated the drum so that all the beans got roasted to the same rich shade of brown. The shop filled up with a heavenly fragrance that completely altered its rhythms. The brisk atmosphere suddenly slackened as customers lingered by the counter, eyeing the shelves as if they couldn't remember what else they had wanted and sniffed the coffee-tinged air.

My favorite sight in the store was the breasts of a housemaid—let us call her Eva. I don't remember when breasts had gotten so alluring. It happened as naturally and as imperceptibly as you grow out of your clothes. You simply notice one day that the sleeves of your shirt are too short or that your old shoes pinch, and one morning I suddenly realized that the spectacular breasts of the housemaid had a powerful hold on me. They were large and firm, and I carefully choreographed my movements around the store so that I could brush up against them.

Eva was a simple girl from the hills, which gave me a chance to get my hands on what I'd had my eyes on. One afternoon, I saw her sneaking her boyfriend into the storeroom in the back of the shop. Uncle absolutely forbade strangers in there, so I told Eva that there was only one way I wouldn't tell on her. She allowed me to slip my hand into her blouse and fondle the springy mounds of her breast. I felt like Rodin molding the most beautiful sculpture from the most pliable clay in the world. Eva endured my artistry with a vacuous look in her eyes and a pouting expression on her face. I wondered how come my touching did not do anything to her, but I thought I'd better not ask.

"That's enough," she decided after a while.

"No, I said both tits!"

"Well, hurry up!"

I switched sides, though not hands, but I never managed to make any impression on Eva with my fondling, whereas her warm, milky, smooth breasts made a huge impression on my puberty-crazed hormones. She was a girl of principle, however, and she refused to let me slide my hand under her skirt no matter what I threatened to tell my uncle about her.

I didn't push my luck. I was hugely excited and happy.

I learned much more than blackmail in my uncle's care. I drank in the atmosphere of the shop like a sponge and later drew on it for my first full-length film, *Black Peter*.

Before I came to Náchod, I had only lived with my family, so I had to figure out how to act around other people and Uncle Boleslav gave me one of the most formative lessons of my life. It happened at a chessboard. Uncle Boleslav was a good player and he played a lot of chess with me, but I could never beat him, which made me furious with myself. I felt I was failing the family tradition since my brother Pavel had once played with José Raoul Capablanca, one of the all-time greats of the game. Back in the thirties, after the Cuban genius had lost his world title to the hard-drinking Alexander Alekhine, he traveled around the world, making a living off his mastery of chess, and he stopped in Čáslav to pick up some pocket change. My hometown fielded thirty of its best players for a simultaneous game, and Capablanca defeated twenty-nine of them in short order. Only one Čáslavian gave him any trouble, and he was just a kid. In the end the champion was forced to offer the kid a draw.

That kid was Pavel, my own flesh and blood, and for years I day-dreamed about the event because it allowed me vicariously to touch true greatness. I suppose that I calculated that if my brother, as a teenager, could hold his own against the best in the world, then maybe one day I could do it, too. I wasn't particular and didn't really care what I became a champion in, just as long as I wound up on top of the heap somewhere, anywhere, in anything.

Meanwhile, however, I couldn't even beat Uncle Boleslav in chess. I got so frustrated by constantly losing to him that, one day, when he stepped away from the board, I moved a rook pawn up a square. It hadn't been my move, but I needed every bit of an advantage and I figured he'd never notice this inconspicuous flank move. Uncle Boleslav came back and sat down. He glanced at the board. He eyeballed me for a beat. He lowered his forehead and stared at the game for another beat. Suddenly, he swept all the pieces off the board with an angry swish of his hand. That was the last time I got to play chess with Uncle Boleslav. He never offered me another game and I was afraid to ask him, but I never again tried so blatantly to cheat either.

I'd lived with Uncle Boleslav for a year when he lost his old tenants in the tiny apartment across the hall from where we lived. He no sooner stuck a FOR RENT sign in the window than he had a delicate situation on his hands. A couple of young Germans showed up to look at the place, and they quickly agreed to pay much more for it than Uncle Bole-slav had been getting. He didn't dare to turn them down, and they moved in.

The Germans had hardly any furniture, and they often didn't come home at night. Perhaps they were gay lovers, perhaps they had been planted there by the Gestapo. Anything was possible and Uncle Bole-slav was worried, so my Náchod relatives got together and decided that I should go live with Aunt Anna for a while. I packed up my suitcase and moved to the other end of Náchod.

The course of the war had changed that year. By the summer of 1943, the German Sixth Army had surrendered at Stalingrad and the Allies had launched their invasion of Italy. Central Europe still re-mained firmly in German hands, but there was less and less to eat in the Protectorate of Bohemia and Moravia and a growing kid was a considerable drain on a family budget, even though no one ever said a word about it to me.

I have nothing but love and gratitude for Uncle Boleslav, Aunt Anna, and their families.

Anna was my father's sister. She married a druggist named Sládek, and they had five children; three of them were grown and only the two youngest boys, Jiří and Jaroslav, remained in the house, so I had a bed of my own to sleep in again.

The family owned an apothecary, which was no less a holiday for the nose than Uncle Boleslav's grocery store. The shop didn't yet have the antiseptic aroma of modern drugstores because it sold more herbs, teas, and spices than synthetic medicines, so I loved just ambling around the shelves and crossing the zones of delicious smells. It was like floating through a tumbler of an elaborate tropical cocktail. I wanted to spend more time in the apothecary, but I wasn't given the run of the place as I had been at Uncle Boleslav's shop. Mr. Sládek handled the whole business alone, and he still had the time to take an hourlong nap every afternoon, which turned out to be a good thing for me. While Mr. Sládek napped, everyone in the small house had to find something quiet to do. I'd stretch out on the sofa and I'd read. I read all of Jules Verne in Náchod, and I read all sorts of adventure stories. I remember a book called *The Deckhands of Captain Bonteco* that really caught my fancy. It was about boys stowing away on a ship to Africa. I also read Mark Twain and Victor Hugo. I learned to appreciate books and to love stories.

The war kept squeezing Europe tighter and tighter, and one day Anna, too, asked me to pack up my suitcase. She had tears in her eyes as she told me that I'd be going back to Čáslav, where some people wanted to help take care of me. They had more money and could afford to feed me better.

I arrived back in Čáslav in the fall of 1944, but not to live in our old house. I'd never live there again. I was an orphan now, and I was taken in by old friends of the family, the Hluchýs.

Mr. Hluchý was a part-time hockey referee and a full-time director of the gasworks. His apartment lay inside the plant, so I spent a lot of time just wandering around its grounds and taking in the fascinating sights. There were huge ovens with flickering vermilion cracks in their armor, house-sized piles of coal, intricate networks of pipes curving and twisting around the buildings, giant water containers.

A great deal of work and energy passed through the place, but at night it had to be absolutely dark. All the ovens and all the windows had to be screened so that not a single ray of light escaped because the American planes had started to bomb the factories and industrial sites of Bohemia and it was clear that the Germans were going to lose the war. I couldn't wait.

Living out of a suitcase in households where they secretly felt sorry for me, passing from one kind relative to another, I quickly realized that it helps in life to make yourself liked and it helps if you don't give people unnecessary trouble. I made sure that I did well in school, and I tried to see things from my benefactors' perspective now and then. I helped out in the households and in the shops, and I was careful not to cause problems.

I found out that being a rebel and raising hell is a huge existential luxury, and I suppose that I grew up to be more of a diplomat than anything else. I learned to read people's moods and to understand what they felt even if they didn't fully understand it themselves. I noticed that people don't always believe in doing the things they do, that there often is a gap between who they think they are and who they really are.

I didn't know it at the time, but I see now that living out of a suitcase gave me a very good training for my future trade as a director.

ROLE MODEL

With the Gestapo looking for him, brother Pavel couldn't stay in one place for too long. He was not on any of the Germans' most-wanted lists, but he had to avoid situations where his papers might get closely compared to stagnant police files. He solved his problem by hooking up with the East Bohemian Operetta. He designed and built sets for this traveling company and then helped lug them around the underheated auditoriums or dusty gyms of small towns, where the company put on old musical chestnuts, such as *Die Fledermaus, The Polish Blood,* or *The Pearls of Madame Seraphine.*

One day Pavel showed up in Náchod with his troupe and took me to their opening night. I don't remember anymore what I saw that evening, but I know that the show enthralled me. I didn't want it to end and then I longed to see it over and over again, but the following night my brother took me backstage, which turned out to be even better. I was still a kid and no one paid any attention to me there, so I found a chair in the corner, sat down quietly, and took in the scene. It was tremendously exciting.

Gorgeous young women darted around me in bras and garter belts and panties. They thought nothing of flashing their white breasts and buttocks as they hurriedly changed their frilly costumes. There were a lot of jokes and camaraderie and chaotic energy, the lovely music was pouring in from the stage, and I didn't know what to focus on first. The erotic charge and the atmosphere alone would have been enough to suck me into show business for life, but there was more. There was also the fragrance of theater makeup. I'd thought I wanted to keep my nose around roasting coffee beans, but I didn't know a thing.

Backstage at the Operetta, there were such glorious swirls of feminine, fruity, flowery, sexy smells, such heady washes of cheap perfumes, of violets, of unwashed bodies of young women, of lipstick, of drooping lace and rouge, of starch, steaming iron, mothballs, of liquor and cherry and pie, of ballet slippers and sweaty blouses and faintly pissy skirts that I decided on the spot that I was going to spend my life there.

The only thing I wasn't completely sure about was what job in the theater I was going to go after. I knew I didn't want to be an actor because I saw that backstage, in contrast to the auditorium, the leading men of the operetta were all treated like little boys. I was just thinking that maybe I'd have to become a playwright or a composer when an older man stormed into the dressing room. He was gruff, dressed in a wrinkled suit, balding, and yet all those beautiful young women suddenly perked up. They started tripping over each other to make him notice them. He didn't even seem particularly sober, but they put on smiles that wouldn't quit. They flirted with him. They gazed into his eyes. They would have done anything to please him, which was just where I, too, wanted to have them one day.

"Who's that?" I pointed out the old man to Pavel the first chance I got.

"Oh, that's the guy who directed this thing," Pavel said.

"Is he good?"

"He's real good with a bottle, yeah, the old alkie." My brother wasn't very impressed with his troupe's theater director, but I knew a role model when I saw one. The East Bohemian Operetta stayed in Náchod for a week, and by the time they left I knew what I wanted to do with my life.

In 1944, I got to see Pavel's troupe again in Čáslav, where I was now living at the gasworks. Pavel was still with the Operetta, so he gave me a ticket to their performance of *The Polish Blood,* a classic of light musical entertainment. I'll never forget that evening in the Dusík Theater. The place was packed. I'd never known so many people could fit in it, but it was no wonder because the musical was lovely. I was quickly drawn into its well-made plot, and I loved its comedy and laughed at all the jokes when suddenly, in the third act, in the middle of a lighthearted quartet, all four singers broke into sobs. They struggled to go on with quavering voices, but their voices kept giving out. They finally fell silent and just stood there on the stage, weeping.

The orchestra stopped playing, and, reigning throughout the building, you heard a silence as hard as a diamond. It seemed a snatch of a bad dream, but when I glanced around me, I saw only intent faces. No one stirred, no one seemed confused, as if they somehow understood something that had escaped me.

The four singers on the stage wiped their eyes and composed themselves. They didn't look at all ashamed. The conductor gave them a nod, the orchestra started back at the top of the quartet, the singers intoned their music and resumed dancing, but not for long, because soon their voices were skipping under the mysterious emotional strain, soon they were sobbing again, soon the conductor stopped the music. Now the entire house stood up and stared in silence. I rose, too. I didn't understand what was going on, but I could feel the powerful currents of repressed emotion coursing through the theater.

A somber-looking man appeared onstage and announced that the artists wouldn't be able to continue and that the evening's performance was over.

"I apologize to everyone," he said, "but given today's situation, I hope you'll understand."

I didn't know it, but I'd just witnessed the end of culture in Bohemia.

I hadn't been reading the newspapers or paying attention to politics, so I didn't realize that on that day, with one decree, the Germans had closed every theater, ballet, orchestra, and movie house in the country. They had ordered all the actors, stagehands, musicians, dancers, and conductors in the Protectorate of Bohemia and Moravia to report to the factories and put their shoulders to the stalling wheel of Germany, but it was too late for the Third Reich.

MY BACTRIAN CAMEL

A few days after Hitler committed suicide in his Berlin bunker and shortly after the Red Army passed through Čáslav, I looked out of my window in the gasworks and saw a wonder no less amazing than the fact that the war was finally over. The factory stood on the edge of town, so the view from my room was of bright-green field running to the horizon.

In this field, calmly grazing on the sprouting wheat, stood a two-humped camel.

The animal population of the countryside had been decimated by the war, I hadn't seen a pig in months, dogs were a luxury, and here was this exotic animal from the deserts of Asia cropping the lime-colored wheat under my window. I threw my clothes on and sprinted outside, fearful that I was seeing a mirage, but the Bactrian camel was real. I cautiously advanced to his side. He seemed comfortable around people and went on gorging himself on the luscious wheat, so I ran off to get my buddy Karel Bochníček and a couple of other friends. They were all excited by my discovery. How did the exotic beast get there? It was absolutely incomprehensible. But there was a good reason, as we found out later.

"Let's take him to the zoo!" someone suggested.

It was a fine idea, which had only one thing wrong with it. The nearest zoo lay in Prague, some eighty kilometers away, and the country was in chaos. The trains weren't running. Red Army convoys criss-crossed the country, confiscating watches. Wehrmacht stragglers were still trying to slip through and make it back to Germany. The roads were full of people displaced by the war as the prisoners, the concentra-tion-camp survivors, the forced laborers were all heading back home on foot, on carts, in coal-burning cars, on army trucks.

The only way to get a camel to Prague was to lead him there on foot, so a camel relay was organized over the telephone. We Čáslav boys would take the camel to Kutná Hora and hand him over to the local Boy Scouts chapter, which would walk him to Kolín and so on, all the way to the pen in the zoo.

Karel, two other boys, and I tied a rope around the camel's neck and dragged him out of the wheat field, which was a big job. We discovered that it took all of us to pull the creature onto the main road and that if he saw a leafy bush, there was no stopping him. You had to wait till he slurped the foliage off a few branches, and only then could you yank him away. The animal was as strong as he was stubborn.

We had pulled the camel halfway to Kutná Hora when a long convoy of Russian trucks and tanks swung up on the horizon. When we moved to clear the road, the beast refused to budge, even when all four of us hung on the rope with all our weight.

The first Russian to reach us was an officer riding in a *gazík*, the Russian jeep. He stopped and watched for a while, so we got suitably frantic, but the camel held his ground and now the military trucks were starting to pile up behind the jeep, blaring their horns. The officer got out. I thought he would help us get the animal off the road, but he had a better idea. He pulled out his service revolver and aimed it at the camel's head.

I hadn't thought we could try any harder than we were already trying, but the funny thing about guns is that they give your energy an incredible boost. Half hysterical now, we started kicking the animal, twisting his tail, pushing and pulling him, yelling wildly, but it didn't help. The camel just leaned back and kept on chewing in the middle of the road, so Karel ran and knelt down before the Russian and begged him not to shoot. For a long while, neither the Russian nor the camel were impressed with our effort, but then, suddenly, the camel burped and a mass of green fodder flew out of him. The stream of dense and vile liquid caught me square on the head.

I stank from the horrible camel vomit for a week, but it didn't matter because the Russian officer had cracked a smile and put his gun away while the unburdened camel, too, had come back to life and let us drag him off the road.

The officer jumped back into his jeep and the Red Army convoy set into motion again and roared past us. Behind it marched a weary infantry batallion, followed by a pair of horses pulling a khaki field kitchen. I never knew that camels and horses had a problem with each other, but the moment the horses saw our camel, they panicked. They were so spooked that they jumped over the ditch and tore away down the field on the far side of the road. I can still picture in my mind the clanging field kitchen, bumping down that field, the utensils bouncing off it. The first to go was its short chimney, then the pot covers popped off, and after that everything went, all the pans and dippers and kettles and cans, strewn all over the weedy field.

We handed the camel over to the Boy Scouts in Kutná Hora, but I don't know if it made it to the Prague Zoo.

In May of 1945, the wonder of this exotic beast showing up under my window, coming out of nowhere, a symbol of peace, my two-humped dove, completely overshadowed any sense of history being made for me. But then I found out that my symbol of peace hadn't come out of nowhere.

Toward the end of the war, a small German circus had gone to Russia to entertain the depressed troops. When the Eastern Front started turning into a rout, the circus raced back to the Reich and put on shows in villages, performing for provisions. One paid with a chunk of bread or an egg or a bale of hay to see the few acrobats, the dressage of some scrawny nags, the toothless bear, the monkeys, and the two-humped ship of the Gobi desert.

The end of the war stranded the circus just outside a small Czech town not far from Čáslav. The Czechs there had been waiting for six years to take revenge on Germans, some Germans, any Germans, but they didn't dare mess with the Wehrmacht tanks and the army trucks still streaming west in long convoys. They did collect enough courage to attack an exhausted circus troupe.

They killed all the circus people and shot their bear, too. Man, woman, child, beast, they were all Germans. They slaughtered the horses and ate their meat, but in the confusion of the skirmish, the Bactrian camel got away and he kept running till the delicious spring wheat stopped him under my window.

LEDGER OF A SUMMER HOTEL

The chaos of the end of the war subsided in a few weeks, and as soon as the railroads slapped together a provisional schedule, my brothers and I headed to our summer hotel at Mácha's Lake.

Rut was a scene of desolation, its windows shattered, its doors broken, the furniture looted or busted, the walls charred by fire, piles of turds in every room. How did the possessions in which we took such pride wind up in such a state?

"May you live in interesting times," says a wise old Chinese curse, so let me show you the ledger of all the occupants of a small summer hotel in the most interesting period in Central European history.

When Rut was built, Stalin was wrestling with Trotsky on the Soviet politbureau and Hitler was still giving buffoonish speeches in beer halls. Czechoslovakia was a democratic country, so for a dozen years my parents happily ran their summer hotel for profit.

By the late thirties, Hitler had grown so strong in Germany that a local architect who had done some rebuilding work on the hotel for my mother decided to get as far away from him as he could. He was Jewish and prescient; he moved to South America.

In the fall of 1938, at the Munich Conference, Hitler took the part of Czechoslovakia where Rut stood and the borders of Germany jumped over its roof. For a while, our hotel lay in a different country.

A half year later, Hitler annexed the rest of Czechoslovakia, so once again we didn't need a passport to go to Rut, but it didn't matter. We didn't fit into the landscape anymore, and the Germans soon requisitioned the hotel. At first they ran it as a retreat for German mothers and children. Later in the war, they restricted the invitations to war widows.

By the end of the war, the soldiers of the Red Army were using Rut as their barracks. They made a bonfire in the living room, behaving inside the hotel as if they were camping outdoors.

As soon as we got the place back in the spring of 1945, my brothers immediately set out to repair it. There was an acute shortage of materials and most of the skilled craftsmen were busy elsewhere, so the project took a lot of sweat and ingenuity. I stayed with them all summer, helping however I could. I was thirteen years old and I badly wanted to have the old pension back, though I realized that it was never going to be the way it had been. Nothing was.

The Sudetenland was an odd country after the war. All the boys who had tried to stone me so dispassionately, and all the girls who had looked on, had been deported into what was left of Germany. The teacher who had tried to protect me from them had had to go, too. In fact, all the Germans were gone.

They had left the country on very short notice, so Czech opportunists were moving in to seize the houses, the farms, the furniture, the tools, and anything else the Germans had hastily abandoned. Many of the new owners were takers, looking only for a quick score and a way out. They cruised around the deserted villages, taking what they could carry. They didn't have the time to wait for any paint to dry.

My brothers and I saw the future differently. We put on one coat of paint after another. We didn't cut any corners on the family hotel.

In a couple of years, it would turn out that the opportunists had had a better read of the political situation in the country. In 1948, Rut would be "nationalized" by the new Communist government, which called our summer hotel a Recreational Center and sent in their cadres and shock troops. Because I was underage and had no other domicile, I was allowed to keep a room there till 1953. When I came of age, I lost the room, and our last tie to the family hotel was broken.

The building was later acquired by some factory, and, for decades, its employees took their vacations there, but in 1991, after the Velvet Revolution of 1989, the old two-story building was "privatized" and returned to the family again.

But I am getting far ahead of myself here.

Back in 1945, while I was fixing up Rut with my brothers, someone brought me a newspaper clipping. It described a school for war orphans that the government was setting up in the town of Poděbrady. The place was to be an all-boys' establishment, modeled on the English public schools. The students would live in dormitories, get a good academic education, learn practical skills in various shops, and develop their bodies on sports fields. The school seemed to have my name on it, so I sat down and wrote a letter that got me an invitation to an interview.

I liked the sleepy town on the river Elbe right away. Czechoslovakia had seen no battles in the war and little American bombing, so Poděbrady was untouched by the war. There was a large spa for cardiac patients who sipped their Poděbradka, the mineral water rich in iron; they circulated around parks and promenades and dozed off at open-air concerts. The town's famous son, Jiří, the King of Bohemia in the fifteenth century, sat on a bronze steed on the main square and peered down on dirty buses that belched oily smoke.

The school was housed right in the King's old castle, which over-looked the river and the bridge that spans it. I was anxious to make a good impression on the cheerful founder of the place, Mr. Jahoda, and I must have succeeded, because he invited me to come back in the fall.

When I reported there in September of 1945, I was shocked to learn how many of my new schoolmates in this institution for war orphans still had both parents. Some kids there had lost their families in the war as I had, but many of them had daddies who were ministers, diplomats, offspring of old Prague money, even high Communist functionaries.

I later learned that shortly after the liberation, when Mr. Jahoda proposed to the Ministry of Education that he set up a school for boys who were victims of the war, all the political parties lined up behind his irreproachable idea. Grants, subsidies, and donations began to pour in, and Jahoda was given a free hand in choosing his professors. It quickly became obvious that he was putting together the best school in the country, and both the new Communist elite and the old capitalist money scrambled to slip their sons in with the orphans.

Clearly, I had stumbled onto a very fine education.

HERO

The dumbest game ever invented in Poděbrady Castle was called the "cap game." The idea was to pin your cap against a wall and hold it up there for as long as you could. The only catch was that you couldn't use your hands. You had to keep the headgear on the wall with your head, shoulders, or your back, so you twisted your body around the wall and waited for everyone else to get bored with the sheer nonsense of this contest and drop out.

All it took to win the cap game was determination; it was a contest I couldn't lose.

One afternoon, I got myself into a cap game that lasted right through dinner, something that had never happened before. By then, I was only up against a slightly built boy with alert eyes, because everyone else had dropped out of the contest hours before. I'd seen this kid around and hadn't paid much attention to him, but now that I looked at him closely, I suddenly wasn't so sure I could take him. I struck up a conversation with him to size him up. He didn't sound as if he were ever going to quit, which was fine by me, because neither was I.

Our roommates came back from dinner smacking their lips. They stroked their bellies and described the heavenly delicacies we had missed. My stomach was growling, but the kid and I said we weren't hungry anyway and went on pressing our caps against the cold bricks.

The other boys ran out to play soccer in the courtyard; now we had to shrug off the sounds of pounding feet and the excited yelling below as well, which should have been sheer torture, but it wasn't. We went on talking, and it slowly dawned on me why I didn't mind missing out on the game. The kid was the best raconteur I'd ever meet in my life. He was quick-witted, sarcastic, and didn't miss a thing.

His name was Ivan Passer.

As lights-out time drew near and our shoulders grew sore, we finally negotiated to let our caps drop on the count of three. The cap game wound up a tie.

After that game, Ivan and I arranged to live in the same dorm. Soon afterward I found myself, in the dead of night, throwing a Wehrmacht dagger across the dorm at a locker. The dagger was a find from one of our nature walks and the object of this stimulating game was to sink the dagger into the wooden door of a locker. You got a point for each time the knife stuck, and you kept on going till it was deflected and dropped. The game was a lot of fun, but it could only be played late at night, after the professor with night duty had gone to sleep.

Ivan had a knack for throwing knives. He was the man to beat, and he was on a roll this particular night, racking up points and gouging the locker with each flick of his wrist. There was a line of boys behind him waiting for their turns, but everyone got so caught up in Ivan's string of perfect throws that no one was paying attention to the door.

Suddenly, Professor Krista was standing among us.

Krista was a tough teacher with a sadistic streak, so everyone dove for his bed. Ivan had been the focus of all the attention and, with the lights blazing, he never stood a chance of getting away. He was poised for another throw, too, holding the dagger by its tip near his ear and aiming it at the locker. While the others scrambled around him, he simply let his arm down. He didn't even bother hiding the knife.

Krista sauntered up to him.

"Let me see that," he said.

Ivan handed him the dagger, and Krista weighed it in his hand. "Oh, made in Germany, huh? That's nice!" He strolled to the locker and examined all the nicks and holes in it. "Oh, yes, this is nice, too! This is a thing of beauty!" He moved back to glare at Ivan, who stood there in his pajamas, barely reaching the burly professor's shoulders. "So who else has been throwing this knife with you, Passer?"

The question was purely rhetorical. Krista had seen enough to know that all of us had been involved. Ivan said nothing.

"I asked you a question, Passer!"

"Nobody," said Ivan.

The right hand of Krista shot up and caught Ivan across the face. The blow was so hard that it knocked him off his feet. I cringed just watching this. I knew how Krista hated it when people stood up to him, and Ivan should have known it, too, and if he didn't know it before, then he sure knew it now, but he certainly didn't act accordingly. The fool picked himself up off the floor and looked Krista right back in the eye.

"I am going to give you one more chance, Passer. Who else was throwing this knife?"

"Nobody," answered Ivan without missing a beat, and I realized we had a goddamn hero among us, just as Krista's left hand came out of nowhere again and knocked Ivan off his feet once more.

Ivan stood up and looked at Krista as hard as before, and now Krista, too, realized he was not going to beat anything out of him, so he turned to the rest of us.

"Okay, so let's do it the other way around then. Which one of you has been helping Mr. Passer here vandalize school property?"

A deep silence.

"Okay, fine. I see you're a bunch of heroes. Line up by the door, heroes."

This we did, hastily, and Krista marched us out into the courtyard, where he ordered us to stand at attention till "the other vandals" confessed.

We stood there shivering till dawn.

I don't think that the summer was far off at the time, but I remember being chilled to the bone and working my big toes and sniffling and watching the eastern sky turn pale and then pink and finally light blue, and freezing there in my pajamas. I wound up figuring out a few important things that night. I realized, one, that I was no hero; two, that I didn't care if I was a hero or not; and three, that the real heroes, the kind that clearly couldn't help themselves, were wonderful, even though they caused a lot of unnecessary pain around them.

Ivan came from a family that was so rich that some of the bank notes in circulation bore the signature of his grandfather. This, of course, was the worst possible background to have with the Communist revolution only a couple of years away. He was also half Jewish, so his family had just passed through hell in the war. He was very bright, but in school he always acted the consummate rebel. He disdained doing his homework, and he was very principled in breaking all the rules he could possibly think of, so he languished in endless study halls.

My friendship with Ivan has lasted all our lives. He'd later go to the same film school as I did, collaborate closely on my Czech films, and wind up in America with me, directing films like *Cutter's Way*, *Law and Disorder*, and *Stalin*. But long before that, back in the midsixties, he'd make *Intimate Lighting*, a gentle, generous, perfectly observed film that firmly belongs on my list of the ten best movies ever made.

SLAVE

While Ivan was the hero of our dorm room, Ferda was the "slave" in its pecking order. Ferda was no better or worse than anyone else, but he never stood up for himself. He was frightened of everything, and you sensed the perpetual panic in him right off.

We had some tough and scrappy schoolmates, boys who had survived the war on the streets. They read people at a glance and knew no mercy, so Ferda wound up cleaning our room, mopping the hallway, even polishing other boys' shoes. It was his job to turn out the lights at night after everyone else had gone to bed. He ran errands for the bullies. And he got pushed around for his trouble. He didn't dare to complain, never hit back, always just ate the contempt, the taunts, the slurs, the punches, the trip-ups.

The only person that Ferda ever fought in Poděbrady was his best friend, Zach. Zach was the "slave" of the boys next door, and, periodically, always late in the evening, in scenes straight out of Jack London, with sweaty audiences, shouting, excited bets that were never honored, angry tears, and blood, Ferda and Zach were forced to slug it out.

These fights began one winter night after someone had secretly borrowed the boxing gloves from the gym. Ferda and Zach were bullied into putting them on. They shared the same lot in the dorm and they had become friends, so even after they had been shoved into the mean circle of boys, they tried to go easy on each other. They pulled punches, jabbed at each other's gloves and forearms, signaled their slow-mo blows. But they couldn't maintain the pretense for long. They were goaded on by the quickened bullies, ridiculed, pushed from the back to slam into each other until, all of a sudden, they were punching for real, grimacing with hate, hitting to hurt, bloodying each other's noses, trading low blows, putting all their suppressed feelings into the ugly beating while the onlookers shrieked with animal excitement.

I didn't like to watch Ferda's unending humiliation, and yet I never stood up for him, though I held considerable authority in our room. I didn't make him clean my shoes or carry my books, but I looked on while other boys did.

One afternoon, strolling through the game room, I saw Ferda sitting in the corner, scribbling something on a sheet of paper. I wouldn't have paid any attention to him had he not looked up as I was walking by, with a look of tremendous guilt on his face. That expression stopped me cold. As I halted right above him and peered down at his face, he turned visibly pale. Now he had me thinking that he was penning some sort of a denunciation.

"What're you writing?" I asked.

"Nothing!" he whispered, stiff with panic.

"Lemme see."

"No!"

"Come on, Ferda, I'm gonna see it either way."

"Please, no! Don't do it!"

"Give it here."

By then I was sure that Ferda was ratting on someone, so I made him show me what he'd been writing. It was a letter that went something like this:

"Dearest mother, please accept my fondest greetings. Do not worry about me and please stop reproaching yourself for sending me here. I love the school, and all the boys here are really wonderful to me. I have so many friends here, more than I've ever had before, and they all like me a lot . . ."

Ferda was standing in front of me, just humming with fear of a new humiliation, but it was I who was feeling deeply humiliated now. I handed the letter back to him, and I ran.

"Sorry, Ferda," was all that I could get out.

After that, I tried to help Ferda, though I'd still only do it surreptitiously so that no one would make fun of me for it. I'd get out of bed and switch off the lights before the other boys got on Ferda to do it. I mopped the floor for him a few times, but only when it was my turn to do it anyway. I still didn't confront his bullies.

I've been sorry about it to this day.

THEATER OF THE SMITHY

As soon as I got my bearings in Poděbrady, I started looking for a way to get into theater. A couple of years had gone by, but I was still thinking back to the backstage thrills at the Operetta, and my attraction to it went beyond the erotic titillation, the music, the smell of makeup. I was drawn to its make-believe world because I instinctively felt that it showed the truth of the heart much more clearly than any sincere confessions, wise explanations, or learned analyses.

I quickly found out that the castle housed the Theater of the Smithy in the wing that had once sheltered the blacksmiths of the royal cavalry. It seated some three hundred spectators, and our school produced one play each year under its proscenium arch.

During my stay in Poděbrady, the school theater was run by Professor Sahula, the art teacher. Every year, I auditioned for the biggest roles in his productions; he cast me as the bridegroom in Gogol's *Marriage*, Harpagon in Moliere's *The Miser*, Hadrian in a comedy called *Hadrian of Roam*.

We not only acted in the plays, we also sewed the costumes, built the sets, worked as stagehands during the one-day run of each show. We would perform it for the student body on a Saturday afternoon and then again for the parents that evening. Both audiences laughed generously at all the jokes we managed to pull off and shrieked at all the mishaps we couldn't avoid. They shouted wisecracks, had a great time, and gave us standing ovations.

I liked being onstage, but I liked putting on makeup even more. I had to transform myself into old men for the roles of Harpagon and Hadrian, and I couldn't wait to get my hands on the costumes, the greasepaint, the ludicrous wigs.

I completely forgot about this thrill, but then, in 1983, I watched F. Murray Abraham transform into a very old man for *Amadeus*. It took three hours to add the three score years to his character of Salieri and the astounding metamorphosis brought back the old surge of excitement I'd once felt in the dressing room of Poděbrady Castle.

There were two other amateur theaters in Poděbrady, and they booked the Theater of the Smithy whenever the school wasn't using it, so I was always hanging around the stage. One of these groups was leftist, while the other featured the local pharmacist, butcher, and doctor in its casts, so its politics were right-of-center, but both theaters relied heavily on their prompters and I saw little difference in their performances or their choices of plays. I tried to join both of them, but basically they were not interested. I finally did manage to land a small part in a village drama put on by the leftist group. I played a kid who gets embraced by the flirtatious heroine, and now the only recollection I can pin on that experience is that, on the opening night, the aging ingenue smelled strongly of garlic.

The biggest event in the Poděbrady theater of the forties was when the bourgeois group hired a famous actress to guest-star in one of their shows. Vlasta Fabiánová was a beautiful woman in her late thirties and a famous member of the National Theater. She was lured to do her star turn in a role she had made her own in Prague so that it would be a cakewalk for her. She showed up in Poděbrady for only a single re-hearsal and frankly treated the whole thing as a payday.

I went to see both of her sold-out shows at the Royal Smithy, and what I saw shocked me. Fabiánová had all the other actors in the show so intimidated that, for the first time, the Poděbrady cast had learned all their lines by heart. Not only did you not hear the standard hissing of the prompter and the odd pauses it entailed, but the timid and frightened amateurs gave the performances of their lives, though they didn't even know it.

Fabiánová sold all her lines, punched them out for a much larger house, and constantly drew attention to herself. She looked phony and artificial, and the Poděbrady amateurs were so scared of her that they didn't dare to act at all. They simply existed in the play as if they had forgotten they were standing on a stage, as if they really lived the situations of the plot. I'd never seen anyone behave so naturally and so truthfully in a theater before. Beside the shopkeepers of Poděbrady, the star of the National Theater stuck out like a busted wire out of an umbrella.

Before that performance, I'd never have dared to question the artis-try of the acclaimed actress, but that night I realized that the critics, the popular wisdom, the whole theatrical establishment could be com-pletely wrong and that I'd better think for myself. I remember that moment, the sudden illumination of this revelation, both frightening and exhilarating.

I suppose, too, that I'd already begun to develop my civil, naturalistic sensibility. I still dislike grand manner, operatic emotions, pathos, still distrust gestures and attitudes that are larger than everyday life. I believe that if you look at it carefully, ordinary behavior packs more than enough drama.

ON THE FINS OF LOVE

It was in the Theater of the Smithy that I managed to snare my first date. The bright and witty Marta F. was one of the Poděbrady girls who went to school with us, and she had been distracting me in class for years. She had light chestnut hair, a pretty face, great legs, and a maturely shaped body. The problem was that she was constantly getting propositions from upperclassmen, and they were already shaving.

"Hey, Marta, what do you say we go for a walk?" I'd corner her in the hallway from time to time.

"With you?! Tsss!" She always turned up her nose.

But then she got cast opposite me as the ingenue in one of our school plays and, suddenly, she agreed to go out with me, though she still couldn't resist making it a dare.

"I could meet you at six-thirty," she said, knowing that the gates of our castle got locked at six o'clock. She lived at home in town, so she didn't have to worry about any curfews.

"Fine." I quickly took her up on it.

I knew of a window in one of the stairwells in the castle that opened on the ramparts and figured that I'd crawl out on the high wall and then climb down into the open courtyard below using the streetlight that jutted out of the wall. It was shaped like an old lantern and hung over the gate. Though it was late winter, the weather was unseasonably mild. The dusk was falling as I lowered myself from the ramparts onto the rod of the lantern. Just then, the light turned on in the lamp under my feet. Before I could get over the shock, the gate creaked and swept wide open beneath me. I froze. Two professors strolled out and halted on the sidewalk, their heads a couple of feet from my shoes.

"So where the fuck is the old bitch?" sighed one of them.

"Maybe she forgot again. She's really been getting senile lately, did you notice?" said the other one.

My heart sank. It was only a matter of time before they saw me, and once they realized what language I'd heard them use, I would be a tiny footnote in the school yearbook. But I was trapped and didn't even dare shift my weight. I thought out every breath I took. Time passed. A delivery truck rattled out of the back of the courtyard, heading for the square. The driver just stared straight at me, his face level with mine. He looked stunned by the strange sight of a kid crouching on top of two calmly talking gentlemen, caught in his headlights like an incubus.

He drove on, but one of the professors looked up. He squinted right up at me, so directly and so long that I prepared to jump down when, incredibly, he glanced away again and it dawned on me that the brilliance of the lamp had screened me from his view. But he must have sensed me hovering over him because his eyes floated up again. This time, he would have surely found me in the light, if the creaking gate hadn't saved me.

The professor of history stepped out. She was an older lady, and she moved with the fluttery motions of a small bird.

"I'm so sorry! I thought I'd get out of there faster," she said.

"Oh, no problem! Not at all!" the two hypocrites smiled, and the three of them finally shuffled off to the square.

It was now almost six-thirty and I was supposed to meet Marta in an old deer park on the far bank of the river, so I sprinted across the square, rounded a corner to the bridge, and barely stopped myself at the foot of it. At the center of the bridge, yapping with the pretty instructor of Czech, stood Professor Sahula.

I spun around, peeled into a doorway, and cursed my luck.

Marta was never going to give me the time of day if I stood her up, but there was no other bridge in Poděbrady, no ford, no ferry. Then I remembered the rowboats moored under the bridge. I dashed down to the water. The heavy boats lay on the cement bank, their tarred bellies up, chained and padlocked to huge iron rings.

There was only one way to get to Marta. I stripped down to my boxer shorts, shoved the clothes under the boats, and waded into the powerful current of the river. The freezing water cut my skin like razor blades. The force of the river was pulling me right under the professor's eyes, so I had to strain against it. It took me forever, but somehow, on the fins of lust and fear, I made it to the far bank. I scrambled out of the water and ran to the neglected deer park.

Through the bare trees, I saw Marta before she saw me. She was standing near the gate and eyeing the road nervously. She had on a tight skirt and a warm jacket, and she had pulled her hair back. She had dressed up for me and had never looked better.

I dragged myself toward her wearing only the pair of dripping boxer shorts. My teeth were chattering, my knees knocking, all the hair on my body bristled with the cold. She finally glanced back in my direction. For a moment, she stared at me as if I were some sort of a vision, then spun around and marched right out of the park.

"Wait, Marta! You won't believe what I've just gone through! Marta!"

She never even looked back. Not an auspicious beginning to my love life, and yet some forty years later I found a way to make use of it.

When you can connect a scene in a movie to a moment in your life, you have a chance to make it more truthful, to get it to resonate more deeply. I've never made a nakedly autobiographical film, but my films are full of indirect and oblique connections to obscure events in my life. In my 1989 film *Valmont*, there is a scene where the hero tries to impress a woman he is seducing by flopping into a lake. He pretends to drown, but the ploy doesn't work. The woman flees and afterward, when he gets back to his room, dripping water and covered with pond weeds, he finds himself face to face with another woman who may just be the love of his life, a wet and ridiculous man ringing with a distorted echo of my aborted seduction of Marta F.

GIRL ON A TRAIN

The only thing I didn't like about Poděbrady was the boring Sundays there, so I soon invented a destination that sprung me from the castle on weekends. Every Saturday, after the morning classes, I'd get on a train and head to the small house my brother Blahoslav and his wife, Boženka, were renting near Rut. I had to change trains three times, and, if everything went well, the journey took five hours, but there were times when I missed one of the connections and then it got to be midnight by the time I greeted my brother and his wife. In the morning, I'd have a long breakfast with them and stroll back to the train station so that I could make my ten o'clock curfew in Poděbrady.

I rarely missed a weekend visit, even in times of friction between my oldest brother and me. Blahoslav was fourteen years older and a teacher by profession. He naturally tried to assume a kind of parental responsibility for me after the war. I resented his attempts to supervise my upbringing. I just didn't see the point of losing a brother to gain an ersatz father, but Blahoslav felt responsible for me and kept worrying about what I'd do with my life, so he never stopped asking me if I'd decided yet what I wanted to be. I was fourteen or fifteen years old, and my future profession was the last thing on my mind. I did have my secret fantasy about the theater, of course, but I didn't dare apprise my practical brother of that. Blahoslav was relentless, however, so one day to get him off my back, I finally blurted out the first thing that popped into my mind: "I dunno, maybe I'll study chemistry or something."

That Christmas, I received about ten books on chemistry, a huge chart of the table of elements, and a biography of some famous scientist.

Blahoslav meant well, and even though his attention got to be suffocating at times, I made for his house every weekend. I must have longed to be attached to a family again, to steal the last few moments of family warmth, even while I told myself that my weekends were nothing but getaways from the castle.

The truth is that I liked even my arguments with Blahoslav.

But I also loved the railroad journeys and couldn't get enough of watching people on the trains. I'd find some drunks playing cards and watch them fight. I saw a sharp-witted old lady flip into doddering senility every time the conductor showed up because she didn't have a ticket, which she could clearly afford. I watched a pickpocket work his mark. I listened to all the different voices, shy, obsessive, drunken, self-loving, goading, shrill, musical, and I spent a lot of time studying young women. I'd try to catch their eye. I was pumping with hormones, so I'd daydream about seducing them and hope they had the sort of schedule that would put them on my train every Saturday afternoon.

One afternoon, I wound up alone in a compartment with a pretty girl in a blue-gray skirt. She had short brown hair, and she was a couple of years older than I was, probably about seventeen.

The old Czech trains had compartments with two benches facing each other and a pullout table under the window. I was sitting by the table, and the girl sat in the far corner of the compartment. If I peered into the window, I could faintly see her reflection in the dirty glass.

I was racking my brain for something witty to say when she casually got up. She opened the top part of the window and looked out at the passing fields. She stood right in front of me, leaning into the chess-board-sized table, her mound of Venus right on top of it, clearly traced in the tight skirt. I lifted my right hand and rested it on the table. She paid no attention to me, so I brushed my hand up against her skirt, as if by accident. She just stood there, so I started lightly touching her underbelly. She went on taking fresh air.

I still remember how the tight fabric gave way when I started stroking her skirt. The telegraph wires went dipping under the horizon and rising above it again, as I massaged the thick pillow of her pubic hair. I was getting extremely aroused, but she remained still and never once glanced down at me.

Maybe it was minutes or maybe hours before the train pulled up to the village station. Suddenly, she came to. She slammed the window closed, grabbed her bag, and headed for the door. I tried to catch her eye, but she wouldn't look at me. She opened the door of the compartment, and she was gone.

I slid the window down and stuck my head out in time to watch her step off the train. She never glanced in my direction. She kept her back to me as she walked along the tracks. I stared at her ass, grinding in the tight skirt. The train jerked into motion and pulled me right past her. I was just a couple of yards from her face, staring as hard as I could.

She marched on, swaying her syrupy hips under the tight blue-gray fabric, peering straight ahead, and I wondered if she was wet between those firm thighs, and I smelled my fingertips and there was the faintest scent of girl fragrance and I thought how strange everything was in life, how odd that this girl who had just shared the biggest erotic thrill of my life wouldn't even glance at me.

VÁCLAV HAVEL

One fall in Poděbrady, I was appointed an adviser to a group of young boys. They were four years younger, and I was supposed to be their older brother and their tutor. I couldn't wriggle out of the job, though playing papa was the last thing I wanted to do.

My new roommates still hated girls. Their lights-out conversations bored me to sleep. Their interests and enthusiasms got on my nerves. They seemed so naive, so needy, such little kids that I tried to spend as much time away from my dorm room as I could.

Among my charges was a roly-poly kid with an air of intelligence who struck me as being decent and polite to a fault. I figured that he'd soon end up being the "slave" of the room, but the kid turned out to be no Ferda. In fact, as time went on, I noticed that his roommates treated him with friendly respect.

His name was Václav Havel, and he must have already possessed the inner strength that he would later draw on to survive the many years in tough jails, the decades of surveillance and harassment by the Communist government, and the rigors of a democratic presidency.

One year, some booster donated a bicycle to our school, and we learned to ride it after our lessons. You got on the heavy machine in the courtyard of the castle, rode out onto the square, made a U-turn around the statue of King Jiří, and returned to the group of boys, waiting impatiently for their turn and yelling wisecracks. The whole loop came out to less than a hundred yards.

I'd never sat on a bicycle before and I almost crashed as I rounded the limestone pedestal of the King, but it was a wonderful feeling, this miracle of precarious balance and speed, and I immediately got back in line for another spin.

Soon after me, Václav Havel climbed on the bicycle, which a couple of boys held up for him. He was younger and the bicycle seemed too big for him, but the helpers shoved him forward and he managed to set the machine in motion. He wobbled across the courtyard and out the gate and on, right past the statue of King Jiří.

He didn't make the prescribed U-turn and kept pedaling furiously across the square. He was clearly riding off on the booster's bicycle, and we looked on in awe. The last I saw of Havel, he was moving quickly and unsteadily in the direction of Nymburk.

Professor Hofhans, the man in charge of the lesson, was talking to the janitor and didn't realize what was happening until someone started a mock chant that we all joined in: "HA-VEL ES-CAPED! HA-VEL ES-CAPED! HA-VEL ES-CAPED!"

Hofhans owned a motorcycle, but he was a professor, so he couldn't just jump on it and take off after the escapee. A professor had to do everything by the book, so he told us tersely to stay put and he made for the castle. He showed up some ten minutes later wearing leather pants and a leather jacket, a helmet, goggles, and gloves that reached to his elbows. He unlocked his motorcycle, rocked it off the stand, started it up, slipped the goggles over his eyes, and set out after the booster's bicycle.

By the time Hofhans caught up with him, Václav was halfway to Nymburk. The professor pulled up alongside him. "What're you doing, Havel! Stop and get off that bicycle immediately!"

"But, sir, I don't know how to turn or anything!" Havel pleaded with him. "I tried stopping a couple of times already, sir, but I can't reach the ground! What am I going to do?"

Havel's legs were too short—he was scared to turn and even more scared to crash, so he just kept going. Hofhans had to ride ahead, dismount his machine, and catch him. Modern Czech history owes him an enormous debt.

A few years later, in Prague, when our age difference no longer mattered, Václav and I became friends. Havel came from old Prague money, so after the revolution he hadn't been allowed to go to the university. He was scrambling to get a high school diploma by taking some evening classes. Still, he seemed to know everybody in the arts. We were both penning poems in those days, and Havel took me with him to visit two of the great Czech poets of this century, Vladimír Holan and Jaroslav Seifert.

Of these two awed visits, I remember the afternoon at the Holans the best.

Vladimír Holan lived with his wife and daughter on the island of Kampa, under the medieval Charles Bridge, in the heart of Prague.

"He hasn't stepped out of his apartment in years," Havel informed me on the way to his house. "He just won't set a foot out so long as other poets are sitting in jail in this country."

On a bright spring day, the raven-faced poet received us in a room with closed shutters. It was lit by a single lamp, which threw expressionistic shadows on the walls. Holan reminded me of a badger, but he was friendly and interested in what we were doing. When we got up our nerve and shyly asked him if he would read something for us, he seemed flattered. He recited his intricate, tough-minded, deeply spiritual verses plainly, without any theatricality or bombast, with a great power of suggestion.

I recalled the powerful impression the intense poet had made on me later when I read Seifert's poem in which he recapitulates the deaths of all the poets of his generation who were dear to him. Of Holan, then only recently deceased, Seifert wrote:

> In that damned bird cage of Bohemia,
> he threw his poems about with contempt,
> as if they were chunks of bloody meat.
> But the birds were afraid.

Over the years, as we periodically reminisce about the old days in Poděbrady, I've discovered that a curious fiction has lodged itself in Havel's memory. It goes back to the days when I was still his adviser.

One morning of that year, Havel got called into the principal's office.

1 Riding my favorite
Christmas gift, age three.

2 With Mother and my dog
Rek, the killer of Liliputian hens.

3 *Top* The last happy
summer at Mácha's Lake
(*from right*): Father and
myself, Mother, Uncle
Boleslav, and brother
Pavel.

4 An instrument of fate –
pension Rut, before the war.

5 *Top* The family after Father's arrest (*from left*): cousin Jaroslav, myself, Mother, brother Pavel, cousin František, and brother Blahoslav.

6 Playing a Paris alderman in *Ballad of Rags* in Prague, 1949.

7 The mandatory May Day parade of 1953 – stuck carrying the Soviet flag for the Czech TV contingent.

8 *Opposite, top* As the second assistant director on the set of *Grandpa Automobile,* 1956.

9 Alfred Radok on the set of his *Grandpa Automobile.*

10 My wedding with Jana, 1958: brother Pavel is standing on my right,
the best man Radok is second from the right and the director of *Puppies*,
Ivo Novák, is fourth from the left.

11 Pavla Martínková, the female lead in *Black Peter*. The town of Kolín is in
the background.

12   Mrs. Matoušková offering her delicious *buchty* to Vladimír Pucholt, the movie star who later escaped to Canada to become a pediatrician.

13 Playing a coin-tossing game with Ivan Passer and Vladimír Pucholt on the set of *Black Peter*.

14 Věra's and my wedding
ceremony, 1964.

15 Věra pregnant with Petr
and Matěj.

16   *Top* Directing
my ex-sister-in-law
Hana Brejchová in
Loves of a Blonde in
1965. My hand is
screening the girl
from Zruč.

17   Working the
clapper on the closed
set of the very racy
Loves of a Blonde.

18   The "blonde," Hana Brejchová, and the "blonde killer" Vladimír Pucholt.

19 *Top* Vrchlabí volunteer fireman Debelka runs the beauty pageant traffic in *Fireman's Ball*, 1966.

20 The cold gray morning after the dance in *Fireman's Ball*.

21 Tailoring a shot for *Fireman's Ball* with the cinematographer Miroslav
Ondříček and the writer Jaroslav Papoušek (*right*).

22 "Say cheese, man" (*from right*): Sidney Lumet, James Ivory, Jerzy Skolimowski, Ján Kadár, and myself during the New York Film Festival, 1964.

23 *Opposite, top* Landing in New York in 1967, with Ivan Passer and Maurice Ergas, Carlo Ponti's assistant.

24 *Opposite, below* Linnea Heacock, the girl who ran away from home in *Taking Off*, kneeling before David Gittler, the master of pauses, 1970.

25 *Top* With my "repertory actor," Vincent Schiavelli, who taught the middle-class parents how to smoke marijuana in *Taking Off*, and who later appeared in *One Flew Over the Cuckoo's Nest, Amadeus,* and *Valmont*.

26 On the set of *Taking Off:* Buck Henry (*center*) and Lynn Carlin (*right*).

"Mr. Havel," Jahoda told him stiffly. "It's been brought to my attention that you've been immoral with yourself."

To this day, Havel remains convinced that, as his adviser, I must have turned him in, but I didn't. Not only have I never informed on anybody in my life, I was being immoral with myself, too.

One night in our dorm room, I overheard Havel telling somebody what a swell place the Café Mánes in Prague was. It was a remark in passing, but I filed it away in my memory. Havel was from a rich, sophisticated family, so he knew about these things, and a little knowledge of smart cafés in Prague had always gone a long way in impressing the provincial girls. And it's often the offhanded remark, the tiny perception, the accidental gesture that changes the course of your life.

Sometime later, perhaps in 1947, I missed my Saturday train to Mácha's Lake and, on an impulse, marched down the main road to the outskirts of Poděbrady. I thought I'd try to hitch a ride somewhere. It didn't matter where.

I got lucky. The truck driver who stopped took me all the way to the center of Prague. Prague was a big city, but there were only two things there that I had any emotional connection with. One was my Bactrian camel, the other was the swell Café Mánes.

The Prague Zoo had a whole herd of Bactrian camels, and they all looked alike, so I took a streetcar back to the center of the city and started searching for Café Mánes. It proved very easy to find. The magnificent coffeehouse on the bank of the river Moldau had a clean, modern look. There were pretty waitresses, ladies in furs, little girls in white socks, and flowers on the marble-topped tables, so it truly was a swell café. I had just enough money to order a small plate of Russian eggs. They were delicious. I ate a couple of salt horns with them, as slowly as I possibly could, savoring every chunk of the peppery salami salad that the hard-boiled eggs came on. Twenty minutes later, I wiped my lips into the thick cloth napkin and headed back to Poděbrady, feeling extremely worldly.

For many weekends after that I shivered on the gravel shoulders of district roads and cursed the passing drivers. It took hours, sometimes the whole day but somehow I always made it to the marble and damask of Café Mánes for my twenty minutes of high glamour. I never went back to the zoo, never figured out anything else to do in Prague. But from then on, the city's bright lights drew me like a moth and I knew where I was headed once I finished the school in Poděbrady, understood that there was no other place for me in the world.

A MAN AT LAST

The Communists took power in Czechoslovakia in February of 1948. Stalin was consolidating his grip on all the territories that the Red Army had liberated during the war, so the Czech politicians were supervised by Soviet advisers.

In Italy, Vittorio De Sica was cutting his *Bicycle Thief.*

In Prague, the Communist minister of culture Václav Kopecký, who would cross my path several times in the coming years, roared at the Czech bourgeoisie in a speech transmitted over the national radio: "We'll cut the vein right by your balls!" He was setting the tone for the political discourse of the next forty years.

In Poděbrady, one hardly noticed that a revolution was under way. It didn't show up in the streets and I didn't own a radio, so the only thing one could point to was that the seniors in our school suddenly got Communism. They began holding passionate meetings, signing proclamations, waving placards, speaking about the end of the exploitation of man by man.

I was only a couple of years younger, but in my crowd, oddly, no one got carried away by such notions. We surveyed the theatrical enthusiasm of the older boys with a cold eye. It just didn't seem plausible that everyone would suddenly work according to his ability while earning according to his need, that the strong would suddenly be happy to stay even with the weak, that the revolution could change the very competitive nature of man.

That spring, along with every other hotel in the land, Rut was nationalized as a capitalist tool of exploitation of the proletariat. It didn't matter that we had no employees and that the place was only seasonal. I had no other address, so I was able at least temporarily to keep a room there.

When the school year ended, I headed to Rut alone. Both my brothers had settled in the area, so I wasn't going to be very far from them. I was free from their supervision, however, and I could get on with my project for the summer of 1948, which was to lose my virginity.

The first thing my brother told me when I arrived at Mácha's Lake was that our Rut had been commandeered for a two-week crash course in "socialist modeling." I couldn't believe my luck. I hurried to the building and found it crawling with young women. The catch was that, under socialism, the fashion models were picked not for their looks, but for their political maturity.

I sat in my window for hours on end anyway and watched their classes. The homely girls would do some calisthenics and then sit down to discuss Marxism-Leninism. They were groggy with boredom, so I easily engaged the prettiest of them in a staring duel. She was a short, tomboyish girl with firm thighs, short brown hair, nice skin, and an ordinary face, and she boldly stared right back at me. If I grinned at her, she'd crack a smile, so I'd mime invitations for her to come up into my room. She discreetly gestured that she'd like to, but couldn't.

She wasn't lying. The Communists were puritanical, and the girls had strict curfews. Their plump, acne-skinned instructors watched them like the spinster aunts of Sicily. I tried prowling the hallways late in the evening and early in the morning, but I never managed to exchange more than a few words with my socialist model. She was sixteen like me, came from a small town in Moravia, and hoped to go to school in Prague in a couple of years. She said that she'd love for me to show her around the area, but she just didn't see how she could slip away, even for a short walk.

The smiles and the short conversations were enough to inspire me to write a poem in which I called her my "Moravian Eyes," but before I had a chance to show it to her, the two-week course in Marxist-Leninist modeling drew to a close. On the last day of the course, I cornered one of the instructors. I was going to tell her about my lyrical feelings for Moravian Eyes because I didn't know what else to do. The instructor had a hairy upper lip and an overbite, but she was older and more experienced, so I didn't have to spell it out.

"Are you kidding me?" she teased me. "You've been sitting in that window like a lizard!"

She made fun of me, but promised to bring Moravian Eyes to the bench by the lake at eight o'clock that evening. I was supposed to play cards with some older buddies that night, so I rushed to give them my regrets.

"Sorry, guys, but I've got a date."

"No shit! Who?"

"You know that model from Moravia?"

"Maybe she'll finally make a man out of you, huh?" they kidded me. "Stranger things have happened!"

"Maybe."

I wasn't leaving anything to chance. I washed my sweatpants, my T-shirt, and my tennis shoes and got to the bench half an hour early. Eight o'clock came and went. I watched the sunset. I slapped the mosquitoes off my neck. I recalled how boldly Moravian Eyes had looked at me and couldn't imagine that she would stand me up.

It wasn't until nine o'clock that I finally saw a shape coming down the path from the hotel. The figure moved like a girl, and my heart began to race. But it was only the go-between, the instructor, descending to tell me that Moravian Eyes was sick and wouldn't be coming. I was so crushed that I didn't notice that the teacher was wearing a dress and smelling pretty with a vengeance. She was on the far side of twenty, so I saw her as an older lady; it hadn't even occurred to me that maybe she wasn't sorry that my Moravian Eyes was sick.

We started talking. It didn't take long for me to confess that I was a virgin, and, in no time after that, I no longer was one. I lost my innocence on the sandy forest floor covered with dried pine needles, with mosquitoes buzzing my ears and the teacher of socialist modeling expertly taking care of all the details. I didn't have to struggle with her bra or fumble between her thighs. I didn't get to lay with my love, my inspiration, my Moravian Eyes, but I was rather proud of myself anyway.

The following morning, while I slept late, the models packed up and left the hotel.

I was feeling very manly, but didn't know how to face either Moravian Eyes or the instructor, so I stayed in bed and listened to the footsteps in the hallway and the banging of doors. I stretched and went over all the details of the night before in my mind. At last I heard the bus pull up to the front of the building. There was a surge of excitement in the hallway and the engines roared and then the hotel grew quiet again, and my life as a man began. There was another card game that night, and I arrived early.

"So how did it go?" my friends asked me. "Did she give you any?"

"Of course."

"You're kidding! You mean you're not a virgin anymore?"

"Of course not."

"Oh yeah? With that chick from Moravia?"

"Of course," I lied, because I didn't dare tell them about the last-minute switch.

I might have never known that Moravian Eyes hadn't been sick at all if I hadn't run into her a few years later in Prague. I spotted her in a crowd of people, strolling down the street, as tanned and fit and short-haired as ever. She was now a university student and lived in Prague. She had never done any modeling, thank God, she said, because all that had just been nuts anyway. We talked, and I brought up our bench date that wasn't.

She had no idea what I was talking about.

The go-between had never told Moravian Eyes anything about the date. In fact, on that last night, the instructor never let her out of her sight. She actually made sure Moravian Eyes was in bed at curfew.

I couldn't believe that anyone would be capable of such naked perfidy, so we went to a café to go over the small print of the instructor's betrayal, and that started a fitful sequence of events that led to Moravian Eyes conceiving a baby, but I don't want to get that far ahead of myself here.

"GET LOST AND LEAVE NO TRACKS"

I returned to Poděbrady a man of the world, but I found that the whole school was tense. Several new faces had appeared on the faculty, and they were all Communists, sent in by the Party to take hold of an institution that had been patterned on the English system of capitalist education. We also got new books in our classes, new dates in history, new names in literature. The older professors struggled to orient themselves in their courses, though all the changes were quite simple: Churchill and Woodrow Wilson were out, and Stalin and Lenin were in. Ibsen and Whitman were out, and Gorky and Stalin were in. Religion and God were out, and Marxism-Leninism and Stalin were in.

That year, I was sitting next to Zbyněk Janata in class. Janata was a Poděbrady boy who didn't live in the castle with us. I liked him a lot. He was quiet and modest, and he had a sense of humor that was similar to mine, so we got along swimmingly. He later somehow checked out of my life. I am not sure why, maybe he transferred to a different school, but in any case I didn't hear about him again until 1953 when he was tried for high treason by the Stalinist courts.

As I later found out, over the intervening four or five years, Janata had become a member of an anti-Communist underground cell, organized by the Mašín brothers, who had also been our schoolmates in Poděbrady. Their father had been a general in the Czech army and the brightest hero of the war resistance, a man who remained defiant even as the Germans tortured him to death.

The Mašín brothers had clearly inherited their father's genes and, for several years, they ran a tight, effective group that committed various acts of sabotage against the Communist government. They were young and fearless and believed Radio Free Europe, so they kept waiting for the Americans to come and wipe out Communism. Meanwhile, they set fires and attacked police stations to get arms. They killed several policemen in the process.

By 1953, the Americans hadn't made any moves and the Communist State Security was starting to nose around their group, so the Mašíns decided to defect to the West. They were going to join the American army and parachute back into Czechoslovakia when the cold war finally grew hot and the country was liberated from Communism.

The Iron Curtain had come down by then, making the western borders of the country nearly impregnable, so the Mašíns decided to head to the United States through Berlin. They took Janata and two other young men with them when they crossed the border into East Germany. Things went quickly awry, but the group was armed and determined not to be taken alive. They had to shoot their way out of a provincial train station in Uckro, killing a couple of German policemen and wounding several more, so they became the targets of a massive manhunt. Some twenty-four thousand East German VOPOs and Soviet soldiers combed the countryside for them, finally pinning the group down in a small forest. The Mašíns killed two more Germans and escaped again. They doubled back and waited out the searchers, and then, five weeks later, miraculously, both of the brothers and one of their three buddies made it to Berlin.

Janata and the other friend weren't so lucky. My old schoolmate had hesitated briefly when the bullets started flying in Uckro and got caught by the furious East Germans. He was returned to Czechoslovakia and sentenced to death, so a person I'd shared a desk with was marched to the gallows and hung. His body was cremated, and his ashes were scattered over a garbage dump. But this is a flash-forward to 1953.

Back in the late forties in Poděbrady, I had to learn the hard way just how interesting the times had gotten with the revolution. It happened in the fall of 1949, and the agent of my enlightenment was Eda V.

Eda's old man was a Central Committee member of the Party and the editor of the biggest literary journal in the country, *Literární Noviny,* but Eda was clearly not going to follow in his footsteps. He was a clumsy kid of gross personal habits and very dim intellect. He couldn't keep up with the rest of the class, so we all felt that he had no business going to school with us. Nevertheless, Eda was passing all his classes. His father had made it a habit to show up in Poděbrady and visit with the Party cell at the castle. He flattered our comrade professors with the flotsam of high-level gossip, and they took care of his son.

Not all the professors liked what was going on with Eda. Some got openly sarcastic about his staggering ignorance; still, they didn't dare fail him. They extended no such mercy to other kids who deserved to flunk out, so pretty soon the glaring double standard caused all the kids in our class to hate Eda's guts.

I am not sure that the good-natured Eda ever noticed. He constantly misread what was going on around him, and we hit on the perfect way of expressing our contempt. The class took hot showers twice a week. A group of us would surround him in the large tiled hall. We waited till he soaped up his face, and then we pissed on him.

Eda stood under a stream of warm water, so he didn't feel anything. To divert him even more, we'd horse around with him. He was flattered to be the center of attention. He had a big booming laugh, and he laughed right with us, though he had no idea what was so funny. If Eda was ever happy at the castle, it was while being pissed on in the showers.

I was pissing on Eda's knee one afternoon, hooting with the crowd of boys around me, when I suddenly realized that the other kids had fallen silent. They stood stiffly staring behind my back, and I got hit by the sobering shock that grips you whenever you get yanked out of the protective anonymity of a crowd.

I shut up because now I could feel a cold draft surging over the wooden slats on the floor. The door behind my back had been thrown wide open. Standing in it, still, like a reptile, and looking straight at me was Professor Masák. He eyeballed me for a long, hard beat, and then he slammed the door and was gone.

The man was one of the new party cadres at the castle. That night, I didn't get much sleep. I was preparing my speech, which turned on the basic injustice of Eda being tugged on the coattails of his Party daddy to places he had no business being.

The following morning, I sat in my classes waiting to be called out, but no messengers showed up. A few days passed, and I started to relax again when I got word that I was to go and see the director. Mr. Jahoda waited for me behind his big desk. He looked me over in silence. He pointed at a sheet of paper on his desk. I picked it up and read a statement that had clearly been prepared for my signature: "I hereby resign from my studies . . ." I put the sheet back down.

"I can't possibly sign this, Mr. Jahoda. I don't deny that I've done a pretty terrible, pretty disgusting thing, and I accept that I should be punished for it, but I think that it should be viewed in a wider context . . ." I never even got to finish my speech. Mr. Jahoda peered at me for a moment, and then he said softly: "Let me give you some good advice, Miloš. Get lost from here and leave no tracks."

His quiet words gave me the feeling, for the second time that week, of being yanked out of a dream. It suddenly hit me that Jahoda was absolutely right: this was no boy's game anymore. Professor Masák was a Party heavy, Eda's Red papa was a heavy in Prague, and paranoia raged everywhere. Only a few months before, the boys in another dorm had set a pillow on fire while screwing around with matches. One of them grabbed it and threw it out the window. He saved the castle from a fire, but the smoldering pillow landed a few feet away from another new professor, who immediately read a vicious counterrevolutionary attack into the incident. The State Security was called in. The pillow bomb quickly snowballed into a big investigation with interrogations, depositions, background checks.

In a couple of years, the Party chairman himself would hang for being a CIA agent and for heading subversive operations that spread potato bugs and put nails in the nation's butter.

I bent down to the resignation sheet and scribbled my signature on it.

"Thank you, Mr. Jahoda."

"No need to go back to your class," he said.

"Oh. Right," I stammered.

I backed out of the office feeling light-headed and headed to my dorm room. It was deserted, and I pulled out my battered suitcase and started throwing clothes and books into it.

I'd later find out that comrade Masák had accused me of ridiculing the Communist Party by urinating on the leg of the son of one of its guiding lights.

I was packed up in ten minutes, but I had no idea where to go. Jahoda had told me to get lost without a trace, so heading to one of my brothers was out. But I didn't have anyone else in the world I could turn to. I walked out into the hallway and stood by the window, looking out, thinking, searching for some sign. All I needed was a direction, a point on the compass, but I couldn't come up with any. A kid I knew was walking down the hallway. He was supposed to be in class like everyone else, so to this day I am not sure what higher power had sent him my way. He took one glance at me and stopped.

"What's the matter?" he asked.

He happened to be one of three or four people in Poděbrady whom I could talk to about anything, so I laid it all on him. His name is Jan Klíma, he is now an esteemed surgeon in Prague, and, on that morning in 1949, he calmly considered my predicament.

"Look, just go live with my mom in Prague for a few weeks." He shrugged his shoulders. "Then something will come up." He jotted down the address and a note for me to take to his mom.

I still had all my winter things locked away in a box upstairs, but I didn't even bother searching for the janitor. I thanked Klíma, grabbed my suitcase, and hurried out of the castle. I didn't say good-bye to anyone. I made for the train station and caught the first train to Prague, as I'd known for a couple of years now that one day I would.

PART 3

PRAGUE

LOYAL COMMUNIST

For a teenager coming from a boarding school with a six o'clock curfew in a two-story town, Prague was something completely new—always lighted, always in motion, busy, exciting around the clock.

I didn't have any money, but I was happy just walking the streets in the center of the city and looking around. There were the streetcars I'd dreamed about as a boy, beautiful women, foreigners, taxis, sports stars, the sleek black limos of the politicians and the secret police, museums, classy prostitutes, cafés, and theaters.

Mrs. Klíma was clearly on the side of the angels. She took one look at Jan's note and showed me how the huge chair in the small study unfolded into a bed. I wound up sleeping on it for two years.

My second priority in Prague was to find a gymnasium where I could finish my senior year in order to go to the university; I had to go to the university so that I wouldn't be drafted for a two-year stint in the military. A few doors got slammed in my face, but then the avuncular principal of the gymnasium on Bílá Street glanced at my last report card and told me to come back in the morning.

The next day, I met Tomáš Frejka. He was the only kid sitting alone in my new class, so I was seated beside him. I'd later find out that no one wanted to share his desk with Frejka, whose father was some sort of Party official, high and obscure, though I don't think that was why the other kids shunned him. I never really understood why they didn't like him. He seemed a little odd maybe, too reserved and too unassuming, and he rarely took part in the normal give-and-take of the class, but I didn't care. I'd let him copy my answers on a test now and then, and I left him alone.

One day toward the end of the school year Frejka surprised me.

"Hey, you wanna come to my house for a party tomorrow?" he asked me out of the blue. "I've got some new records and stuff."

"Sure," I said, because I was curious to see how his family lived.

I assumed that Frejka was talking about some sort of a birthday party.

It didn't even occur to me that we would be celebrating May Day of 1950. I'd never heard of anyone celebrating state holidays in earnest before.

The Frejkas lived in a sumptuous villa whose gate was guarded by two beefy men in plainclothes. They eyed me suspiciously as I rang the bell, but Frejka came out and nodded to them, so they let me in.

Frejka had a large room of his own, a record player, and a splendid collection of American jazz records, which he was playing for three or four other boys and a couple of girls. I'd never seen any of them before. They were all seventeen or eighteen, too, but they behaved with a tongue-tied formality. A woman brought in a tray of open-faced sandwiches. I assumed she was Frejka's mother, so I introduced myself. She turned out to be the maid. I didn't know that people could still have maids after the Communist revolution, so I shut up. We looked at some books. Someone smuggled in a bottle of cheap wine. We swilled it straight from the bottle, two slugs apiece, not enough to take the starch out of the mood.

Meanwhile, the house started to ring with voices as other people arrived for the main party, to which ours was just a sideshow. A few older gentlemen in suits stopped by to greet us. More stocky young men with low foreheads milled around the hallways.

"Let's go see the movie," said Frejka.

This was another unheard-of luxury; the Frejkas had a projection room right in their house. A projectionist screened some sort of a nature film for us, only a one-reeler, but interminable. It was now past midnight, and I was dying to go home. I said my good-byes, and, waiting for my coat by the door, I watched the unbuttoned adults drift into the projection room for their own screening. A couple of the men were drunk enough to stagger. Suddenly, I recognized a face I'd seen in magazines.

The bald and meaty head belonged to Václav Kopecký, the minister of culture. He, too, was tipsy and bleary-eyed. A bodyguard handed him a large envelope. Kopecký stuffed it into his back pocket, grabbed the messenger by the shoulders, and dragged him off into the projection room with him. As I was leaving, I heard a burst of movie music and voices speaking in English.

Frejka told me later that the Party functionaries had watched Rita Hayworth in *Gilda* that night. He said the envelope for Kopecký contained the May Day speech that the hungover minister delivered to the nation the next morning.

I was never invited to the opulent villa again, but then the Frejkas probably didn't throw too many more boring parties there either. The elder Frejka was soon arrested by the State Security and, in 1952, ended up being one of the fourteen men tried in the largest show trial of the fifties. The case centered on the chairman of the party, Rudolf Slánský, who had himself set the wheels of Stalinist justice in motion. All fourteen defendants had been broken by ceaseless interrogations, weeks of no sleep, brutal threats to their families, and psychological torture. They confessed to being CIA agents and other preposterous crimes. They were all high Party officials, and they were all Jews. Their trial was broadcast on the radio and widely reported in the newspapers.

The papers also published a lot of resolutions of worker's collectives, letters from readers, and opinions by public figures. They all barked for blood.

I'd long since lost contact with Tomáš Frejka, but I'd think of him every time I glanced at the revolting newspapers. I felt sorry for the hell that Frejka was going through.

One day all the newspapers in the country published an open letter to the chairman of the State Court:

Dear Comrade,
I ask for the highest penalty for my father—the penalty of death. I've only now come to see that this creature, who cannot be called a human being because he never possessed even a shred of feeling or of human dignity, was my biggest and most inveterate enemy.

I pledge that wherever I shall work, I shall always carry on as a loyal Communist. I know that my hate for all of our enemies, and especially for those enemies who wanted to destroy our ever richer and ever more joyous life, and most of all my hate for my father, will always give me strength in my struggle for the Communist future of our people.

I ask that this letter be forwarded to my father or that I myself be allowed to tell him so.
                                        Tomáš Frejka

Three of the fourteen men on trial were sentenced to life imprisonment, the others all received the death penalty. Frejka senior was hanged shortly after the letter came out.

"DO THE STRUGGLE FOR PEACE, COMRADE FORMAN"

In the fall of 1949, I was in full command of my life. I figured that I'd graduate in a few months, go to the Academy of Dramatic Arts for four years, and become a theater director. The fact that there wasn't a play shown in the city that I wanted to see didn't give me any pause.

Czech theater had entered the dark period of socialist realism. The only productions allowed by the government were by-the-numbers pieces of agitprop. Most of them were Soviet and dealt with the joy of building dams in Siberia or reforming lumpen proletariat or surpassing the production plan. The many theaters of Prague played mostly to empty auditoriums, which didn't matter financially because they were fully subsidized by the government now.

I longed to work in the theater anyway, so I hooked up with Jaromír Tot and a few other stagestruck teenagers of Dejvice and we quickly put together an amateur production of a prewar musical. The piece was called *The Ballad in Rags*, and it was a modern update of the life of the great French poet François Villon, who, on the eve of his scheduled execution, composed a quatrain about it:

> *Frank, being a Paris boy has no truck*
> *with these folks. They don't give a fuck.*
> *Soon they'll slip a noose around your neck,*
> *which end of you is heavier to check.*

The musical had been written by Jiří Voskovec and Jan Werich, two actors who had run the most popular theater in Prague between the wars, but now their names were banned in the country because they had spent the war in capitalist New York, so we credited it to Jaroslav Ježek, who had only composed the music.

We were so young and green that nothing was a problem. We thought big and wound up with a small orchestra, massive dance numbers, and elaborate sets. Everyone did everything, and we put the production on its feet with a great burst of energy. The opening night in the auditorium of our school was a delirious success, so we started looking for a place to mount the play for a longer run.

The fact that I sought to engage one of the largest houses in Prague, the Theater of E. F. Burian, will tell you everything you need to know about our naive self-confidence. I went there on a Saturday night and saw a performance of a collective-farm play. Here and there in the huge, cavernous hall, a body broke up the linear patterns of upright seats. They belonged to retirees who hadn't come to watch, but to save money on heating their apartments. I felt sorry for the actors. There were more people on the stage than in the auditorium, so the performance was painful and rushed. At last, the heavy curtain dropped and the smattering of spectators got up quietly and shuffled to the exits. A few minutes later the building was empty, the lights turned out.

I decided that the theater was perfect for what we needed, and somehow we charmed its director into renting it to us for a string of Monday nights. Looking back now, I don't understand how we pulled it off, but we stole permission forms at the district cultural department, forged stamps and signatures, even bribed the poster man to put our ads over the notices of the National Theater.

That first Monday, the large hall nearly sold out and the people laughed uproariously. You could almost feel the sad building perk up. The word of mouth was going to be fabulous. A bunch of high school kids soon had one of the most popular shows in Prague, which shows how desperate the city was for some entertainment. We even began touring smaller cities and towns with the show, and, for the first time in my life, I was making money.

Fifteen years later, when I was casting my third film, *Loves of a Blonde*, I remembered two of the kids with whom I had worked in *The Ballad in Rags*. Ivan Kheil had become a dentist by then, and Jiří Hrubý was selling furs in the largest department store in Prague. They hadn't been onstage in all those intervening years, but they looked perfect for the roles of two middle-aged reservists on the prowl and I knew what they could do. They both took leaves of absence from their jobs and became our characters or rather got the characters in *Loves of a Blonde* to be who they were. They are simply wonderful in the film.

Of all the performances of *The Ballad in Rags*, I most clearly recall our show in the small town of Slaný. The day had the makings of a catastrophe from the start. We were amateurs, so if someone didn't feel like acting, he simply didn't bother. That afternoon, we were taking a rented bus to the theater, and four of our actors didn't show up. They were nowhere to be found. The show had to go on, so I decided to take on another role while our stagehand and someone's girlfriend bravely promised to plug up the remaining holes in the cast. It took a while to sort all this out, so we got a late start. We rehearsed the stand-ins on the bus. They gave us no reason to relax, so we spent the ride cutting lines and rewriting the show.

When we got to Slaný, we discovered that, in all the confusion, we had somehow left our main set in Prague. It didn't seem to matter anymore, so we dragged out something from the Slaný theater's shop and set it up onstage.

The show started and the curse held. Actors proceeded to enter too early and leave before they had spoken all their lines. They bumped into one another. They groped to cover up other people's early exits. And then the whole improvised set crashed down.

The Slaný audience had come to watch the energy and enthusiasm of late adolescents acting their hearts out. They sensed the disarray on the stage right off and began watching for miscues. They were soon having the time of their lives. They gasped for breath and ached from laughing at us.

Behind the shaky set, hysterical with embarrassment, we hissed and swore at each other. The intermission was a long-drawn-out string of recriminations. Finally, the band started to play the overture to the second act. The curtain hadn't gone up yet when an explosion shook the stage. It was answered by a volley of uproarious laughter from the auditorium. The spectators were dying to see whether the set had collapsed again or what other calamity had befallen us. They started clapping, then stomping their feet and chanting: "O-PEN CUR-TAIN! O-PEN CUR-TAIN! O-PEN CUR-TAIN!"

Behind the curtain, our stagehand lay unconscious on the floor in a pool of blood. He'd been trying to fix some light when he touched a naked wire. The shock had knocked him off the tall ladder and caused the pandemonium among the cheering theatergoers. The show received a long standing ovation, and the stagehand wound up in the hospital for several weeks, which only confirmed that life was a tragedy cut with a comedy.

In the late spring of 1950, while *The Ballad in Rags* kept selling out, I took my talent exams for entrance to the Prague Academy of Dramatic Arts. As part of the audition, you were given a situation, such as "fire," and you had to use the other applicants to dramatize it, so you assigned the roles of a smoker who falls asleep, the firemen playing cards in the firehouse when the alarm goes off, the mother who has to pitch her baby off the roof into a net, the heartless onlookers, and you directed your skit for the talent judges.

Stepping before the professorial panel of talent judges, I was confident and relaxed. I knew I was brimming with the rare commodity they were looking for. The chairman peered down on me as if he could sense my disposition.

"Comrade Forman, why don't you do 'the struggle for world peace' for us?" he said very casually.

I started sweating rivulets. "Oh, sure. Yes, of course," I stammered. I went back and sat down to think.

I had half an hour to prepare my presentation. I sat there as if I'd just gone through a complete frontal lobotomy. Not a brain wave stirred in my head. I don't remember what inanity I put together to illustrate the struggle for world peace. I am not sure that I could remember it the next morning. I'd completely mastered the art of forgetting by then.

The talent exam shook me up, but the sound of the previous Monday's applause was still ringing in my ears. I felt like a veteran of the theater. I'd been through bribes, con jobs, and electrocutions onstage, and the more I thought about it, the more I was sure I was bound to be accepted by the academy anyway, so I left for another wonderful summer on Mácha's Lake.

Late that summer, I received a rejection letter from the Academy of Dramatic Arts. I'd made no fallback plans, and most of the universities had closed their enrollment. I was headed for two years in the army if I didn't find something quick.

Only three university branches were still accepting applications. One was the department of mining and engineering, another the law school, the last the screenwriting program at the film academy. I applied to all three.

I took my first entrance exam at the film academy. It lasted all day, and all I remember is that I had to write some sort of composition. I sat on a very tight muscle and wrote my guts out and, that very evening, I was told I'd been accepted.

The feeling was a high so tremendous that winning an Oscar has nothing over it.

The Prague Film Academy ran on old-fashioned ideas. I was in the dramaturgical department, so in my four years of study I never got to touch a camera or talk to an actor, though I had to learn all about exposition strategies, dialogue, character, and catharsis. We penned reams of screenplays, treatments, and short stories. We also saw a lot of films and got to flog them to death, frequently deep into the night, in heated arguments with grandiose claims and cigarette butts spilling out of ashtrays.

The school gave us a chance to develop our sensibilities and personalities under the tutelage of some of the best Czech artists. Many of them were the kinds of writers, directors, and film professionals who should have been too busy with their own careers to teach, but they had been purged by the Communists and had no other way to earn a living. Looking back on my education now, I'd say the most important thing I got out of it was the same thing my teachers got out of it, a chance to weather the raging storm of Stalinism that was wreaking havoc on everyone in the country.

My youngest professor there, Milan Kundera, was only a few years older than we were, but he'd already started to make a name for himself as a poet. He was handsome, witty, and a proclaimed libertine, so he drove the female students to distraction. He taught literature at the academy, giving lucid and ironical lectures on his beloved French writers.

One day, he made us read an epistolary novel written by a man who had served Napoleon as a general in one of his Italian campaigns. It was called *Les Liaisons Dangereuses,* and, in those days when I was thinking about sex all the time anyway, its frank discussion of sexual intrigues, escapades, and power games made a huge impression on me, so huge that, some thirty years later I'd make a film of it.

But French literature also almost got me kicked out of the film academy. One day, my close friend Zdeněk Borovec and I got carried away talking about the cursed poets in class. We both greatly admired Baudelaire, Rimbaud, and Verlaine, and we knew a number of anecdotes from their lives.

A few days later, the dean of the film academy called us into his office. Miloš Kratochvíl, our professor, walked us there and listened dutifully while the dean lectured us on how important the ideological purity of his institution was to him.

"I am not going to tolerate any Francophile 'decadents' in this school!" the dean concluded his diatribe.

"Yes, you're right, Comrade Dean," Kratochvíl agreed with him. "This indeed is very serious."

"So what do you propose to do about it, comrade?!" The dean jumped on Kratochvíl. "It's your class we're talking about!"

"Well, I think the political honor of the entire class collective is on the line here," said Kratochvíl.

"This is true," said the dean. "So let's give some serious thought to expulsions, shall we?"

"Absolutely," said Kratochvíl.

Everyone knew the dean was a party hack, but Miloš Kratochvíl was a great teacher, a fine writer, and a person of surpassing kindness. He had personally been very friendly to me in the past, but when the dean dismissed us, Kratochvíl marched away from me with a curt good-bye.

I stumbled home with visions of crew cuts, uniforms, machine guns, and tanks dancing before my eyes. Several young Communists in our class adored Comrade Stalin, and I was afraid I'd just handed them a cheap chance to show they could be more Stalinist than Stalin himself.

A few days later, Kratochvíl called for a session of the "court of honor," suggesting that our class collective meet at the Vikárka restaurant of the Prague Castle. The place was known as the favorite eatery of the Communist President Antonín Zápotocký, so no one raised any objections, even though these rip-and-maul sessions normally took place right in the classroom. I didn't understand Kratochvíl's odd suggestion, but I was scared and didn't give it much thought.

That night, our class collective was shown into a private salon decked with medieval tapestries. Rococo marble clocks ticked on occasional tables with spidery legs of mahogany. A killer chandelier sparkled overhead. There were upholstered chairs, crystal decanters, damask tablecloths, silver spoons, and an imperial waiter.

My honor-court judges came mostly from working-class families. All their lives they ate their dinners without a napkin in sight. For silverware, they often made do with a tin spoon. They slurped their soup out of a deep plate, then heaped the dumplings into it and watched the porous dough sponge up the residue of the soup. That was how *I* ate at home, anyway.

At the Vikárka, we tiptoed into the salon and just sat there, intimidated by the sheer splendor of the room. No one dared say anything. There were too many forks by each plate.

The only person who remained himself was Professor Kratochvíl, who calmly proceeded to steer the collective to give Borovec and me another chance, a chance to reform, a chance to grow, a chance to overcome our decadent tendencies.

We were in and out of the Vikárka in an hour.

It wasn't until I was walking home that I realized what Professor Kratochvíl had done. With his brilliant mise-en-scène, the sweet man had completely taken all the righteous emotions away from our "judges." I hadn't known it was possible to direct life with such confidence, or even that the buttons he was pushing existed. But when I finally understood the subtlety of his methods, the delicacy of his touch seemed almost diabolical.

REACTIONARY SWINE IN ETHER

While I went to the film academy, the Communists stood the Czech economy on its head: making money was considered immoral; education and achievement counted as strikes against you. The state ran everything, paying truck drivers more than doctors or scientists. Fashion models were picked for their politics, not their looks. Artists got fat, but only if they stopped expressing themselves.

As time passes, however, the strange becomes ordinary, and then it becomes the norm. All the jobs I had in Prague in the early fifties were in some way peculiar. *The Ballad in Rags* gave me my first steady income only because the Czech theater had been decimated by the doctrine of socialist realism, but if I indirectly benefited from the revolution there, I soon paid for it on my next job.

Toward the end of my first year at the academy, a list of *brigada* openings went up on a board in the dean's office. These summer stints of drudgery on farms and in factories were supposed to bring the students closer to the heroic proletariat. They paid next to nothing, but only "antisocial elements" didn't sign up, so everyone scrambled to get a farm: The idea was at least to get a suntan out of the deal.

On the spur of the moment, I put my name down for the mines. The miners were the pride of the regime and the papers were full of apocryphal stories about them, so I was curious to see what these people, their life, and their underground world were really like.

I was sent to Rakovník, a small town where they mined *lupek,* a gray, slatelike stone that was ground up for fireclay. I was going there for a month, and I figured that for a mere four weeks I could even handle Devil's Island.

My idea of the *brigada* was that I'd go down into the pit for eight hours every day, get into wonderful shape by doing the hard work, take in the infernal sights, learn what made those people tick, come back up, put on a clean shirt, and make for some working-class bar. I'd devote my evenings to cold beer, card games, stories, and provincial girls.

I knew that I'd made a big mistake as soon as I reported to the mine.

I was shown into a large room with twenty-five soggy mattresses lying right on the filthy floor. Scattered among them were chairs, lockers, open suitcases, and boxes. Work clothes, dirty boots, and empty bottles were everywhere. The dorm for seasonal workers didn't have a shower or a bathtub; you washed in a metal sink in the hallway in the stink of the only toilet in the drafty building, which was almost always clogged up and overflowing.

At six o'clock the next morning, a group of bleary-eyed miners and I piled into a rickety cage and went down into the pit. A foreman who stank like a brewery handed me a pneumatic digger and showed me how to put it to the stone wall. It was a heavy and mean instrument, and I danced the St. Vitus' dance with it for eight hours. At the end of the shift, every muscle in my body ached and my hands shook with exhaustion. I declined overtime and went back up. I didn't care that the sun was still shining and that I was filthy. I stuffed myself with dumplings, collapsed on my mattress, and slept like a dead man until it was time to get up and go back down into the pit again.

I never even began to have a life in Rakovník. Something always hurt, and I slept away all my free time. I ventured into town only on Sunday afternoons, when I'd have a couple of beers in the smoky tavern, which seemed darker than the mine, and fall asleep right there on the table, holding my head in my palms.

I tried different jobs around the pit, but it seemed that every time I got a new assignment, I'd traded down. To get away from the pneumatic digger, I became a loader of the tiny railroad cars that carried the *lupek* to the surface. The work quickly cost me half the skin on my hands. I didn't have the calluses it took to lift the sharp-edged chunks of slate out of the streams of cold and dirty water that gurgled through all the mine shafts. I nicked and jammed my fingers and wound up with sore and bloody hands, so I volunteered for the grinder.

This roaring machine worked up on the surface, crushing the slate, so I figured that I had it made when my transfer came through. I wound up standing all day in a gigantic cloud of rough-particled dust. The visibility around the earsplitting machine was about twenty feet, and we were given no masks or filters to breathe through. The job dried out your mouth so badly that you had to wash it out before you could eat. After you blew your nose, the gray handkerchief weighed more than a pocket watch.

After their shifts, the miners would all eat something that stuck to their ribs and hit the sack, but late in the evening they revived and started drinking. Around midnight, our dorm would ring with peals of laughter, the clinking of bottles, the smacking of cards. Then the yelling and the singing would begin. It would all end with cursing and fighting and vomiting. The miners didn't quiet down until dawn, when everyone dozed off again, for an hour or two, just before the shift started.

My roommates were all going to die miners. They came from different corners of the country and were staying in Rakovník only for the summer, but it wasn't clear they had anything anywhere else that they missed. They seemed moved only by a desperate longing to raise some hell and snatch a little fun out of the endless ass-busting, but the only entertainment they ever came up with was alcohol and fights.

I kept to myself in the dorm, and no one bothered me. The miners didn't understand me, and I was afraid to get too close to them. But in the end, the summer job in Rakovník made the impression on me that it was supposed to. I hadn't really appreciated the sheer toughness of the proletarian life before. I'd had no idea.

But I was also convinced that I never wanted to get near it again and that I didn't have what it took to survive it anyway.

When I came back to Prague at the end of the summer, I moved into the Arts Academy dormitory, where I was assigned a room with a music student by the name of Ševčík, who majored in conducting and minored in percussion instruments. He was preparing for his final exams, so he conducted classical records most of the day. He'd wave and jab at the wall with the baton, while his record player blasted away. He worked up a sweat doing it, and when he was finished conducting he'd drag out his drum set and bang on it till the building's designated quiet time at ten o'clock.

I couldn't trade roommates because I was lucky to be in a two-person room. Most of the students at the academy shared their space with three or even five other people. I was always trying to write, but I couldn't get anything done in the dorm. I looked into renting a room of my own, but I quickly learned that even a tiny room in someone else's apartment was impossibly expensive.

During that year, I heard that Czech television was looking for someone who loved movies to host a new show, so I asked for an interview. I figured I'd use the position as a stepping-stone to the job of a radio sports announcer, which seemed like the best career in the world back then because sports announcers got paid a lot of money to watch soccer and hockey games, and even got to travel abroad.

Czech television was just getting started in the early fifties. There were only a few hundred TV sets in the country, and no one understood the power of the medium. I'd only seen the huge box with its tiny, round, black-and-white screen a couple of times myself before I applied.

During my job interview, I was told that the show paid only a few hundred crowns and promised no end of headaches. Other than that, it was a great part-time, entry-level position.

A week later, I had my own TV show, a sort of a Czech socialist-realist "Thursday Night at the Movies."

My show had its mandated quota of Soviet movies, but I tried to put on good Czech prewar films by directors such as Otakar Vávra and Martin Frič, who hadn't been banned after the revolution, or foreign works by "progressive" filmmakers such as the Italian Neorealists. I'd brief the audience on the background of the work or interview an actor who was in it, and then I'd roll the film. I'd end the show with a short quiz for film buffs. I'd run a clip from some classic, asking viewers to identify the film and actors in the scene. The viewers would mail their answers to me, and I'd announce the names of the winners on the next show and send them a picture book about Prague.

All the broadcasts aired live. The technology was still primitive and allowed for no taping of the shows, no prerecording, no five-second lapse. The words and images flowed straight "into the ether," and the Communist government was so terrified of this spontaneity that every word had to be cleared by the censors first. They called themselves the Press Administration, and you had to fill out a form in duplicate and enclose a detailed script of your show. The censors stamped the form and sent the original back. They kept the copy, and when you went on the air someone somewhere closely checked what you did against what had been approved.

There were, of course, no teleprompters, so everything had to be read or memorized, but if you flubbed a line or even just transposed words in a sentence, the censors reported you, and you had to answer for it to the management.

My boss at the studio was grooming me to step up to the variety show, so one day I was assigned a broadcast with a group of jugglers. I asked them to put down on paper for me anything they said during their performance.

"We just juggle is all," I was informed. "We don't say boo."

"They don't say anything," I reported to my boss.

"I don't care," said the boss. "We've got to send something upstairs."

I went back to the jugglers with the Press Administration form and told them they had to give me something. They returned the sheet to me with a big grin.

"Hey! Hoy! Wow! Wowie! Yuy! Hop, hop, hop!" was what they had put down.

"Thanks, guys," I said, and turned it in to my poker-faced boss.

A few days later the original came back with the requisite stamp.

Another time, before some Russian war movie, I was told to interview the chairman of the Czech-Soviet Friendship Society. His name was Homola, and he was a big and busy comrade, but he agreed to squeeze me into his schedule and share his thoughts. I sent him the five or six questions I was going to lay on him before the camera, asking him to send his ideas back to me. I got no reply. I called and left messages. Homola ignored them. The show was fast approaching and I didn't know what else to do, so I went to see my boss. I was secretly hoping that the censors would allow Homola, a comrade beyond suspicion, to jam on my themes. My boss, however, came up with a different solution: "Write the answers for him, then send a copy upstairs and another copy to Homola."

I composed a set of answers to my own questions and wrote an apologetic letter to Homola. I explained that though I didn't want to put any words in his mouth, I had to turn in something, so I was enclosing a few suggestions. I also made it clear that while Homola was free to rewrite my composition, he was expected to be familiar with whatever answers he wished to give because the interview was going to be live and had to be approved first.

I didn't hear back from Homola. On the day of the show, he showed up late, just before we were to go on.

"Comrade Homola, I'm sure you know those answers by heart, right?" I asked him as politely as I could.

He began stammering. "Well, I . . . The problem was . . . Well, I have the answers right here, don't I?" He pulled my letter out of his breast pocket.

"Yes, but this is supposed to be a spontaneous interview."

"Well, I'll just give you these answers." Homola blew me off.

I didn't dare warn anyone about the impending disaster. There wasn't time enough, anyway.

In the studio, with the red light on, I posed my first question to Comrade Homola pretending, as I always did, that it had just occurred to me. Before I finished "developing" the train of thought, Homola pulled my letter out of his pocket, haltingly read off a concise answer to the question, folded the sheet, and put it away again.

I didn't know what to do. I stared at him. Finally, I did what I'd always done in these interviews: I pretended that I'd just thought of another question. For a long moment, Homola fumbled with his breast pocket and then read another perfect response to my "extemporized" probe. The rest of the interview went the same way, in the pure spirit of Dada.

The next morning, I was called upstairs and yelled at by a roomful of superiors. They accused me of ridiculing the Party and its leadership and called me a "reactionary swine." They didn't fire me, however, so I kept scheming to set up an audition for sports announcer. It took over a year, but one day I was finally told to report to the Štvanice Stadium for a hockey game. As I walked there, I did voice exercises. I was greeted by the great announcer Staňo Mach, whose temperamental, rapid-fire description of the action wildly exaggerated what went on in the ice rink.

I recorded five minutes of commentary. I gave it everything I had, but I never heard from the sports desk again.

PART 4

APPRENTICESHIP

DIRECTOR LAUGHS

In the early fifties, the Party aestheticians wrestled with an ulcerative problem. With Communism and its perfect society looming, where, they asked, will our writers get their dramatic conflicts? Under capitalism, with its unceasing struggle between good and bad, writers had it easy, but now the free ride was over.

Many a literary symposium got nowhere with this thorny dilemma. Finally, Comrade Zhdanov, one of the Party's foremost aesthetic philosophers, came up with a solution. The socialist realists, he decreed, would henceforth write about the conflict between good and better.

I undertook to implement Zhdanov's maxim by writing a comedy called *Leave It Up to Me*. The idea for the plot wasn't mine, but it had to do with a very fervent comrade who takes on too many responsibilities in his zeal to do good works for the Party. He is all heart, but he simply can't physically handle all the jobs and positions that he volunteers for, which leads to sundry comic predicaments and disasters. In the end the comrade learns from his mistakes and scales his zeal down to the disappointingly human level of his energy.

I wouldn't want to reread the screenplay now, but I am glad I wrote it because it gave me a chance to work with Martin Frič.

It all started when I met Jana Nový, the daughter of the most suave leading man in the history of the Czech cinema. The way Oldřich Nový spun the flaps of a swallowtail coat simply floored my mother's and grandmother's generations, so I was curious to see what he was like in person and Jana introduced me to her family.

Mr. Nový proved to be a polite, reserved gentleman, but his debonair wife decided that I was to become her son-in-law. It didn't faze her in the least that Jana and I were just good friends. As part of her grooming me for the position, she took me to see the legendary director Martin Frič. On the way, she mentioned that she had an idea for a fabulous screenplay.

Martin Frič had started his long career between the wars. He shot some wonderful films that made no money and then made money with some commercial trash, all the while downing awe-inspiring amounts of booze. Through the war, Frič kept drinking and making movies. When the war ended, the regime changed again, but Frič stayed on in the director's chair. When he was shooting, the first order of business for his assistant was to stop at the liquor store. The normal purchase ran to four bottles of red wine, a case of beer, and two bottles of vodka.

Frič dispensed drinks to anyone who showed up on the set, and he drank what he didn't give away. You couldn't tell if Frič was getting drunk or not, but at about three o'clock, he'd usually make his first mistake of the day. Sometimes he'd forget to say "Cut," and the actors would run out of lines and have to improvise nonsense till he realized what had happened. He'd then get up and slap his hands.

"Good night, everybody," he'd say.

His crews loved him because he always knew what he wanted, so they would get home early from the set and the pictures were always on schedule.

Then came the revolution and everything changed: the liquor, the liquor store, the assistant, the industry brass, but somehow Frič hung on, though he couldn't drink anymore. His doctors had warned him that even a single drink might very well kill him, and his health had been deteriorating so fast that he listened.

By 1954, when I met him, Frič had made more than sixty films under three completely different governments, and as always he was looking for something new to work on, which was where I came in. As a young man from the academy, I had the know-how to put Mrs. Nový's story idea on paper.

Frič talked to me for a few minutes about the movies I liked.

"All right," he said suddenly, "so you'd like to write this script?"

"Oh, yes! Yes!" I said.

"Okay, so can you come by Monday morning?"

"Of course."

"If you could maybe try to write the opening scene by then, it would give us something to talk about."

On Monday morning, with the first scene in my notebook, I took a streetcar to the outskirts of Prague. Frič had a large villa in a stand of tall pines where he lived alone.

Our collaboration was strangely detached and rather mysterious to me. Every morning I'd read to Frič what I had written the day before, which usually amounted to a scene. He would listen to me without saying a word. I'd finish reading and shut the notebook. Frič made no comments, offered no suggestions. He sat there as if his mind were somewhere else.

"So what are we going to have next?" he'd finally ask.

I told him what I thought I'd write in the afternoon. Frič heard me out, again offering no ideas or criticism. "Don't make it too long," is all he would ever tell me. I'd go off and write another scene, trying to keep it as short as I could.

Our working mornings quickly acquired their routines and rhythms. Frič always welcomed me with the same question: "What would you like to drink, Miloš?" If I said I wanted a soda, Frič went and got it, but if I asked for a beer, he would send me for it myself. The big refrigerator in his kitchen was always nearly empty. I never saw any food there, but the largest shelf supported a spectacular bottle of French cognac. The image was pretty arresting, and I wondered about it every time I opened the refrigerator. We didn't talk about personal things, but I finally asked him anyway.

"Why do you keep that bottle of cognac, Mr. Frič?"

Frič knew that everyone knew that he wasn't supposed to drink, and he shrugged his shoulders. "One day I won't give a damn about anything anymore," he said matter-of-factly, "so I'm just going to pour me a big shot of wonderful cognac."

I just hoped it wouldn't be my screenplay that would drive him to uncork that bottle. Our script was done in three weeks, and when I finished it Frič seemed satisfied. Mrs. Nový got the credit as my coauthor, though she hadn't even bothered to read the thing as far as I could tell. I didn't care because I was paid 3,000 crowns when the project was approved for production, which was more money than I'd ever had to my name before.

I didn't hold on to it for long.

A few months earlier, I'd visited Moravian Eyes in the small town near the Beskydy Mountains where she lived. When I ran into her on the street in Prague, she'd given me her address, but when I showed up unannounced at her house, she wasn't home. Her mother told me to go look for her along the shore of a nearby river. It was a hot summer day, and I spotted her lying on a blanket, alone, sunning herself. I laid down beside her and spent the afternoon trying to charm her.

We didn't have tons of things in common, but I managed to talk her into taking a walk through the forest with me. I think she may have been intrigued by the same sense of a missed connection, of what might have been, of a chance to go back and fix the past, because she let me seduce her. I was no longer a virgin, but I might as well have been, that's how quick it all was, a matter of seconds. I walked her home, got on the train to Prague, and didn't see her again until the end of that summer.

"I'm pregnant," Moravian Eyes announced the next time I saw her.

"Oh, God."

"It's your baby because it couldn't be anybody else's," she said.

I tried to sit her down to talk it over, but she had everything figured out. She was getting an abortion. She had a friend who knew a doctor who could take care of it. The only problem was that it cost a lot of money.

I was only too glad to hand over the money I'd just made on *Leave It Up to Me*. I was grateful that she had been so independent and taken care of business so promptly. In those days, if you were single, every official abortion had to be approved by your street committee, which was invariably a nest of boot-tough lady comrades who had no patience for immoral behavior. They were only too eager to see to it that young people bore the consequences of their lewdness.

Moravian Eyes reported to me later that the pregnancy had been terminated, that everything had gone well, and that she never wanted to see me again.

By then Frič had begun shooting my script with Oldřich Nový in the lead. Sometimes I'd drop in on the set because I was curious about how movies were made. It always surprised me how matter-of-factly and smoothly everything ran. The film crew set up the camera, lighted the set, and called the actors. Frič looked on while the actors did two or three takes, and then everyone moved on to the next shot. Hardly a word was said.

The Barrandov Studio pros had no illusions about the movie, so they kept everything simple. It was just another job, but it beat documenting the heroism of our workers in a steel mill somewhere.

One evening I went to watch the dailies. I expected to see the same silent, tough-minded professionalism, and I got the surprise of my filmmaking life. Frič laughed so hard at every take that he soon had the hiccups. I barely recognized the man. I'd gotten used to a reserved old gentleman who wasted not a word, and here he was almost falling out of his chair. I just couldn't believe it.

I waited to see what the problem was with the old man. Everyone around him just sat there and peered at the screen, but Frič kept slapping his thighs and gasping for breath. He seemed so alone in the detached crowd of his crew that his behavior bordered on madness, and suddenly I didn't like those old-pro, seen-it-all mugs around me. I'd grown fond of the old man, and it touched me that he was so intensely behind what he was working on, that he was able to enjoy it so much.

Now that I've been through the whole grinding process myself, I am even more impressed by Frič's laughter in the screening room that evening. It also helps me to understand how he could have made more than seventy films in his life, an astonishing number, and he probably still had a couple more in him when he died. He was still going strong, still looking for new material, still directing when the Soviets invaded the country on August 21, 1968. The next morning, as the Red Army tanks rumbled through the streets of Prague, Frič was found dead in his villa. On a table stood a half-empty bottle of cognac and a snifter.

MESSY LIFE

In 1955 I was working as the second directorial assistant to Alfred Radok, who was to become my mentor for several years, on a film called *Grandpa Automobile.* I haven't met too many geniuses in my life. Our language is driven by salesmen rather than poets, so the term has been weakened by their inflation of words, but I am convinced that Radok was an authentic genius, though most of the evidence was lost in the ephemeral works of Czech theater. He was only allowed to make a handful of movies in his life, but his first film, *Distant Journey,* remains one of the undiscovered classics of the world cinema.

Radok was a survivor of the German concentration camps, and *Distant Journey,* which he shot in 1949, is pulsing with his war memories. It deals with the fate of the Jews in the war, combining documentary footage from Nazi propaganda films with several stories of concentration camps inspired by historical events, such as the infiltration of Maidanek by the Polish Resistance, and the female orchestra of Theresienstadt. The film dramatized how people defied transport to death camps by committing suicide, what the end of the war in a depopulated camp was like, and other horrors of interesting times. This work of extreme, feverish images and brilliant formal ideas alarmed Party critics in Czechoslovakia so much that they banned it for twenty years, though Radok was allowed to work in the theater.

I first met the man while I was still at the academy. I'd approached him with a screenplay idea, but nothing came of it, except that Radok remembered me, and, in 1955, when he needed help with a script, he called me. He said that the screenwriting credit had already been signed away to the big-name author whose book the screenplay was based on, but if I rewrote the script with him, he would give me the position of second assistant director.

I grabbed the offer, and Radok and I started working on *Grandpa Automobile,* a comedy about the first turn-of-the-century car races. Its fantasy and playfulness remind me of the Hollywood motion picture *Those Magnificent Men in Their Flying Machines,* which came later.

Radok must have appreciated my anonymous contribution to the final script, because one morning in Prague's Stromovka Park he handed the set over to me. I was to direct a scene that reproduced an old movie-journal report on the sighting of a fantastical six-seated tricycle in early-twentieth-century Prague. The machine was about ten feet high and it had caused a near riot in the park, so I had a mass of extras in period costumes to play with. For the first time in my life, swelling with self-importance, I took charge of a movie set. The skeptical attention of the veteran crew only egged me on to show them I could handle the job.

I tested the crew that rode the contraption and saw that they could maneuver it with casual elegance, so I decided where the camera would go, deployed the extras to create a Sunday in the park, took a long look through the camera lens, stepped back, and gave the order that set it all in motion. The six riders leaned into their pedals, and the gentlemen in top hats, the ladies with parasols, and the urchins in rags all surged toward them in amazement. I looked on, and everyone had done what I'd told him to do, but something seemed off.

I wasn't sure what it was, so I ordered another take. It took a while to get everyone back to his original spot. I spent the time trying to picture the scene speeded up with the jerky motions of the old films that would be added to my shot later, but that didn't get me anywhere either.

I watched the second take as intently as I could and got the same sense of something not being quite right, so I requested still another take.

"It looked pretty good to me," grumbled the veteran cameraman.

"Yeah, sure did," agreed a gruff chorus of old-pro voices around him.

The setup was fairly laborious, and they were afraid they had a novice director on their hands who was going to drag them along on a chase of impossible perfection. They sensed that I didn't know exactly what it was I was after.

"I'd like to shoot it again, please," I insisted.

Grudgingly, they obliged me, but they took their sweet time chasing all the extras back to their starting positions. Finally, everyone was ready for another take, so I quickly set the scene in motion, but as the extras swarmed to the odd machine, some guy suddenly had had enough of this filmmaking nonsense. He spun around and walked away from the tricyclists, passing directly in front of the camera, probably going for a beer.

"Cut!" I yelled. Now I knew precisely what it was that I hadn't liked. The scene as I'd directed it was too perfect, too conceptual, too theoretical: in all the movie journals I'd ever seen, there were always folks strolling right past the main attraction, no matter how shocking or titillating it was.

I ordered one more take, but now I planted a few alienated citizens around the park and ordered them to stroll away from the knot of commotion. They did, and they gave my tidy scene the messy life that had been missing from it.

It was a brief moment, a tiny perception, and a massive revelation for me. It showed that the life on the screen is made truer by those who deny its logic.

SO GODDAMN YOUNG

When you direct a movie, you have to hold the whole film in your head so that in the end all those hundreds of tiny bits of film can hang together as a whole. It's as if you were trying to balance a house of cards on your palms for three months, and it takes immense concentration. When I shoot now, my life stops. I could never manage a love affair while directing a film.

But *Grandpa Automobile* was Radok's house of cards, and I was very much his lowly assistant. I had to put in hard fourteen- and sixteen-hour days, but I didn't have to take the job home with me at night and I packed the energy of a healthy twenty-three-year-old, so I still managed to have my heart crushed by a real, honest-to-goodness, flesh-and-blood French girl.

It's now difficult to imagine how cut off from the world Czechoslovakia was in the fifties. Only a few sports stars and politicians got to go to the West, and very few foreigners came to Prague. Our script called for several foreigners in the cast, and when we started shooting, suddenly, a bunch of Frenchmen appeared among us. Their arrival had the feel of an invasion of extraterrestrials.

I tried not to gawk at them, but I immediately took note of a fragile-looking girl with large green eyes and long black hair. She was beautiful, and she boldly returned my smiles. Her name was Sophie Sell, and I soon found out that she didn't work on the film. She had come to Prague with her film-star parents, Raymond Bussières and Annette Poivre, our principal actors, who had also brought a grandma with them for their working vacation in Czechoslovakia.

Sophie and I started taking long walks together. We had a great time just trying to communicate simple things. We both spoke just a few words of English, so I tried my twenty lessons of French on her and Sophie worked her twenty words of Czech on me. She was twenty-one and acted her age when we were alone, but after we became intimate, she insisted on meeting me only secretly. I didn't understand why Sophie was so nervous about people seeing us together and she never gave me an explanation that made any sense, but I didn't push her. Her grandmother liked me, so she helped us steal some time together, and I gradually realized that I was falling in love with Sophie.

One evening, we had a late date at my brother Pavel's painting studio. Sophie was going to sneak out of the hotel after her parents had gone to sleep, but she was late. I'd been waiting for her for over an hour when her grandmother rushed in. She was very upset.

It took me a while to understand what the old lady had come to tell me: I was never to see Sophie again. I couldn't exactly understand why because the only reason Grandma gave me was that her father had found out about us.

"Yes, all right, but what's wrong with that?" I asked.

My French was so terrible, the old woman never understood enough to give me an answer that made any sense to me.

After that nocturnal visit by Grandma, I hardly ever saw Sophie on the set. When she came in, her father kept his eye on her even while he was in a shot. She avoided me when he was looking, but she gave me long, soulful looks behind his back.

Finally, one afternoon, I managed to snatch a moment with her.

"What is the matter with your father, for God's sake!" I demanded.

Sophie looked at me with those huge eyes, and then she began to explain, very slowly, so that I'd understand.

"My father loves me."

"So what, Sophie?!"

"He is not my father. He is not my blood."

Bussières had married Sophie's mother when Sophie was a girl, and lately he had gotten incredibly possessive about her. When he found out that she was in love with me, he threatened to walk out on the movie. I was shocked by the news. Sophie had tears in her eyes and had to run off again.

We never had another moment together. I got scared and stopped pursuing her. I imagined what would happen if Bussières really quit the film and *Grandpa Automobile* never got finished on my account. It was one of the biggest Czech productions of the decade; I'd never work in the movies again. And I was too much of a coward to risk that.

When Bussières and his wife finished shooting all their scenes, they prepared to drive back to Paris. Radok and several other people went to see them off from the Hotel Ambassador. It was easy for me to tag along with the production group, so I was able to say a strained good-bye to Sophie. I found that I couldn't handle my emotions. When the grandmother and Sophie started climbing into the backseat of the car, I had to walk away quickly. Tears the size of jelly beans rolled out of my eyes. It took a stiff drink to get my composure back.

I wrote Sophie several letters, and she wrote back to me a couple of times. Then her letters stopped. I finally got someone to help me write a polite letter to her grandmother, asking what had happened to Sophie.

Sophie had gotten married. She had met a Moroccan banker and was living in North Africa. A few years later I heard that Sophie had had a terrible accident. She was pushing a Jaguar to its limits somewhere on the Riviera when she skidded off the road. She very nearly killed herself. She had to have a number of operations and wound up staying in the hospital for months.

In 1963, when my *Black Peter* began to play the film festivals, I finally got a chance to go to Paris. I tracked down the grandmother, and she told me I was in luck. Sophie just happened to be in town.

We had a very touching dinner together. Sophie was still only in her late twenties. She hadn't changed much. She was still very beautiful, but I could sense the terrible accident in her. There was a beat of hesitation at times, an odd movement, a deeper perspective on things, a certain aura around her. It all made her seem more fragile than ever.

We drank a lot of wine. We were both thinking how different our lives might have been if one or two things had not happened the way they did, but we didn't talk about it. Then, out of the blue, Sophie told me about her car accident.

"I was so bored. You can't begin to imagine what the life of a rich banker's wife in Morocco is like," she said. Her big green eyes were brimming with tears. "And I'm still so goddamn young."

We both were.

PUPPIES

The woman who replaced Sophie in my heart would become my wife, and I met her in 1956 through an old screenplay called *Puppies*, which I had written back in 1954 as my graduation thesis at the film academy.

Professor Kratochvíl liked the script so much that he took it to Barrandov Studios, where he ushered it through various committees for two years. Finally, in 1956, after *Grandpa Automobile* wrapped, one of the production teams at Barrandov asked me to come and talk to them about *Puppies*, so I introduced myself to Jiří Šebor of the Šebor-Bor film group.

I liked him immediately. Šebor was a tall, athletic man in his forties, an old Communist, but he had an air of common decency about him. He'd also lived in England during the war, so he had an experience of the wider world, which was then fairly rare.

"Who do you think should direct your screenplay?" Šebor asked me the first time I met him. I would have, of course, ideally wanted to direct the screenplay myself, but there was absolutely no chance of this, and we both knew it.

"Ivo Novák," I said, because I thought this young director who'd had some bad luck would let me keep a hand in the project.

"I'll look into it," said Šebor.

In the end, Novák directed the film, and I stayed at his elbow through the whole production. I wound up with the credits of screenwriter and assistant director, so *Puppies* is the first film for which I can take some responsibility.

The story came straight out of the problems of my everyday life. The young hero is dating a girl whom the government has just assigned to a dreadful job in the provinces, so she needs to get married to stay in

Prague. Her city boyfriend is willing to help, but he's still living with his parents and they don't like the girl. He decides to marry her anyway. The wedding is a secret, on-the-run affair. The couple has nowhere to spend their wedding night, so the hero smuggles his new wife into his room, where his parents discover her, and so on, in the rhythms of a situation comedy.

Puppies would be released in 1957, the year the Russians shot up their first *Sputnik*, but it changed my life a long time before that. Ivo Novák and I were still in preproduction when a couple stepped out of the lovely Art Nouveau Café Slavia on the banks of the Moldau. I was standing by its entrance with a group of buddies, and we all shut up and stared at the woman. She looked just like a box of nougats. She was quite young, but exquisite. I realized with a start that the guy she was with was an actor I knew, so I quickly struck up a conversation with him. He didn't introduce me to the young lady and she didn't say anything, so all I could do was stretch the banal conversation and let my eyes stray to her now and then. The more I looked, the more I liked what I saw, but the guy soon led her away.

"Who the hell was that?" I asked my friends while we watched the stir she created on the sidewalk.

"That's Jana Brejchová," someone said.

They didn't know much about this Brejchová. They thought maybe she'd just been in some movie, still playing some teenager, but Jana had, in fact, completed a couple of movies by then.

"I saw somebody yesterday we ought to look at," I told Ivo Novák first thing the next morning, because we were still casting the film at the time.

I loved the audition Jana Brejchová gave, though I'd probably have been smitten if I saw her feed the grinder in a *lupek* mine. I sat there and smiled. When she finished, I followed her into the hallway and asked if we could have dinner sometime.

"Sometime maybe yes," she said.

Jana was simply too beautiful to play the heroine in our pedestrian film, but she got the role of the girlfriend. She seemed very real on the screen, and not just to my love-struck eyes, because she went on to become the best leading lady of her generation by far.

We had our dinner and we began a courtship, and I don't know if it was art imitating life or life imitating art, but like the lovers in *Puppies* we had nowhere to go. I was making money now and renting a room in the apartment of a tailor in Skořepka Street, but like all the other landlords in Prague, he had a no-visitors rule. Naturally, I tried to smuggle Jana into my room anyway. We waited until after the tailor's bedtime, then levitated into the apartment, or so we thought. As soon as we started undressing, the tailor was banging on my door. "That young lady has to go away! That young lady has to go away! That young lady has to go away!" he kept repeating as if his brain were stuck on a single wave.

Jana rented a no-visitors no-exceptions room from an old lady in Jesenius Street, but at least the old woman was hard of hearing and the room was on the first floor, which gave us something to work with. Around one o'clock every night, I'd start pacing the sidewalks under Jana's room. The house stood across the street from a small park, which helped me stay inconspicuous. I could whistle at the bushes and pretend to be walking an imaginary dog. Once the old lady was safely asleep, Jana quietly opened her window.

That window was so high that I was never sure if I'd make it in. Somehow, I always managed to climb up, but you could read the frantic kicking of my feet on the wall. I put scars into the gray mortar and scuffed up the tips of my shoes. I had to move fast because people jump to conclusions when they see a pair of feet dangling out of a window in the middle of the night.

Jana and I would get an hour or two of sleep, with an alarm clock under the pillow. It was set for five o'clock—the landlady was old and didn't need much sleep anymore. I also wanted to be out the window before the sidewalk below came to life, because I couldn't afford to be mistaken for a robber. After the night in Jana's arms, I didn't have the energy to run away from a bank clerk.

This makes for romantic memories, but at the time it was a profound drag, though later, in *Loves of a Blonde,* I constructed a scene out of the experience.

A few months went by and *Puppies* and another film with Jana, *Wolf Trap,* were released. She started getting stacks of letters from adoring fans. In cafés, mothers pushed their effeminate sons before her and made them stammer their names. A well-dressed gentleman offered to pay a lot of money for her underwear, as long as it wasn't clean. She still couldn't take her boyfriend into her room, however, so, again like the young couple in *Puppies,* we decided to get married. We would then be able to rent a room for two.

We wanted to spend at least one luxurious night together, so we decided to splurge on a one-night honeymoon in the most expensive hotel in Prague. No one in the country would take more money from us than the Hotel International, so we booked its presidential suite for an even 3,000 crowns a night, a sum that lingers in memory because at the time the average salary in Czechoslovakia ran to about 2,000 a month. The building in the shape of a wedding cake was a gem of Stalinist high-rise architecture and featured waiters in black tie, but in the morning Jana saw a massive bedbug crawling over the sheets.

I speared him on a pin, and we lingered over the sumptuous breakfast. We'd paid all this money and didn't feel like going anywhere, bedbugs or no bedbugs, but soon it got to be check-out time anyway.

On the way out, we stopped at reception. "Excuse me," I asked the officious clerk, "who had the presidential suite before us?"

He knew the answer right off. The hotel was brand-new, and, before us, there had only been two guests unbalanced enough to dish out three grand a night: some dignitary from Asia and the Soviet minister of communications.

"Well, one of those two parties has left something behind," I said, and set the pin with the bedbug on his counter.

The clerk shrugged his shoulders and went back to his paperwork.

DERANGED LANDLADY

When Jana and I finally got a room of our own, we were giddy with happiness. It was only four walls in somebody else's apartment, but now we could stay in bed together all day if we wanted. We could even hang up a few pictures.

We rented a furnished room from the Placek family. It had belonged to their only daughter, but she had just married a gym teacher, and they didn't need the space.

The Placeks went to bed early, usually no later than nine o'clock, which was not uncommon in the city that rolled up its sidewalks long before midnight, while Jana and I rarely got home before ten. All the lights in the house would be out, all the doors closed. We'd flip on the switch in the hallway, tiptoe into our room, and not dare to turn on the radio.

In that house, if Jana turned a page too abruptly, I jumped at the sound.

One night, we came home and all the lights were on, all the doors thrown open, but there was no one around. We'd never seen the house like this, but it didn't seem as if it had been robbed. The rooms hadn't been ransacked, the beds were all neatly made, so we put it down to some family celebration and went to bed. I'd just drifted off to sleep when doors started banging all through the house. Several people had come into the living room, and some woman was laughing hysterically in the kitchen.

"Sounds like they really tied one on," I said to Jana.

"Good for them," said Jana.

The woman kept laughing and laughing, just hiccuping for air.

"That can't be the landlady, could it?" I asked.

"I think so."

Slowly, we realized that no one else was laughing with her.

"Jesus, is she going to be okay?" said Jana.

"I don't know. This is so odd," I said.

As we went on listening, mesmerized by this relentless laughter, the lonely sound of it got weirder and weirder.

"Miloš, she's not laughing." Jana suddenly gripped me. "She's crying!"

Jana was right. I'd never noticed before how indistinguishable the two choking, air-sucking sounds are. Some horrible tragedy had happened. We lay there for several more hours, now unable to sleep, while the sounds of grief drifted in and out. At one point, Mrs. Placek stepped out into the hallway. Someone was trying to comfort her, but she was inconsolable. We could hear her fight for breath, breaking into crying jags as she spoke.

"Oh, she was sitting there just looking at me . . . She seemed so alive . . . And that wedding dress . . . Oh, my little doll, oh, my baby . . . Just like she was going to stand up and say, Hi, Mama . . ."

The facts came later. Mrs. Placek was talking about her daughter whose room we were renting. The young woman's marriage to the gym teacher had fallen apart sometime before. The gym teacher had a girlfriend, and he had just about moved out of their apartment, but once a week he would still show up for dinner, which was a long-standing family tradition, and act out a happy marriage for his in-laws.

This went on for some time, but lately the gym teacher had begun to tire of the charade. With her tenuous hold on him slipping, the daughter probably resolved to make a final, drastic play on his sense of guilt. She put on her wedding dress and set a chair opposite the front door. When she saw the gym teacher coming from the window, she turned on the gas and composed herself perfectly on the chair, figuring that her estranged husband would be upstairs in a couple of minutes, save her, come to his senses, and "marry" her again.

The gym teacher walked into the building and started trudging up the stairs. Evidently, he dreaded the dinner, the smiles, the small talk, the hypocrisy. He had been in turmoil over the situation for weeks now, and, on that day, a few steps away from the door, he finally decided that he couldn't go on with the lie anymore. For the first time, he found the strength to turn around, run down the stairs, and walk away. He was through with the marriage, the wife, and her whole family.

The Placeks showed up only minutes later. They were on time for the weekly dinner, but when they rang the doorbell there was no answer. They banged on the door and got no response. Then they smelled the gas. They called the landlord, who had to break down the door. There, sitting on the chair in her wedding dress, her eyes wide open staring right at them, was their daughter. She was dead.

All these circumstances came to light only after our life in the Placeks' house had become a nightmare. One morning not long after the tragedy, I swung open our door and it hit something very hard. I pulled it back and saw Mrs. Placek lying on the floor beside an overturned chair.

"Oh, my God! I'm sorry, Mrs. Placek!" I rushed to pick her up, but the landlady gave me a look of utter incomprehension, tore herself out of my arms, and skittered off into the kitchen. It was a very strange reaction, as if she were a little out of her mind. I lifted the chair, which belonged in the dining room, stood it by the wall, and went on to the bathroom.

On the way back, the chair was gone.

Jana was just getting up, and she'd heard the commotion in the hallway. "What was that?"

"I don't know. It was really odd. It was almost like the old lady's been listening behind the door or something."

After that we could peek out the keyhole at any time and nearly always see Mrs. Placek sitting outside our room on the chair, her eyes closed, her head cocked slightly to the side. We never heard her approach, but she'd sit there for hours on end. If we opened the door, she'd look away, grab the chair, and quickly walk off. She didn't seem in the least embarrassed, but we were.

I think that Mrs. Placek had become unbalanced by her grief and was using the noises we made in the room to bring her daughter back to life. She heard us moving around, listened to Jana's muffled voice, and thought that it was her daughter fussing in her room.

Our life in the grieving house became impossible. The landlady was lurking behind our door at all hours of the day and night. We lost all privacy. Raising your voice in an argument was out of the question. Stepping out of the room became a skit. I'd grab the towel, get behind the door, raise my voice, and say to Jana, "Where is the towel? Did you see the towel? I wanna go wash off."

Sometimes this wasn't enough to send the woman away; then I'd have to pump the door handle a few times. That would tear the landlady out of her deranged trance, and she'd hurry away, but we didn't dare step out of the room without looking through the keyhole first.

And minutes after Jana or I returned, Mrs. Placek would be back in the hallway, leaning forward on her chair, listening with her head cocked, her eyes closed.

We had to get out of there.

Meanwhile, Jana had made *Wolf Trap,* and it became a huge success. After it won a prize at the Venice Film Festival, Jana had to give a press conference there. The Western journalists grilled her on what her life was like. They wanted to know all about this beautiful oxymoron, this socialist film star. Did she have domestic help? How many rooms were there in her villa? What flowers did she like on her dining-room table?

"Orchids," Jana told them.

DOOR KICKER

I used Jana's press conference in Venice to make a push for an apartment of our own. You could not simply buy an apartment in Czechoslovakia in those days, even if you had the money. Apartments were assigned solely by bureaucrats, so it was strictly who you knew, and I'd gotten to meet some influential people in my new job.

I was working for Alfred Radok again, helping him with a mixed-media show that the Ministry of Culture had commissioned from him. The piece was called *Laterna Magica,* or *Magic Lantern,* its inspiration and name taken from an ancient entertainment. "Magic lanterns" had once been used to shine through drawings and project the first flickering images ever seen, so they were precursors of the movies. Our task was to create a showcase piece about Czechoslovakia, a propaganda coup

de théâtre that would put the country on the map at the World Expo
'58 in Brussels.

The influential person I'd gotten to know was Zdeněk Mahler, a very
decent man who had daily access to the minister of culture as his
speechwriter. I took Mahler out for a drink and explained to him the
predicament that Jana and I were in. Mahler thought our living situa-
tion at the Placeks' ridiculous. He convinced his minister of this, but
being in charge of culture, Comrade Minister Kahuda had no apart-
ments to hand out. All he could offer was an office that his ministry
would decommission for us.

We jumped at the chance and moved in one afternoon.

The office was in a large building on Všehrdová Street, near the
center of Prague, and it was one of eight rooms on our floor. Five of
them were working offices while three had been turned into one-room
apartments by the ministry to house its emergency housing cases.
Mahler himself lived in one of the rooms, another was occupied by a
clerk of the passport department, and Jana and I got the third.

We were enchanted by our new home. It was large and had plenty
of light from a window high over a busy street. There was no landlady,
and since it was a former office, the room even had a telephone. We put
in a bed, a writing desk, and books, bought a hot plate and a mirror,
and began entertaining our friends there.

The biggest downside of our new place was that it had no bathroom.
There was only a common room with a toilet and a couple of industrial
sinks off the hallway. A thin wooden door separated our room from the
working office next door. You could clearly understand everything that
was said there, and we quickly discovered that the clerical staff oversaw
all the exhibits in Prague. They handled everything from fine art to
trade shows. All day long, the phones rang and the old manual typewrit-
ers chattered.

After five o'clock, when the noise died down, the office became a
boudoir. The clerks and their secretaries suffered from the same lack of
privacy as everyone else, so they conducted their romances right in the
office. They knew that we lived behind the thin door, but it didn't
inhibit them in the least. We could hear them on the floor, in the chair,
standing by the filing cabinet, sitting on the desk, and could soon classify
the different bureaucrats according to their sighs and whispers, the
passionate pounding, the thrashings or the soft whimperings of their
orgasms.

The clerical lovemaking nearly always ended with a long silence.
Then the door handle clicked, the hallway rang with the pitter-patter

of high heels, and then came the sound of the rotary phone being dialed in the office.

"Honey, I got swamped with work today," said the men, "but I'm finally getting outta here. D'you want me to pick up anything on the way home?"

The next morning, I'd pass the lovesick clerks and the lovesome secretaries in the hallway, and there was no way to connect their sounds to their faces, so I nodded my greetings and wondered.

Many mornings, strangers knocked on our hallway door, mistaking it for one of the working offices. The light in the hallway was usually out and our room lay near the staircase, so the visitors started their search for the proper bureaucrat by knocking on our door. This was especially galling after a late night at work. I'd have a pillow wrapped around my head, and I'd be trying to sleep through the typewriter salvos when there would come the inevitable knock on the door. If I tried to ignore it, the timid knocking would quickly escalate to fist pounding, so I'd have to get up and send the stranger away.

I began leaving the door of our room unlocked. That way, the supplicants would knock, try the door handle, stick their head inside, see a bed with a couple sleeping in it, and make their way down the hall.

It didn't always work that way, however.

One morning we were still in bed. We heard someone knock, try the door, and quickly close it again. As we eased back to sleep, the door slowly opened again. Someone strolled in and cleared his throat.

"Good morning, comrade," said a very polite voice.

I peered out of the bed and saw an elderly gentleman in a long black coat thumbing a wide-brimmed hat. When he saw that I was looking at him, he pulled a chair up to my bed. He began unfolding some drawings.

"Excuse me, comrade, if I could just interest you in glancing over this blueprint," he said very softly, not daring to glance at Jana. "This won't take but a minute and then I'll be out of here."

He had put glasses on and was ready to explain the blueprints to me when I realized what he was thinking: he had been dealing with the Communist bureaucrats long enough to come to the conclusion that there were no limits to what they were capable of. It wasn't even beyond them to stick a bed in their office and conduct official business right out of it—a girlfriend at their side.

I didn't have the strength to explain to the old gent that this was no office, that this was my apartment.

"All I'd like to do, comrade, is take down this wall between the closet and the library," he went on, flipping the blueprint over, so I'd see it better. "That wall's not bearing any weight. I had an architect check it out."

I could barely keep my eyes open. I wanted him gone. "Go ahead," I said.

He seemed stunned. "May I have your name, comrade?" he said after a moment.

"Miloš Forman."

"Thank you! Thank you, Comrade Forman!" He was very happy. Perhaps his house was protected by the historical society and they'd had him in a vise. He quickly rolled up his drawing. He put his hat back on. He tiptoed out of my room. He probably took his closet wall down and no one was the wiser.

I shut my eyes and went back to sleep, thinking that now I'd seen it all.

But for every comical distortion of the strange life under Communism, there were a number of tragic stories. One of the more poignant belonged to our neighbor in the third decommissioned office.

His name was Pepík, and he was undone by his success in the new order of Czech society. He had been a fine tile man in a small provincial town, but after the revolution, the Communist Party pulled him out of his world and made him its "working-class cadre" in the Ministry of Culture. He could have been a happy, respected man in his native town, with a trail of gleaming bathrooms behind him, but the party gave him a big job in Prague and it wrecked his life.

One afternoon, I was standing in the hallway, talking with Mahler, when a short, thin, sickly looking man tried to slink by us. Mahler intercepted him. "Pepík! Come here, let me introduce you to our new neighbor!"

Pepík shook my hand, glancing around nervously, and then he scampered away. He never collected enough courage to look me in the eye.

Pepík worked in the passport office of the Ministry of Culture, deciding which one of us "cultural workers" would be allowed to go abroad. I couldn't see the powerful job in the man and Mahler explained to me that Pepík was in over his head at the office. He didn't comprehend the bureaucratese. He hated to say "no" to people, which was the essence of his job. He missed a lot of things that other people got. His subordinates mocked him, but so subtly that he couldn't get mad at them. His nerves were shot, and he drank heavily to make it through his days. He had no wife, no friends, no respect. He was lost in Prague.

A few days later, in the dead of night, there was a knock on our door and the muted sounds of sobbing. I looked at my watch. It was past two o'clock.

"Who is it?" I asked.

"Open up!"

"Who is it?"

"Open up!"

I cracked the door open. Leaning against it, convulsed with sobs, was our timid neighbor Pepík. I invited him in. He staggered to a chair, almost toppled it over sitting down, then launched into a slurred lament.

"You guys are so wonderful! You're artists and everything! But look at me! What am I? Me, I'm just a turd! You know my mother's just nuts about your wife. She thinks she's an angel. She's so proud of me just because I know you! Can you imagine that? Proud of me?! Yup, proud of me. Proud of a turd."

"Okay, okay, Pepík, why don't you go sleep it off. It'll all seem better in the morning, I promise."

But he went on and on till five o'clock when he finally passed out and I carried him off into his barren room. As drunk as he was, he never even dared glance at Jana.

At seven o'clock, my bladder about to burst, I staggered down the hallway to the bathroom. I heard Pepík's door open behind me. I stopped and looked back in time to see him leave for work. He wouldn't look at me, but he seemed chipper, smelled of cologne, stepped lively. I'd only drunk a fraction of what he had put away, but I was massively hung over so at that moment Pepík seemed like a superman to me.

Three nights later, at midnight, another storm of blows woke us up. This time he was kicking the door, so I let him in again. He could barely talk. "Those goddamn assholes! I'm gonna show 'em! I don't care! I'm not afraid of those bastards. I know how to handle them! I've been learning from them! I know their ways!"

No matter how drunk Pepík got, he never uttered the words "Communists" or "comrades." I don't know what horrors he got to see on the job, but he was terrified of his party.

He hollered for a couple of hours, wept, and passed out. I lugged him to his room. At seven o'clock in the morning, somehow, he repaired to his office. This went on for months, only more and more often. If I saw Pepík in the hallway, he skittered away from me, but a few hours later, transformed by alcohol into a snarling, hurting, slobbering door kicker, he didn't care if he tore the house down. I didn't know what to do about him. We'd already tried to pretend that we weren't in the room when he showed up, but he could just smell us right through the door like a bloodhound.

One night, I let him kick the door for an hour. He raged and pleaded till he finally tired himself out. "You're just like everybody else! The same son of a bitch!" was his parting shot. The abrupt silence in the hallway soon got to be so unnerving that I dragged myself out of bed to check on him.

I smelled the gas as soon as I stepped into the hallway. His door wasn't locked. Pepík lay sprawled on the bed, his eyes wide open, the gas burners hissing. I grabbed and slapped him. I was really angry, and I took it out on him. I kept pummeling him until he snapped out of it and started shivering with fear.

He stayed away for a couple of weeks, but when he resumed kicking our door, I always got up and let him in.

One night, he showed up waving a gun.

"I'm gonna waste 'em all! I'm plugging their guts! I'm pumping them fulla lead!" he slurred, but he was not pointing the gun at his Party tormentors, he was aiming it straight at me, and he was swaying as if he were standing on the deck of a rocking ship. I suddenly got the feeling that it was only a matter of seconds before he accidentally squeezed the trigger, so I dove at him, knocked the thing out of his hand, and punched him as hard as I could. I'd had enough. I dragged him off to his room and threw him on the bed. I then turned off the main gas line in the hallway, shoved his gun under my bed, and went back to sleep.

For the next few days, I was too nervous to give the gun back to Pepík and he was too sober and nervous to ask for it. But the possession of a firearm was a serious political offense in Czechoslovakia, and Pepík had gotten his pistol only because he was a trusted member of the *milice*, the party paramilitary unit on his job. I didn't want Pepík to have the gun, but I knew that if, for any reason, it were found in my room, I'd be in big trouble, so I had to do something.

I stayed up all night, waiting for Pepík to head to work in the morning. I caught up with him in the hallway. He was sober and wouldn't look me in the eye. "Pepík, I don't know if you remember it anymore, but you came by my place with this," I said, and I showed him the gun. He glanced at me, glanced at the gun, and dropped his eyes again.

"Oh, yeah, right," he mumbled. "Thanks." He took the pistol and hurried away, and we never talked about it again.

Over the years that followed, Pepík's alcoholism slowly became an embarrassment on the job. He got demoted a couple of times and made less and less money, so instead of vodka he started drinking cheap wine. He didn't need anything stronger anymore anyway.

He had the shakes in the morning by the time he met his future wife. She was no longer young, but she was pregnant and needed a father for the baby. One day, Pepík moved out of our building and the ministry reclaimed the office.

HOLE IN THE MARRIAGE

With time, Jana and I stopped being happy with our office. We had forgotten what it was like to be haunted by a deranged landlady and began talking about starting a family, but a drafty room lacking a simple sink and ringing with typewriter salvos was no place for a baby, so we decided to make an all-out push for a real apartment.

Our campaign would finally prove only that we didn't have the instincts to survive under socialism, even though it opened with a great deal of promise: Mahler convinced his minister that the Czech film industry's first lady and her up-and-coming screenwriter husband merited a bathroom of their own, and Kahuda set up an appointment with Václav Kopecký for us.

The loud drunk who had watched Rita Hayworth in *Gilda* to celebrate May Day at Frejka's house was now the deputy prime minister, and he could grant apartment keys. He remained the most colorful personality among the Communist leaders, famous for his earnest, rousing speeches: "People always ask me: What will Communism be like when we reach it? First of all, comrades, everything will be automated! You'll step up to a machine, punch a button, and out pops a roast pork with dumplings and sauerkraut. You punch another button, and out pops a cold beer. Another button, and you get shoes, still another, clothes, and so on. And we'll put such a machine on every street of every town! And every village! Every last hamlet in the country, comrades!"

The comrades went wild and cheered for minutes on end.

Kopecký invited Jana and me to the Hotel Esplanade, where we could discuss our apartment request during the noon break in the session of the nearby National Assembly. He showed up with his side-kick, Ládǎ Štoll, and a couple of bodyguards, looking pale and sweaty. His head sat on several folds of flesh, and he wheezed when he spoke, which was all the time, because in the fifteen minutes that he gave us in a private salon, he never shut up.

He didn't even glance at me. I was clearly a nobody, a tagalong, an accidental appendage. Now and then, Kopecký looked at Jana, who wore her prettiest dress and looked simply stunning, but he didn't speak to her either. He spoke only to Štoll, as he had for years, in long monologues perfected to spare himself all the questions.

"Well, Ládǎ, this is Comrade Brejchová, you see!" Kopecký started explaining to his straight man. "She was just in that movie that we sold all over the world . . ."

"*Wolf Trap*," said Štoll.

"Yes, Ládǎ, yes! And she's from a working-class family, too!"

Kopecký had evidently seen Jana's movies. He talked about them for fifteen minutes straight and then, abruptly, he turned to walk away. It was as sudden as if he had to rush off to the bathroom. He was out the door by the time he shot a glance at Štoll over his shoulder: "So, Ládǎ, why don't you work it all out with our Comrade Brejchová here." And he was gone.

"Okay, comrades," said Štoll, who evidently didn't want to be left behind. "Someone from my staff will call you." And he, too, was gone. Jana and I had nothing to show for our high-level audience, and we didn't know what to think.

A couple of months later, weeks after we had given up on Štoll's promise, our phone rang: "Major Slunský here. So let's discuss this apartment of yours, shall we, comrades?" He said he wanted to meet us in the bar of the Hotel Ambassador, which seemed an odd choice for a meeting. The place was a famous hangout for Third World arms dealers, prurient Western tourists, and the Communist underworld of hookers, money changers, fences, black marketeers, and smugglers, who had to moonlight as police informers if they wanted to stay in business.

We bathed, I shaved, and we put on our holiday best again. When I escorted Jana into the dark bar, all the hookers glared at her while the pimps glared at me.

Major Slunský turned out to be a short, wide-shouldered man in a military uniform, humming with nervous energy. His eyes kept darting around the room while he wrestled with some awkward small talk. He didn't seem to be able to take them off Jana or keep them on her. It was a relief when he finally pulled out a large-format application from his fancy attaché case. We eagerly answered his impossibly detailed questions. The major took an hour to finish the paperwork, putting down everything, including the maiden names of our maternal grandmothers, then zipped up the sheet in his attaché case and was ready to dash off.

"So how do our chances look to you, Comrade Major?" I asked.

"Oh, not bad," said the major. "I don't see any problems. On the other hand, you know the housing situation's terrible . . . but I'll see what I can do, comrades."

"Thank you! Where can we call you if . . ."

"Lemme get back to you, all right?"

"Okay, but if for some reason we should need to get hold of you?"

"No. I'll call you. In a couple, three weeks," said Slunčký, and he trotted off.

So again we knew nothing. All we had to go on was that the man who spoke to us wore an army uniform.

A couple of months later, Slunčký called back and we had another meeting with him, again in the bar of the Hotel Ambassador. Again the spirit of Franz Kafka presided. The major sweated out another sputtering, circular conversation, as if he were preparing to say something big and never could quite get it out. Then he suddenly pulled out the very same application that we had filled out the last time and, item by item, went down the sheet again. I put it all down to Slunčký being star-struck by Jana.

"Well, all right," he finally said. "So let me call you in a couple of weeks, so we can resolve this one way or the other."

I didn't like his remark. I'd thought we were a priority, that our apartment was coming down straight from Václav Kopecký. When Slunčký called again, some weeks later, it was as if he had sensed my fears and decided to calm them.

"So how would the two of you like to see what I've got in mind for you, comrades? Meet me the day after tomorrow, at seven in the morning." He gave a streetcar station in the Břevnov neighborhood as our meeting point.

We got up early, dressed casually, and sardined ourselves into a crowded streetcar that took morose workers to places where they didn't want to be. We got off at the designated station in Břevnov and kept an anxious eye out for the major. Was this where he lived? Or did he work around here? Or if not, was he coming in a streetcar or in a limo?

We never did see him arrive, however. Suddenly, he was crossing the street toward us, his eyes darting around, the familiar attaché case under his arm. He led us down the street, walking alongside the rails of the streetcars. We passed through the next stop on the line, then the next, then the next. Jana and I didn't know what to think. Nothing seemed to have any logic. Conversation once again was sparse, circular, offbeat. Finally, we reached a construction site. No one was working there, though the building wasn't completely finished yet. It was a long beehive of small apartments, with a string of entrances, eerie in its emptiness. There were doors and windows, but the walls hadn't been mortared yet. The major slipped into a stairwell and led us up the stairs, which were covered with piles of cement. When we reached the fourth floor, the major pushed a door open and showed us into a small, two-room apartment. There were no sinks, no toilet, no fixtures, no stove. Wires snaked around the unpainted walls. Wind howled through the windows. Jana and I looked at each other. We both wanted to drop on our knees and kiss the cement.

The major watched the flow of feeling between us, smiling.

"You think you could be happy here, comrades?"

"Oh, and how!"

"I've got you penciled in for this unit." He nodded. "But of course you understand that nothing's easy when it comes to housing."

"Yes, of course, but I thought that since Comrade Deputy Prime Minister . . ."

"Of course, of course. So. Let's talk on the phone in a couple of weeks, all right?"

We went down and admired the construction site as if it were an English park. The major dashed off, and we had a drink to celebrate no more landladies, no more gun-toting door kickers, a real home at last. For me, the first home since living with Mom and Dad in Čáslav. Now we could maybe even start a family.

The major did call a few weeks later, as he'd promised, but he sounded strange. "Well, we can't drag this out forever, comrades," he said sternly. "Meet me at the Vinohrady district office tomorrow at seven o'clock."

Naturally, the meeting location made no sense whatever, but we were there on time. The major marched into the building right past us, barely glancing our way. We jogged after him.

There was an ancient elevator inside, called a "pater noster" in Czech, a dozen cars running in a continuous loop through two open shafts at the center of the building. You waited for a car to rise up to you, hopped on, then stepped off on the floor of your destination. We barely managed to keep up with the major by bounding up onto the rising platform.

"I'm going to talk to the housing chairman," the major announced dryly. "You'll have your answer today." He seemed very remote. As he was about to disappear into an office, he halted, peering at me as if he wanted to say something, but didn't know how. He stood there for a long moment, shifting his weight from one foot to the other.

"All right, so I'm going in to speak with the housing chairman now. We'll just thrash it all out, just me and the housing chairman. It's gotta be decided one way or the other because we can't drag it out any longer. So I'm going in now, going to talk to the chairman." Jana and I both stared at him, bewildered.

"All right, so I'm going in," he repeated, and disappeared inside the office. We waited outside, trying to figure out the meaning of what had just happened. Why was the old shy admirer of Jana suddenly so rude? What did we do? What compromising information could he have found out about us?

We waited by the door for half an hour, forty-five minutes, an hour. The hallway got busy. There were bureaucrats wrestling their coats on or off, supplicants nervously thumbing their headgear, disoriented old people consulting tiny sheets of paper at arm's length.

"Shouldn't you go in and check?" Jana finally nudged me. "It's going on two hours now."

I decided to give it another fifteen minutes when I saw Major Sluncký in the distance at the far end of the hallway. I had to do a double take, but yes, it was our major, stepping out of an office way across the building with a gray-haired gentleman. They had their coats on, but hadn't buttoned them up. They marched to the elevator calmly talking.

Jana and I stood there confused and stared at the major, waiting for some sign from him. As he was about to get onto the ancient open-door lift, the major shot us a quick glance, then gave a little jerk of the head that said, "Follow me." I headed to the elevator, walking as fast as I could. As I got to the pater noster, I caught a glimpse of the major's face disappearing down the elevator shaft. He looked me straight in the eye, but his expression was one of scientific detachment. I didn't make the elevator and I never saw him again. He never called. We never got an apartment, never had any children.

A couple of months later, I described the whole sordid "Kafkárna" to Zdenek Mahler. He peered at me quizzically. "You never slipped him anything?" he asked softly, incredulously.

Instantly, it all fell into place: all those odd beats, the awkward pauses, the shuffling from foot to foot, the sense we'd so often had that the major wanted to say something and never quite could get it out. The major was waiting for me to stick an envelope into his ribs, but Jana and I were just too dumb to realize it. At the time, the going under-the-table price for an apartment was some 30,000 crowns, more than the average salary for a year. It would later go up steeply as the corruption spread, but we had the money. And we would gladly have paid it if only we'd had the brains to read the situation, if only we'd had what it took to reproduce under socialism, but we missed our chance. And it left a hole of disappointment in our marriage.

"JEWISH EXPRESSIONISM"

In 1958, while Aleksandr Solzhenitsyn was writing *One Day in the Life of Ivan Denisovich* in the Soviet Union, the world's largest statue of Stalin, a granite monstrosity the size of a high rise, still towered over the Letná neighborhood in Prague. A couple of years before, Khrushchev had denounced Stalin in a secret speech to the Bolshevik Party, but the Czech Party bosses had made their careers under Stalin with Stalinist methods, so they were not about to permit the Soviet political thaw to undermine their positions. They kept Czechoslovakia completely cut off from the world. Perhaps to overcome that feeling of global isolation, Ivan Passer and I started to go on picnics by the Ruzyně airport. We would stretch out on the grass at the end of a runway, pass a bottle of wine, watch the roaring tonnage of steel lift over us, and guess its destination. In only an hour or two, the plane would be landing in Paris or Rome or London or some other wonderful place that seemed to lie on a different planet altogether. It was easier to imagine growing wings than to picture yourself on a plane bound for the free world, but in 1958 I happened to board one of those planes and the experience turned out to be sheer hell.

Laterna Magica was finally flying to Brussels. Radok had managed to convince the State Security comrades that he needed everyone on his staff at the World Expo and they had found me worthy of their precious passport, so I boarded one of Czechoslovak Airlines' aging Illyushin planes. I had never flown before, and when I was shut up in this iron coffin, when I felt its massive weight lumbering up into the sky, I was suddenly sure I'd never get out of it alive. The body of the Russian plane creaked, hummed, buzzed, vibrated, and threatened to come apart at any moment. The national airline employed military pilots in those days because they were deemed more "politically reliable" than civilians, and our pilot handled the cumbersome Illyushin as if it were a fighter plane. I became violently sick. My first encounter with air travel gave me a fear of flying for life, but then, in Brussels, everything came up roses.

Coming to a Western metropolis from Prague was not unlike coming to Prague from Poděbrady, a transition from forty-watt bulbs to bright neon. The shops were crammed with things you couldn't buy in Prague, such as nylons, blue jeans, and "rustlers," the feathery plastic overcoats that were the rage in Czechoslovakia, and the city was full of fascinating, carefree people.

Laterna Magica won the gold medal at the Expo and became the event's sleeper. Radok was such a wizard of theatrical invention that no one noticed he was saying nothing with his theatrical collage, which offered glimpses of Czechoslovakia and impressions of its culture. There were moments in the show when you watched a cinematic projection and, suddenly, the actress leaped out of the screen and had a talk with her cinematic shadow, which remained there, when the piano player disappeared in midnote with his whole instrument or a line of chorus girls suddenly burst into an empty space onstage. The show's style and wit brought flocks of people to our pavilion. Even Walt Disney stopped by to tell us that he admired our work.

I had been idealizing Hollywood movies and jazz and all things American for years, so I spent most of my free time in the American pavilion. I was completely taken by Ella Fitzgerald, dazzled by Jerry Robbins's choreography, and charmed by Harry Belafonte and many other imperialists whom I couldn't have even dreamed of seeing in Prague.

Nothing impressed the Czech Communists more than a success in the capitalist West, so when we came back to Prague, Radok received the State Prize for *Laterna Magica*. The man had been in and out of political favor throughout the fifties, but now he was immediately hired to create a new edition of the show.

The second edition of *Laterna Magica* was supposed to be entertainment first and propaganda second because there was interest in it in London and other hard-currency markets. Radok asked three of us to be his coauthors in creating the new show. I accepted without hesitation. The show was selling out months in advance in Prague, so stepping up in the credits from assistant director to author also meant that I'd now be making a lot of money on the royalties.

If the original *Laterna Magica* had been a stunning coup de théâtre, its second edition was even better. A section of the show was loosely structured by the rhythms of folk life and centering on a birth, a wedding, and a funeral; it was set in the Bohemian Highlands, where Radok had grown up. This most powerful sequence was inspired by the music of Bohuslav Martinů, an expatriate composer who would die in Switzerland in 1959. The piece was called *The Opening of Springs,* and it was set in a farm's interior, evoked onstage with a few sticks of real furniture and the projections of windows, pictures, and shelves on the walls. Two dancers entered and danced a love duet around a bed, but as they did, the projected images began to blow up in size. After a while, you realized that three boys were peeking into the room through the back window. The lovers went on wooing each other, but soon they were dwarfed by the leering faces of the boys.

In the late fifties, in the Czechoslovakia of Socialist Realism, the scene made you shiver. It was also vintage Radok and one reason people wanted to work with him, even though he was a demanding artist, sizzling with nervous energy. We worked long hours, under constant time pressure, and I saw less and less of Jana. Our second show was undergoing major changes right up to its Party preview, which had to be pushed back several times. I couldn't wait for opening night. As one of the show's credited authors, I thought it was going to open up all sorts of doors for me.

The preview was finally held in the workshops of the National Theater. When I got there, however, the place was crawling with firemen, though there were no signs of fire. The firemen all looked so aloof that I didn't dare ask them what had happened. I headed backstage, where I ran into Radok.

"What's the matter? What's the fire department doing here?"

"What fire department?" said Radok who seemed very edgy. "Go back and look at them, will you?"

The firemen were all State Security agents in drag. The security detail of the Party big shots regularly dressed up as waiters or ushers or firemen, but too many firemen had shown up for our preview, so the general consensus was that something was wrong. The apparatchiks didn't hang around theaters in their free time. They preferred blood sports.

The black Tatra limousines brought a lot of men whose names I recognized from the newspapers and the radio, but whose faces I was seeing for the first time, such as the minister of defense and the minister of heavy industry. Deputy Prime Minister Kopecký and his sidekick, Štoll, walked in and marched boldly to the front row. Minister of Culture Kahuda took a seat a few rows behind them, following some pecking order I wasn't familiar with. The auditorium quickly filled up with the boozy mugs of apparatchiks, though sprinkled among them you also saw famous singers, money changers, divas, hookers, gay hustlers, actors with glamorous girlfriends, and sundry beautiful people. Our show had been eagerly awaited in Prague, so you had to know people to get in.

I took my seat beside Radok, in a small island of pale authors and assistants. I no sooner sat down than Radok turned to me: "Why don't you kick it off, Miloš?"

I climbed onstage, cursing Radok under my breath for setting me up like this, then mumbled some inanities to the crowd which were met with frosty indifference. The lights went down, the curtain up. A silence spread over the auditorium, and it got deeper and deeper. No one laughed at the jokes. No one fidgeted. It seemed that no one even breathed. They all squatted there like stiffs, and I started sweating.

At last, the show ended. Not a single pair of hands clapped. The house lights switched on. Kopecký and Štoll rose and marched up onstage to survey the auditorium. For a long beat, they just stood there and Kopecký nodded his head sternly at Radok as if to say, "Yes, of course, I should have known," then gestured with his finger to call the authors up to his side.

Radok led his gaggle of hand-picked collaborators onstage. He had to face Kopecký and we all tried to hide behind him, an impossibility on the bare stage, so we just stood there in a tight formation and eyeballed our shoes. It didn't really matter because, as always, Kopecký talked only to his factotum.

"Ládă, do you know what we've got here? I got the point of this show! Sure I did! This here is your Jewish expressionism, Ládă!"

Štoll nodded thoughtfully. He was a shaggy-looking man in dark-framed glasses. I can still vividly see how long his pants legs were, so long that he was standing on them with the heels of his shoes. When he shifted his weight, the dirty threads sticking out of their frayed bottoms showed.

"Where are the power plants, Ladislav? Where is that brand-new power plant on the river Elbe? The one that our workers had completed ahead of the plan? How if I were creating this show, Ládă, I'd put that power plant right at the top of it. And I'd show all those atoms circling inside there, too, that's what *I'd* show. So what do these comrades here show us?! They give us Peeping Toms! And did you know whose music that was? Mr. Martinů's, Láďa! Yes! Mr. Martinů's! The émigré who has buried himself in the capitalist Switzerland!"

Kopecký harangued us deep into the night. I sweated right through my shirt. When I finally got home, I drank a gallon of water, took a couple of aspirin, climbed into bed, and didn't sleep a wink.

Ivan Passer, whom I had gotten a job at the theater and who ran our complicated tech board with his customary virtuosity, walked to his house, dropped on the bed, and roared with laughter till his whole body ached. He'd been holding down a volcano of guffaws all night. While Kopecký ran his mouth, Ivan was busting up with great yelps of laughter inside, at times trembling from the sheer effort of keeping them down. He thought he had been able to keep a pretty good mask over his laughing fit, but someone must have noticed it because in the morning he got fired, without explanation, from the theater.

Ivan was the first to go, and Radok was the second. Once he was dismissed, Radok expected his other three writers to quit in order to show solidarity with him. He didn't want anyone to salvage the show; he preferred to see Kopecký and his henchmen shred it to pieces.

I loved Radok much more than the show, but the romantic gesture he was looking for was beyond me. I would have been branded a dangerous nonconformist in my dossier and I simply wasn't enough of a hero to do it, and neither were the others. I don't think Radok ever completely forgave us for it.

HONORABLE HUSBAND

At this point Jana and I had been married for three years, a period of time that, in my experience, is long enough to burn out the rawest of romantic passions. We were still living in our office, but we had stopped pushing for an apartment of our own. I was under a lot of stress and spent nearly all my waking hours reworking the show. We had to drop the Martinů sequence, but we tried to save the rest of Radok's work. The Party canceled our premiere, but the foreign investors were told that their contracts would be honored and that *Laterna Magica* would open in London in three months.

The atmosphere in the theater was fraught with tension, mistrust, intrigues, uncertainty, and rumors. Censors hovered behind the scenes. None of us knew if our jobs were safe. We had to rehearse the understudies as much as the principals in most of the roles because there was no telling who'd be allowed to go to London.

I saw less and less of Jana, and it got to be too tiring to keep her up-to-date on the folly around me. Nothing made much sense, so you had to give a background briefing before you could start simply talking about what your day had been like.

It was then that I began acquiring secrets.

At one point in our show, a line of dancers had to hide behind a satiny curtain, then suddenly pop up in the middle of the following scene. I'd noticed that something always protruded through the satiny material. The dancers would take their starting places and two round and lovely shapes would appear in the smooth curtain. They belonged to one of our prettiest ballet dancers, who happened to have uncommonly large breasts, and I always wanted to run my hands over them. At one late rehearsal, I tiptoed across the darkened stage and gave in to temptation. The dancer knew that it was me, and she didn't pull back.

When we became lovers, I discovered how generous, kind, and tender she was. She never wanted anything from me at all. She knew I was married and had no intention of leaving Jana. She'd see me when I had the time and never complained. She didn't want a family, didn't push me to do something about an apartment, never made me feel guilty. Of course she also didn't have to put up with drunken neighbors barging in every other night. And we had so much in common because our lives revolved completely around *Laterna Magica*.

I thought I loved the ballet dancer even while I still loved my wife, so I did what I thought was the only honorable thing to do: I told Jana. Looking back, I see that it was an incredibly stupid and cruel decision and that it deeply hurt her. Nevertheless she went on living in our decommissioned office with me, with the husband who loved her even while he also happened to love another woman. I was not lying. I didn't understand what was going on any more than the two women in my life did. This situation went on for weeks, with everyone more or less miserable, until Jana slowly built up her emotional defenses against me. She'd get angry at me, want no part of me, act as if she hated me, but then the emotional pendulum would suddenly swing back again.

It all came to a head when *Laterna Magica* finally left for London. I got my passport again, and so did my dancer, who remained as happy, gentle, and unassuming as ever. *Laterna Magica* was no huge success in London, but the show would survive long enough to become one of the better entertainments at the Montreal Expo of 1967. The biggest impact we made in England, however, occurred on opening night. In those days, "God Save the Queen" was played before every performance, so our managing director requested that the Czechoslovak national anthem also precede every performance. The English promoter agreed only reluctantly.

As soon as the *kádrovák*—the political officer of our group—got wind of the two anthems, he demanded that the Soviet anthem be added to the list. The Soviets were our brothers in those days and everyone was conditioned to hear the two anthems together. This time, the English promoter surprised our management by agreeing wholeheartedly. Apparently, he could foresee how the three anthems would be received on the opening night.

That evening, the theater was packed, and when the lights went down, a scratchy tape of "God Save the Queen" resounded through the theater. As was customary, the audience suffered it half-sitting and half-standing, yawning and whispering. They were all back in their seats long before the music ended. After a brief pause, a fresh-sounding version of the Czech anthem came on. It took the Londoners a few beats to realize the meaning of this unfamiliar piece of music, but then they politely rose back up. As soon as they recognized the last bars of the composition, they dropped down. The Czechoslovak anthem had two distinct parts, however, so after a brief pause, the Slovak anthem cut in. There was a noticeable stir in the audience and now the theatergoers straightened up and listened to the spirited tune with wide grins. When they sat back down, the hall was buzzing with comments.

After another brief pause, the Soviet anthem boomed out of the speakers and it was greeted by the biggest laugh that *Laterna Magica* had ever received. The theater was shaking to the foundations and nothing in our show came close to topping this overture, so the following night, our management quietly dropped both add-on anthems.

Meanwhile, back in Czechoslovakia, Jana was shooting a movie. She of course knew that I was living with the dancer in London. One evening she called me at my hotel room.

"I'd just like to say, if you want to stay abroad, Miloš, then go ahead."

"I don't."

"Well, okay, I just wanted to tell you, so you wouldn't be coming back on account of me. Because I found someone else." Her words struck me like a punch to the kidney. At that very moment, I realized how much I still loved her.

Jana didn't owe me a thing the way I'd been behaving toward her, and yet she called me and spoke openly on a telephone that, more likely than not, was bugged. She was taking a huge chance on my behalf, but then Jana always had a lot of character. And now I suddenly saw with a frightening clarity that I'd mistaken desire and physical infatuation for deeper emotions, but there wasn't taking any of it back. I'd been a fool, and I lost her.

Still trying to be fair with everyone, I went and told my dancer what I'd just learned about my murky heart.

"But I knew it all along," she said. If I could have it all back now, I would never have talked about my feelings with either of them.

By the time we came back from London, Jana had moved out of our office. I discovered that she was seeing a German actor whom she had met on the set of her last film. She had started divorce proceedings, and I didn't see her again until we stood in divorce court. She had an older lady chaperoning her there, so we didn't get to talk much. Whatever got said was tinged with sadness. I walked away swearing I'd never get married again.

Everything in the room on Všehrdová Street reminded me of Jana and of my own stupidity. When I couldn't stand it anymore, I went to see Jana's father. He was a truck driver, and I had always liked him and gotten along with him. He welcomed me with a bottle of slivovitz.

"It's all my fault, Mr. Brejcha," I told the old man. "I screwed up."

"It's not your fault, Miloš. Life's screwed up," said my philosophical father-in-law. "I just wish it hadn't happened . . . And to think that she's marrying a kraut now, damnit!"

I was shocked. Jana had seemed so melancholy at the courthouse.

"I'm not going to the goddamn wedding!" continued Mr. Brejcha. "No way. Not only is he a kraut, he's an actor, too."

It took all the eloquence I could summon and the whole bottle of slivovitz to convince Mr. Brejcha, who had come out of the war with a healthy hatred for Germans, that he really had to go to his daughter's wedding. We both knew she would be hurt if he didn't come and he certainly didn't want to hurt her, so in the end he agreed. The wedding was to take place in a fancy hotel in Carlsbad. "I don't know how I'm getting there," said the old man. "I'm sure not driving there in the kraut's hoity-toity car." So I offered to drive him. It was the height of masochism, but I drove my father-in-law to my ex-wife's wedding, though I didn't take him all the way to the hotel. I stopped on the outskirts of the spa town.

"Do you mind walking the rest of the way?" I asked Mr. Brejcha. "You know, I don't want anybody to see me here."

"Of course!" said the old man. "I wouldn't want them to see you either." He got out and, in his black suit and gleaming shoes, headed down the dusty gravel shoulder of the asphalt road.

The marriage didn't last much longer than an average stay in the Carlsbad spa.

Jana and I would become good friends years later, and she would confess that what most drew her to her second husband was that she didn't understand him. She spoke little German and he spoke no Czech, so they hardly knew each other. As soon as they began to learn to communicate, their marriage fell apart.

I was still beat up from the divorce when the new managing director of *Laterna Magica* called me into his office. I didn't know much about him, other than that he was half Russian and a drinking man, because he had only been appointed to the job shortly before Radok's firing. His name was Boris Michajlov, and I quickly discovered that he was nothing if not to the point:

"Comrade Forman, this is now politically a very important institution. I suggest that you resign."

Losing my job was the very last thing I needed at the time, so I sat there for a long while, empty of all thought. I'd never been fired before, and I was in shock. I'd expected this to happen earlier, after Michajlov gave the ax to Radok and Ivan, but now we'd just come back from a trip to London—a trip that hadn't been a disaster—and I'd started to think that my job was safe.

"No, I'm not going to resign, comrade director," I finally announced as firmly as I could. "My conscience is clean."

"You're making a mistake," opined Michajlov ominously.

He let me go that day, but soon called me in again.

"Comrade Forman, where were you on the seventeenth of July last year?"

"How should I remember?"

"That particular day can't be easy to forget!"

I didn't like this at all. I flipped back through my memory to see if I could figure out what he had up his sleeve.

"But I wasn't even here! I was in Brussels in July."

"That's right!"

"I have no idea. It's been half a year."

He glanced at a sheet of paper on his desk: "Does 'Ella Fitzgerald' ring any bells?"

It turned out that Michajlov had the precise dates of all my visits to the American pavilion. The director seemed to have a chart showing where I'd been at any given moment in Brussels, and all of those spots were politically very dubious. They made me seem an imperialist boot-licker. I'd clearly been watched very closely in Belgium, though I hadn't noticed a thing.

I was a goner and there was no reason to drag it out, but my whole life was in shambles anyway, so I didn't give a damn anymore.

"You can fire me, but I'm not going to do it for you," I told the director defiantly.

"That's not smart," said Michajlov.

A couple of days later, Comrade Pokorný, the *kádrovák* of the theater, dismissed me.

"You, comrade, are politically unreliable," he told me.

Shortly thereafter, the other two authors were fired, too, so now all the creators of the second *Laterna Magica* were gone. The next thing I heard was that the whole show was being rewritten to make it ideologically correct, so I was sure it would be butchered. I was wrong though. The big revision turned out to be nearly invisible. You had to know the book of the show by heart to notice that a line had been altered here and there, a snippet of a scene cut, an image dropped. The only significant change was in the credits. There was a new team of authors listed, headed by Boris Michajlov, so I finally got the point of it all: Michajlov had us all fired so that he and his political cronies could get their hands on our royalties. The show ran in Prague for years and it made its "authors" a lot of money. The man even had the gall to cast the deputy prime minister of Czechoslovakia as the unwitting principal of his plot.

Once the shock wore off, I almost had to admire Michajlov. In any case, there was nothing that we could do about it. The whole thing had simply been another day in show business under communism.

I always knew that I wouldn't be with Radok forever because I wanted to become a director in my own right. Even while I was still helping Radok and learning from him at the original *Laterna Magica*, I kept my hand in the movie business by writing a screenplay with Josef Škvorecký.

Škvorecký had grown up in Náchod and gotten the place down on paper in his novels, but he was a few years older than I and we had missed each other in that small town during the war. I met him only after he had become notorious in the country by publishing a novel called *The Cowards*. This great book rendered a jazz-struck teenager's experience of the last few days of the war, and its realistic portrayal of the Russian soldiers had enraged the Communist cultural bosses who idealized them. The novel was quickly banned, but Škvorecký was lucky in that the ban didn't cover his other works, so we were able to start an adaptation of one of his a short stories. It was called "Eine Kleine Jazzmusic" and was about a jazz band during the war.

When Škvorecký and I finished our script, we submitted it to the Barrandov dramaturgists under the optimistic title *The Band Won*, with the tactical subtitle "an anti-fascist musical comedy," but it didn't help. The Barrandov script people didn't think that our screenplay's politics were progressive enough.

Josef and I were still young and naive and we refused to believe that it was impossible to please the dramaturges, so we kept rewriting the script. In response to their suggestions, we turned the jazz band into a symphony orchestra, which later became a brass band. The more we changed the script, the more changes the Barrandov crowd demanded.

Before long, the musicians disappeared altogether and we were writing a war film. Then, at one of the script conferences, someone astutely asked why we were calling our screenplay *The Band Won* when there was no band in it and why it was subtitled a musical comedy when it really was a straight tragedy, so we got wiser and started slipping the old scenes back in. The second time around, these scenes didn't seem to bother the dramaturges at all. They had all but forgotten them and their objections.

We had almost managed to get the screenplay back to what it had originally been by the time the project was approved for production. I was all set to direct it for the Šebor-Bor production group and was eager to seize my chance when word came that the whole project had been scratched. The decision came down from places where they didn't have to explain themselves, so it took me a while to ferret out what had actually happened.

The Party leader, President Antonín Novotný, listened to the radio a lot and apparently one day heard on the news that the Barrandov moviemakers were preparing an adaptation of a short story by Josef Škvorecký. The name rang a bell, Novotný remembered *The Cowards*, and he became furious. He thought that someone was trying to countermand his orders by filming the novel he had banned and immediately decreed that our project be killed.

My sources were sure that Novotný was confusing the two different works by Škvorecký, so I set out to clear up this straightforward misunderstanding. Unlike the earlier novel, our short story had been published officially and there had been no "ideological" objections to it, which armed me with a good argument. I managed to talk my way through several offices up to the secretary of the cultural department of the Communist Party. This somber comrade was a powerful man, but he struck me as a relatively sane Communist. He heard me out with some sympathy, then buried my project with a remark that spoke volumes about the nature of power in our classless society: "Comrade Forman, let me give you a piece of friendly advice: Forget about this whole thing and move on. You may very well be right in your deductions, they're quite plausible. But believe me, even if you're a hundred percent right, there's no one who'll go and tell Comrade President that he is wrong."

ALTER EGO

You go through life collecting incidental observations and tiny understandings and you never know if they will ever fit anywhere. Most never do, but now and then you find that you can get inside a new situation by remembering something that had passed through your head years before. In the late fifties, in a hospital called Kateřinky, which had a large mental ward, I discovered the banality of madness. I wouldn't get to draw on this insight until 1975, when I shot *One Flew Over the Cuckoo's Nest* in Salem, Oregon.

I've always been a hypochondriac because whenever I looked back on my life, I saw only an amazing roll of luck, so I kept waiting to pay for it somehow. If there was a new disease or illness in the news, I always got the feeling, "Aha! This must be it." The next thing I knew, I would have a textbook version of the symptoms.

In the late fifties, the most fashionable medical condition in Czechoslovakia was a nervous breakdown because sensitive people in trouble with the State Security used them to get out of their predicaments. A nervous breakdown absolved you of responsibility for your actions. At that time, nothing was going right for me. I'd screwed up the marriage to Jana, gotten fired from my job, and couldn't get into the movies. For the first time in my life, I felt like a failure, and I wound up with a nervous condition for which I sought treatment at Kateřinky. I had some friends on the staff, and I went once a week for about a month and got some incredibly soothing drug straight into my veins. Maybe it was just Valium, but it sure felt wonderful.

At Kateřinky, there were no private rooms, so I'd come in, change into a hospital gown, and lie down on one of the forty beds crammed into the room. A nurse stuck a needle into my arm, sent the drug dripping through transparent tubes, and I watched the patients.

Observing the mental ward quickly disabused me of the theatrical notion of mental illness I'd picked up watching movies. I had expected the mental patients to act out all kinds of bizarre conceits, but in reality they strove only to be absolutely normal. They just somehow didn't make it. The banality that permeates everything extends even to madness. One day I lay hooked up to the IV in the back of the room when a young man dropped down on the adjacent bed. He was a powerfully built guy in his midtwenties, and he had an engaging smile. He wore a checkered bathrobe over his striped pajamas, but he brushed his greased hair back with a certain flair.

"I hear you work in the movies," he said.

"Well, I have, yes."

"I just want you to know that that's the reason I'm here, the goddamn film industry."

"Oookay."

"Yup! 'Cause my wife's an actress, and she loves me so much that all she wants to do is hang out with me. So they get me locked up in here, so that they can put her in another movie because then they can all fuck her, so that's why I can't get outta this joint for the life of me! But you tell 'em that I'm getting outta here one way or the other and that I know all about how they've been treating her! You tell those sons of bitches that I'm checking outta this fleabag, and once I'm out I'll be looking for them! I love my wife! Do you know her?"

He was so composed that he almost had me believing his story and feeling sorry for him.

"Well, what's her name?" I asked.

"Jana Brejchová!"

I didn't see that coming at all, so I froze and stared at him.

"So you do know her!" shouted the guy. "Do you, damnit?"

"Everybody knows Jana Brejchová," I offered.

"That's right! So you tell your buddies! You tell the whole industry!" he yelled, and he hit the frame of my bed with his fist so hard that the whole thing jumped, then marched away, throwing back menacing looks. I got over my condition in a hurry.

PART 5

CZECH FILMS

HINDSIGHT MANIFESTO

When I look back on my early films, I think they were mostly about trying to see clearly. I didn't realize it back then, but I suppose I was subconsciously reacting to the highly stylized, theatrical, rich style of Alfred Radok. His art brilliantly employed words, music, design, ballet, the latest stage technology. It was as if Radok took you on a trip to the moon: the experience was breathtaking and unlike anything you'd ever been through before, but you had to don a lot of gear to get there. After the voyages with Radok, I merely wanted to go for a walk around the block, look at the old neighborhood, and see it just as it was.

I'd noticed back at the film academy that when it came to the old silent films only the comedies and the documentaries still gripped my attention. It took a film historian to sit through the serious dramas of the silent era, which now seemed mostly preposterous and funny, but a simple documentary shot of a city street, of a woman feeding a baby, of a man cleaning his pipe in the year 1899 fascinated me and I could have watched it for hours.

Even back then I decided that if I ever got to make my own films, I'd try to get them as close to reality as I could. I was going to make sure my characters talked, looked, and acted the same way I saw people around me behave. The paradox is that it was this very idea that steered me away from making pure documentaries. The camera's presence alters most situations that it trails. People become stilted, put on airs, wear masks, show off, get intimidated, so you cannot simply capture the everyday life by documenting it. You have to re-create it.

There is another thing I miss in straightforward documentaries, and that's the story. I believe that we decipher the incoherent flow of life through stories. The stories may not add up to much, they may end abruptly or proceed according to mysterious logic, but my kind of film has to have them.

ASHES

It was while I was still living on Všehrdová Street alone that I came home late one night and found a telegram under the door: "Come to Čáslav. Funeral tomorrow." It didn't say who had died or who was sending the message.

I thought about jumping in the car right then and driving to Čáslav, but it was about one o'clock in the morning already. I went to bed, but didn't sleep a wink.

As I drove to Čáslav the following morning, the day was just breaking. The telegram could have come from several houses there, and it took me a while to decide where to go. I finally headed to the parents of brother Pavel's wife, simply because the Klauses were my oldest relatives in town. I rang the bell. They opened the door right away because they hadn't been sleeping either, but I had the wrong house. It never crossed my mind that death could have claimed my oldest brother Blahoslav.

Blahoslav was still only in his mid-forties then, a young man. His wife, Boženka, was younger, and they had two small kids. But now his coffin was coming from Slovakia on a train that had already begun its journey. This train was due to arrive at two o'clock in the afternoon, and it carried four other coffins.

Blahoslav had inherited our father's love for the outdoors. He grew up as a Boy Scout, and when the Communists disbanded the Boy Scouts after the revolution, he set up a mountaineering club at the secondary school where he taught. The students flocked into the club, and over the years he took hundreds of them on camping trips all over Czechoslovakia.

In May of 1962, he led his last group to the highest mountains in the country. The jagged, snowy peaks of the Tatra Mountains go up to 8,737 feet, and there are many tough climbs and challenging trails. Blahoslav took about twenty kids with him. They were fourteen and fifteen years old, and they had several wonderful days there. They had to wear sunglasses so often that they got raccoon-eyed suntans.

The Tatras are beautiful in May, when carpets of mountain flowers begin to bloom on their slopes. One morning, Blahoslav's group went out on a long trek over a high pass. The sun shone brightly, and there was not a cloud in the sky until shortly after midday. But then the clouds blew in with incredible speed and they were thick and dark gray, so Blahoslav decided to turn around and head back into the valley.

His kids were hustling down the mountain when the snow started falling. Soon it really got heavy. With the roaring wind driving it, the visibility dropped down to a few steps. In half an hour, the ground was covered with drifts of snow. The path descended around ravines and steep cliffs, down rocky slopes where the footing was treacherous, and they were moving into a white wall of snow, so when they reached some pine trees in the lee of the mountain, Blahoslav told his teenagers to huddle under them. He asked the four strongest kids to go with him to get help.

He figured that they didn't have very far to go; in his estimation, their hotel lay only a few hundred meters away. He was right. They were just three hundred meters away from shelter.

The students pressed themselves into a human ball to conserve their body heat, and they waited. Shortly after he left them behind, groping around in the blinding snow on the wind-whipped mountainside, Blahoslav slipped and plunged down a cliff side. He was knocked unconscious in the fall. He never came to again and died of exposure. The bodies of the four kids who had gone with him were all found later not far from his.

The snowstorm stopped as fast as it had started. The group huddling under the trees decided not to wait for help to arrive. They had to brook deep snowdrifts, but they made it down to the hotel in twenty minutes. All the snow was gone again in a couple of days. The storm had been a freak of meteorology. None of the locals could remember such a bad snowstorm that late in the year.

My sister-in-law was crushed, but she acted bravely for the sake of the children. Her kids wore somber faces, but I am not sure they were able fully to comprehend the horrible finality of their father's death. I don't think that children ever really can.

When the time came for the train from Slovakia to arrive, we headed to the station. The train was bringing the tanned survivors as well as the coffins. On the platform, the grieving parents and relatives mixed with those who were relieved that their children were coming back, though they couldn't wait to see them with their own eyes.

The families had decided that all five victims would be cremated together, but Čáslav didn't have a crematorium. The coffins would have to be unloaded, opened so that the bereaved could say their last good-byes to their loved ones, then sealed again and put on a second train that would take them to another town.

The train was running late. I wandered around the small station, down the main platform, in and out of the waiting room. I certainly didn't go up on the catwalk. I hadn't spent this much time at the station since I'd gone there with my mother to wait for Dad to come back from the Gestapo jail. I couldn't wait for the tiny train to appear on the horizon back then, but Dad never got off those trains and now the memories were swirling around me, and Blahoslav who had tried to be my father was coming on a train, too, and he was not getting off it either. All the people in my family dying violently, before their time. There were only two of us left now, brother Pavel and myself. I felt as if the hand on the round station clock, hanging down from the roof at the end of the platform, the same hand that I'd been watching since I was a second-grader, with so many different emotions, was bringing the end of my own life closer every time it jerked.

I'd never dealt with the finality of life so directly before. I'd always put it out of my mind. I'd learned to abstract death from its physical facts as a boy, when I'd lost my parents in such a peculiar way. Never having seen their lifeless bodies, I'd imagine that they'd gone on to live somewhere beyond my horizon. Their deaths had been reported events, so remote that it seemed that maybe they could still linger somewhere somehow and I just couldn't see them. But I was a kid then and I could make myself believe anything. I couldn't do that anymore.

The train didn't get to Čáslav until four or five in the afternoon, so everything had to be pushed back. At last, all the coffins were opened and the relatives were asked to say their final good-byes. I tried to go with them, but was stricken by the sheer horror of it, and my legs literally started giving out from under me. I didn't want to see Blahoslav in death because that image would then always dominate my memories of him.

I still haven't been able to look at anyone whom I loved or have been close to after they have died. The only way I am able to cope with their end, their never being around me again, their being gone forever, their being ashes and smoke or dust and bones, and maybe a few spooky dreams at night, and maybe some thin memories during wakeful hours that are wearing thinner and thinner, the only way I can do it is to avoid carrying the imprint of their lifeless faces in my memory.

When I began my research for *Amadeus,* I was stunned by a letter that Mozart wrote to his father from Paris, where he was staying with his mother. The letter was long and full of mundane facts. In a brief aside, Mozart mentioned that his mother had fallen ill. It was an offhand remark, an afterthought, a triviality, until you looked at the date of the letter: Mozart wrote it three days after his mother had died.

AUDITION

As the fifties ended and a new decade began, I was pushing thirty and not much closer to my ultimate ambition of making movies than I'd been when I graduated from the academy. But I'd been around the business, and that helped me realize that I hadn't even learned the basics of filmmaking craft, which was a mistake.

Filmmaking is a social art and a director tells his stories and makes his images through several intermediaries, so the relationship between him and his cinematographers, editors, composers, and other collaborators is extremely important. All directors, and especially young directors, must legitimize their nominal authority on the set while creating an atmosphere that gives them easy access to the brightest ideas of their collaborators.

There are many ways to earn the directorial chair. Jean Renoir was adored by his crews, Radok respected, others feared. I found that the best way to legitimize leadership is by knowing what you want and not asking for the impossible. But to know the limitations of each element of the craft, you have to be conversant with it.

I had written screenplays and assisted in the casting and directing of movies, but I'd never held a camera in my hand, never matched two strips of film in an editing room, never talked to a composer. I decided that I'd rectify these flaws in my film education and that I'd do it on my own.

I took all my savings and bought a bulky East German camera that had just come on the market in Czechoslovakia. It was loud, but its Zeiss-Jena optics worked splendidly. I dropped 14,000 crowns for it only to find out that there was no film stock to be had anywhere in the country. This was a standard operating procedure for a socialist economy, so you scrambled and made do somehow. It took me a while, but I finally managed to scrounge up a few hundred feet of film from a TV technician who was stealing it on the job.

Next I had to learn how to handle the new pride of my possessions. Ivan knew a great guy who was working as a camera operator and an assistant cinematographer at Barrandov, and one day he showed up with a curly haired dynamo named Mirek Ondříček, who grabbed my camera, and immediately it became a part of him. He just couldn't put it down.

"So now let *me* try it, Mirek, okay?" I'd ask him while we were out in the street fooling around with it.

"Okay, okay! Just a minute! Just lemme finish this shot! This is great!"

"You finished? Now can I try it?!"

"Sure, sure. Just one more thing. One second!"

"Mirek?"

"Oh, shit!"

"What is it?"

"We're outta film."

I hardly got to touch the camera. Ondříček was a total bust as a teacher, but it didn't matter because I'd found my lifelong cinematographer. He has shot all of my films, with the exceptions of *Black Peter* and *One Flew Over the Cuckoo's Nest*, which he had been barred from by the inexorable force of circumstances. His other credits include Lindsay Anderson's *If . . .* and *O Lucky Man!* as well as a number of big Hollywood productions such as *F/X*, *Silkwood*, and *A League of Their Own*.

Fooling around with our new German toy, Mirek, Ivan, and I started making sort of a silent documentary about a pop-music cabaret that was just becoming the hottest thing in Prague. It was called the Semafor Theater, and I'd been friends with its two creators for years. Jiří Suchý and Jiří Šlitr agreed to give us the run of their theater, so we just wandered around the building and recorded its everyday life.

The most fascinating thing I saw at the Semafor was the open audition for a female singer. I couldn't believe the power of the microphone over the girls. They stepped up to it as if it were a magic wand that would endow them with a great voice and beauty. This foot of fat wire got homely young women to vamp shamelessly, tone-deaf singers to wail away at the top of their voices, shy neurotics to put themselves through the torture of public scrutiny. There were moments when the spectacle of the audition became tough to watch. The young women stripped down to the core of their personality and ambition, frequently revealing something so skewed and self-loving that you wanted to look away.

I decided to make a film about an open audition in which I'd never look away. I'd keep looking and make the audience watch with me. My documentary would take an unflinching look at this cruel phenomenon and see it for what it was.

I enlisted Šebor's help, and he set up a minuscule budget at the Barrandov Studios for a documentary called *Konkurs,* or *Audition.* Barrandov gave us some film stock, a one-man lighting crew, a service van, and later an editor. We used my new camera and recorded the sound on an old Grundig tape recorder that I'd brought from Brussels. *Audition* had to be the closest thing to a home movie that Barrandov has ever produced.

We announced a bogus audition for a female singer at the Semafor Theater and then shot it mostly as a straightforward documentary, though I did incorporate a simple story into it. One of the would-be singers, a shopgirl, asks her boss to let her go to the audition, gets a firm no, goes anyway, and bombs. Another girl watches the shopgirl embarrass herself and runs away, even though she has been singing with a rock band and would probably have won the prize.

The rock singer was played by Věra Křesadlová, a young woman I found at the first big rock concert in Prague. The year was 1961, and Khruschev's political thaw had slowly seeped from the Soviet Union all the way to Czechoslovakia. For the first time, rock 'n' roll was allowed in Lucerna, the huge concert hall in the center of the city. The authorities had laid down only one condition: there must be no singing in English, the language of the imperialists.

I went to the concert and was amazed at how much hidden talent Prague had. Groups and singers were coming out of nowhere and rocking the packed underground auditorium. A girl group climbed up onstage, announced that they'd do a song untranslatable into Czech, and belted out an infectious version of "The Loco-Motion." I couldn't take my eyes off the tall, pouty-lipped, dark-haired beauty who anchored the trio. I tracked her down and called and asked her if she would consider trying out for my film, but she wanted to discuss it first.

We got together at a café. She looked very lovely, but she was only eighteen years old and she wasn't impressed by anything. She was cool to my casting proposal and had clearly come to be sold on the idea. I talked and talked until she said yes, she would do it, but only if we'd use her whole group in our movie. A deal, I told her.

Věra acted in the film and, through our fake audition, she landed a real job at the Semafor, where she was acting and singing until quite recently. She also slowly warmed up to my advances, became my girlfriend, and later moved into the decommissioned office in Všehrdová Street with me.

I don't know why, but the shooting of *Audition* became a labor of love for everyone who worked on it. Tough Barrandov pros put in hours of unpaid overtime to help us stay within the budget. Míla Hájek, the editor, was so taken by our material that he buried himself in the footage and worked on the film around the clock, crashing right there in the editing room. He had a nearly impossible task, but he pulled it off. We had shot the film with a camera and a tape recorder that could not be synchronized. We didn't even have a clap board, so all we could hand over to him were reams of unreferenced film and reams of un-referenced magnetic tape. Hájek somehow found and matched the audios with the visuals, but the film immediately began to creep out of sync again, so he'd have to cut a few frames of film here and there just to keep everything lined up, which accounts for the jerky quality of the extant prints. Nevertheless, he single-handedly saved the project.

At long last, we had a rough cut. We invited Šebor and Bor for a screening, and they said that there had never been anything like this in the Czech cinema before, but they didn't know what to do with it.

We had trampled on every movie practicality in the book. *Audition* was too short for a feature and too long for a short subject. The only solution was to cut the film from fifty to twenty minutes.

"But that would be like destroying it!" I objected.

The threat of destruction concentrates the mind splendidly, so I quickly came up with another idea. What if we shot a complementary piece about young people and the kind of music the Communists liked, the brass bands?

I made up a simple story to frame a documentary on brass bands and motorcycle racing called *If Only They Ain't Had Them Bands*. Two young trumpet players in different bands of humorless fogies ask to be excused from a rehearsal for an upcoming band competition so they can go see a motorcycle race. They are turned down, but go to the race anyway. Both get fired for it, but then apply to each other's old bands where new trumpet players are now needed, so they wind up merely switching places and beating the system.

Šebor offered this complementary film to Barrandov as a two-fer because I had in the meantime finally gotten a directing job on a feature film. My first full-length movie was scheduled to start shooting in Kolín, so we proposed that I make *If Only They Ain't Had Them Bands* around it. I'd film it on weekends, using the same crew and the same actors. With all this doubling, the budget for *If Only They Ain't Had Them Bands* was so low that Barrandov had to agree.

I gladly put in the overtime, but the truth is that *If Only They Ain't Had*

Them Bands wound up being a moonlighting job for me. I simply couldn't give it the care I'd give my other films.

In 1963, the two semidocumentaries would be released under the title *Audition*. It was my second film to come out that year; my first feature had gone into the cinemas a few months before.

BLACK PETER

Černý Petr (Black Peter) started with a slim manuscript that someone had brought me. It was written by a sculptor, Jaroslav Papoušek, and he could not seem to get it published. The novella took place in a grocery store shortly after the war, so I knew the world Papoušek was writing about intimately and I saw that he had rendered it beautifully. I liked the minimal story and the characters. In fact, I had a sense that the book could have come straight out of my own life.

I contacted Papoušek to see if he was interested in adapting his novella to the screen with me. We hit it off immediately and wrote the screenplay very quickly, transposing it in a later draft to a supermarket in the present, which meant the early sixties. Our script followed a young man as an older grocer breaks him into the business. A big part of his job is to watch out for shoplifters. He is trained to be a responsible citizen, meaning an informer, and he balks at this. He'd rather think about girls and hang out with his buddies. When he finally does see an old lady steal something in the store, he can't bring himself to bust her. He follows her outside and then lets her get away, exasperating his boss and his father.

When Papoušek and I had a script we were happy with, Šebor started to scheme at Barrandov for a cheap production. He might never have wrung an okay for *Black Peter* from the studio had it not been for the intervention of Vojtěch Jasný, a young man of strangely powerful influence who had studied filmmaking in Moscow and was then starting to make his own films.

I cast the roles of all the young people easily. I'd been waiting for a chance to work with Vladimír Pucholt. I'd found him when we were casting *Grandpa Automobile*. He was very young, but had made an indelible impression during his audition and I never forgot him. He was just a little too old for the protagonist in *Black Peter,* so I cast him as the hero's bricklayer buddy. I made three films with Pucholt, one of the most talented actors with whom I have ever worked.

I couldn't find a father for our grocery trainee for a long time. Ivan Passer was working on the project with Papoušek and me, and one evening he went to check out a bandleader for *If Only They Ain't Had Them Bands.* Somehow he got the rehearsal halls mixed up and saw the wrong band. He came back very excited.

"You gotta see this guy, Miloš. He's a real volcano of humanity."

Ivan was right. I cast the sixty-year-old bandleader in my documentary the very next evening. Jan Vostrčil took the role, but only because he lived for brass music and was willing to do anything for it. I asked Vostrčil if he'd read for the father in *Black Peter,* but he flatly refused me. There were no brass bands in that movie, and he wasn't interested in being some kind of show-off. He had too much going on in his life as it was. I kept talking. In the end, I struck a deal with him. He'd read for the father and if he got cast in the role, I'd find a way to incorporate a brass band into the script.

At first, I wondered if Vostrčil wasn't too old for the role of the father. He could have easily been a grandfather to Ladislav Jakim, who played our young hero. But when the two actors read together, their age difference helped to define the conflict between them more sharply, so I learned that a logical incompatibility often brings out the deeper dramatic truth. In the end, we even made the brass band fit our story.

Vostrčil's wife in *Black Peter* was played by Mrs. Matoušková, whom we found while scouting a location. We'd come to see if her house would make a good home for our grocery trainee. She wanted the money badly and she wasn't taking any chances, so she had baked a whole tray of *buchty,* greasy pockets of sweet dough filled with cottage cheese or plum jam, and she plied us full of them. The house was perfect for us, the *buchty* delicious. And as I watched this alert, stout, gray-haired mama work her crafty magic on us, I had a brainstorm, and asked her, "Mrs. Matoušková, how about playing the mother in our movie?"

"Oh, my God! What do you take me for, some kind of movie star?" The idea gave her a big laugh. "I couldn't do that!"

"Sure you could! You can bake *buchty,* can't you?"

"Well, yes, I can bake . . ."

"But that's all you'll have to do." And we shook hands on it.

Her scene came several weeks into the shoot. She was supposed to pipe in when the trainee and his father had a big argument. On the

morning our crew reported to Mrs. Matoušková's house, they found
buchty everywhere. The poor woman had been up all night baking.
Trays of the sweets were cooling off on the windowsills, the friers were
sizzling, a bucket of batter stood on the kitchen floor. All morning, while
we were setting up around her baking utensils, Mrs. Matoušková forced
her *buchty* on people. They were delicious, but also greasy and filling, so
Mrs. Matoušková was soon a nervous wreck: every time someone de-
clined a *buchta*, she thought she had failed as an actress. I don't think
that she even noticed when her acting career started.

"Mrs. Matoušková? Can you stand over here and just watch how
they argue?" I'd tell her and I'd put her into the shot. "That was
wonderful! Now I want you to tell them what you think about what the
kid's been saying. You don't like it, do you? He's pretty cheeky, isn't he?
Okay, action!"

Mrs. Matoušková took a deep breath and gave the two actors a piece
of her mind. She was absolutely true, fresh, and spontaneous—her
performance in the film was as good as her *buchty*.

I worked with all my nonactors in a similar way, never showing them
the script. I had the screenplay memorized word for word, and I'd start
by acting out the scene for them, explaining what I was looking for. I
made sure they understood what the scene was about and their charac-
ter's attitudes. Then we would go right ahead and shoot the scene. My
nonactors would always remember a few lines of the written dialogue
that I'd used and they would make up the rest. When everything went
well, the performers were merely themselves and the words that came
out of them were right on the money.

But working with nonactors requires a good screenplay. They cannot
perform a scene that is false, whereas good actors are able to hide the
shortcomings of a script. In fact, the better the actor, the better the
cover-up. Nonactors, however, simply can't do things they don't in-
stinctively feel are right. In addition, nonactors can only handle a
limited number of takes per scene. After three or four takes, they will
start to repeat what they'd come up with in the previous takes mechani-
cally and all that wonderful life quickly drains from their performances.
In editing *Black Peter*, we frequently wound up using the first takes.

While a trained actor is oblivious to the people on the set and worries
only about the camera, nonactors are generally oblivious to the camera
and frightened by the crew and the people around them, so I learned
to save time by allowing only familiar faces on location. I found that you
can work quicker with nonactors than you can with professionals that
way.

We shot both *Black Peter* and *If Only They Ain't Had Them Bands* in seven weeks for the equivalent of about $70,000—Papoušek, Ivan, and I shared a hotel room and the only catering we ever got were Mrs. Matoušková's *buchty*.

I was so ignorant of the business that nothing seemed impossible, yet during the whole shoot I suffered periodic panic attacks. I'd watch Mr. Vostrčil or Mrs. Matoušková or my teenagers do a take, and it seemed so straight out of real life that it scared me. My God, I'd think, this is so boring! Who's ever going to want to watch this? There was nothing there, just a couple of bored kids shooting the breeze, or parents bitching, or bosses chewing out their underlings. Why should people pay to watch that? All anyone had to do to see the same thing was take a look around.

The scenes seemed so flat, without any redeeming imagination or wit, so stupidly real that I had to hold myself back from juicing them up with some slapstick, jokes, or underlined drama. I kept telling myself that this was precisely the point: you saw scenes like this in real life, but never in the movies. And the final effect was going to come from the sum of the parts and from the context. I had to collect the most "real," that is, the flattest, snippets of life to make a deadly satire of it.

The most difficult scene in *Black Peter* came toward the end of the shoot, and it was a production nightmare. We needed a long scene at a dance, but didn't have the money to hire extras. The only solution was to rent a ballroom in Kolín, throw a free dance on a Saturday night, and shoot the scene with the people who showed up. We'd have from eight o'clock to midnight to get seven minutes of screen time on film. There were going to be no second chances. We'd never get the same people to come again. The scene would require Swiss-clock teamwork from everyone, and I'd have to rely on Ivan even more than usual.

On Thursday morning, Ivan took off on a scouting errand. He was going to find some types, some striking faces, and invite them to our dance because we didn't want to leave anything to chance. Ivan didn't come back all day. He didn't show up in the evening either, so I went to bed furious. I woke up in the morning and Ivan's bed was empty. There was no word from him at reception. I cursed him and delved into all the prep work with Papoušek. We had taken that Friday off the shooting schedule so that we could rehearse the actors, set up the lights, make checklists, put everything in place.

All day I was sure that Ivan would show up at any minute, but he didn't. That night I slept the deep sleep of exhaustion for a few hours, and then I woke up. Ivan's bed was still empty. I didn't sleep a wink the rest of the night. I had speeches running through my head. I was going to tell Ivan just what I thought about his pulling a disappearing act at a time like this, about betraying me just when I needed him most. He had to show up sometime, so I thought he'd be waiting for us on location when we got there but he wasn't.

For all the years I'd known Ivan, well over half of our lives by then, he was impossible to motivate by threats. He never cared. He never got anywhere on time, and he conducted his life strictly on his own terms. It infuriated me, but I secretly admired it, too. This was different, however. My first film, and so my whole career, and so my whole life, depended on this one iffy, chancy dance and the ten pages of script we had to get in the can. For the sake of the film, I resolved that when Ivan finally showed up, I'd try to control my emotions. I'd simply grab him and give him something to do.

That Saturday night remains a blur. We rushed from setup to setup, and somehow we got it all done. We wrapped for the night. Still no Ivan. I was free to kill him now, but too exhausted to care.

Papoušek and I dragged ourselves back to our hotel room at two in the morning. I unlocked the door and saw Ivan sitting at the table. I could feel the blood rush to my face, but before I could let loose with my rage, Ivan gave me that gentle, innocent smile of his.

"Miloš! How could you ever have abandoned me like that?"

I just collapsed on the bed and started laughing. To this day I don't have a clue as to where Ivan was or what he did during the three longest days of my life.

DIRECTOR DRIVES

The first showing of *Black Peter* took place in the small screening room of the Film Club in Prague, and the place was full of old Barrandov hands, their spouses, film buffs, trendy critics, and money changers. I sat down to watch the film, then bolted as soon as it started. Ivan and Papoušek pounded the hallways with me for the duration of the screening, the longest ninety minutes of my life. At last people started coming out. They were subdued, as if they didn't know what to think.

Šebor was worried. "They laughed in all the right places, but at the end they just got up and walked out. They didn't react at all."

Looking back on the film, I can relate to the audience reaction. *Black Peter* doesn't really have an ending. It just sort of stops.

The next day, Šebor called me up, sounding much better. "Something's going on. Every single production group has asked for a screening. I've never known that to happen before."

"Did they say anything?" I asked.

"No, not really, but we're having some kind of a strange impact."

The reviews in the liberal press were wonderful, and even *Rudé Právo,* the Communist Party daily, didn't slaughter us, though, as we expected, its critic didn't see much in the film.

Next came the news that *Black Peter* had been selected for the Locarno film festival. The competition there was stiff and I didn't think I'd have a chance against the likes of Antonioni and Godard, but I was glad to be chosen anyway. I'd finally get a chance to go abroad alone, without a group to slow me down, without the State Security watchdogs.

I'd just become the owner of a car, a British Hillman and a thing of beauty, so I decided to drive to Locarno. I headed there through Paris, which was roughly like going from New York to Montreal via Chicago, but I had to find out what had happened to Sophie Sell.

I arrived in Paris with a map on my knees, my senses dulled from the sheer volume of traffic. After the sleepy streets of Prague, it seemed simply futuristic. I was still wrestling with the steering wheel a bit when I entered my first circular intersection somewhere on the outskirts of Paris. I had no idea of who had the right of way and I got trapped in its inner circle. I went around the central flower bed again and again until a yellow Citroën slammed into me.

There was no question of getting the car repaired. I barely had enough hard currency to get a flat tire fixed, so I arrived in Locarno with the hood held down by a piece of wire. But then the only thing that could make me whole again happened: *Black Peter* beat out all the other films in the competition, including ones by Godard and Antonioni. It was a wonderful feeling, a mixture of gratification and relief, because everything was going to be easier for me now. Any success in capitalist festivals reverberated through the entire Barrandov Studios, and the Locarno laurels were going to boost me up its pecking order. I would definitely be able to make another film, and this time it wouldn't have to be a two-fer.

Barrandov management seemed no less surprised by the prize that I was and quickly entered *Black Peter* in the New York Film Festival. I was elated. I'd longed to see America ever since my parents had dragged me to *Snow White and the Seven Dwarfs,* and now the only catch was that I'd somehow have to survive fourteen hours of torture by airplane.

I got staggeringly drunk for the flight. The propeller plane shook like a washing machine, threatening to come apart at any moment. For fourteen hours I downed drinks and sweated and cursed my stupidity and waited for the wings to drop off and for the icy waters of the Atlantic to swallow us, but the contraption somehow made it all the way to Kennedy Airport, where two lovely hostesses and a huge festival limousine awaited me. I quickly revived.

My head was clear as the black yacht of an automobile sailed onto the runway of a road. I didn't know where to look first. The big cars had fins, and there were house-sized billboards and bright neon signs. Then, suddenly, the breathtaking skyline of New York swung into view. It appeared on the edge of sky, disconnected from the earth, floating on a thin yellow cushion of smog, a panorama of skyscrapers so futuristic and imposing that the tallest buildings were draped in clouds.

When the limo dropped me off at the Drake hotel, just off Park Avenue in the fifties, I strolled to the corner for another magnificent sight. Looking down Park Avenue at Grand Central Station and the Pan Am Building beyond, I was overwhelmed by the sheer scale of the place, its bustling life, the astronomical weight of cement jutting into the low clouds, the streams of gleaming cars flowing by me, the music of vivid colors in signs and clothes and people. It was late summer and the day was hot and humid and I stood with beads of sweat rolling down my back and I smelled the peculiar stink of New York, the odor of exhaust fumes and rotting garbage and loud cologne and sweat and money, an odor that has become the signature of the city for me and which I can never get enough of even now, long after I've tuned out all the spectacular views. I thought then that if one of the zigzagging yellow cabs were to jump the curb and hit me, I'd die a happy man.

I suppose these were the melodramatic thoughts of a little Czech in the big American city, yet I knew I had at last found something commensurate with my ambition, and, from that muggy afternoon on, very privately, in the deepest folds of my consciousness, I started daydreaming that one day, maybe, somehow I'd live in New York for a while, maybe even make it my home.

I must have simply been unhinged by the charms of the capital of the world because there was nothing to justify such musings. *Black Peter* received some nice write-ups in the papers and put my name in the festival Rolodex, but no one from Hollywood called. I still had a lot of work to do before I could begin to catch up to my ambitions, so I returned to Prague and to Věra and to the bells tolling.

Věra and I never talked about getting married. I told her how I'd soured on the institution, and she respected my feelings completely. She was young, carefree, Bohemian, and we were happy together.

"I'm pregnant," Věra announced to me matter-of-factly one day.

"Oh, boy," I said. "Now what?"

"Now we'll have a baby."

She never considered an abortion. Her mind seemed to be made up, and she was comfortable with the choice. I don't recall that she ever even brought up the subject of a wedding. As for me, I simply thought that the baby was her decision.

Věra's stomach began growing, and she started wearing maternity clothes. She sprouted a huge belly, off the charts for her pregnancy stages, and we were both very proud of it.

One evening, Věra's father, Mr. Křesadlo, dropped in for a visit. Věra was singing at the Semafor, so I was at home alone. I liked the old man a lot. A big bruiser of a guy, he was as sweet and tenderhearted as a girl.

"Are you busy, Miloš?" he asked. "Because if you're busy I can come some other time."

I could see that he wanted me to give him a reason to run off, so I was pretty sure I knew what he'd come to talk to me about. I could just imagine the hell that Mr. Křesadlo was catching at home from Věra's mother. In those days, being pregnant out of wedlock seemed like the end of the world to your average Czech, so we had to deal with the issue sooner or later anyway.

"Sit down, please," I said to the old man.

"I won't keep you long," said Křesadlo, taking a chair and a deep breath. "Well, I was just wondering what your intentions are with Věra, now that she's in a family way."

"I love her, and I'll marry her," I said, though I really hadn't been thinking about it much and said it mostly for the old guy's benefit.

He was so relieved and happy that his face lit up with a whole sunrise of emotions. "Miloš, I don't mean to pressure you into anything you don't want to do, you understand. Věra doesn't even know about this."

"Oh, no, of course not."

"Well, I'd better be going," he said, and hurried home to tell his wife so that he could relax and have peace there again.

Věra was very pregnant by the time we got married. And her belly kept growing. Her doctor told her that she was either going to have some huge monstrosity or twins. He couldn't be sure which unless she agreed to an X ray, but Věra resolutely refused.

On August 24, 1964, she went into labor. Back then, fathers were not allowed anywhere near the delivery room. They were barely tolerated in the hospital. The Czech custom dictated that they be out drinking with friends—to "water" the baby so that it would grow—which was fine by me because the whole business of giving birth made me very nervous.

The grand old dame of the Czech theater, Stella Zázvorková, threw a party for me, and I was sitting in her kitchen, "watering" our monstrosity with all my old friends, when I got word from the hospital. Věra had just had twin boys, Petr and Matěj and everyone was okay. In the kitchen, there was a huge toast and sentimental speeches. Another old Czech custom dictated that the father be served a plate of piping-hot lentils onto which a raw egg is tossed. The lentils are money, the egg is gold, and the growing family will never want for anything if the new dad polishes off the plate.

When Stella laid the plate of steaming lentils in front of me, the whole room broke out in happy commotion. Stella took an egg and broke it over my plate. All the kibitzing died out instantly.

The egg had a double yolk.

POSTCARD FROM ECUADOR

I'd lost my father and then I'd lost the brother who would be my father and then, sometime in 1963 or 1964, I got my father back.

While I was still living in the office in Všehrdová Street, I received a letter in large script, as if written by someone who was very farsighted. It came from Hradec Králové and it was signed by a woman whose signature I couldn't decipher. She wrote that she had gotten to know and love my mother in Auschwitz. Before she died of typhoid, my mother had asked this woman to find me if she survived and to tell me something that my mother herself couldn't have told me, but now wanted me to know.

My father, Rudolf Forman, was not my real father. My biological father was someone else.

I remembered the man. He was an architect. He did some work on Hotel Rut for my mother. I liked him as a boy. Not because he showed any special interest in me, but because he had this life force about him. He made people laugh. He was always in motion, always funny, always playing. He disappeared just before the war. He was Jewish, and he'd left for South America just in time to save himself.

My first reaction to the letter was denial. This was some poor crackpot who'd lost her sanity in the horrors that she'd gone through. But the fact was that the woman knew too much, in far too great detail, and it all fit. I'd never looked like my brothers. I was conceived in June, the month my mother usually spent alone at Rut, preparing it for the season. And how could this woman who wasn't from Čáslav even know about the architect? And why did she wait twenty years to relay my mother's message?

But if it was true, a posthumous voice was revealing that I was a bastard, that I was half-Jewish. My life was becoming an incredible melodrama. And if she was right, did my father know that I didn't bear his genes? Did he have any idea? And why did my mother want me to know?

I don't think my father knew. Or if he did, he never let on. He'd never treated me as anything else but his flesh, his son. Rudolf Forman was my true father.

Divining my mother's motivation for the deathbed revelation was more difficult. Maybe she simply wanted to clear her conscience. Maybe seeing the slaughter of Jews by the millions in Auschwitz, breathing the smoke from burning Jewish babies and grandmothers, she wanted to take upon herself their fate. Maybe she wanted to deny Hitler at least that half gallon of Jewish blood that ran through my veins. Maybe she simply didn't want me to wind up an orphan when I really had a father. I don't know what she thought and I never will, but twenty years after her death, Mother gave me a strange and a confusing gift.

It felt wonderful to have a parent after all. I had nothing but fond memories of the architect. He had patted my head a few times, made me laugh once or twice, probably helped my mother steal some happiness. He gave me his genes. He probably survived the war. He was quite possibly still alive.

Once I knew that I had one foot in that wandering tribe of over-achievers that infuriates so many people on earth, I searched for him. I found him easily. The house that Blahoslav had lived in in Staré Splavy still belonged to the architect, so my sister-in-law had his address. I didn't tell her why I wanted to know, but I learned that my supposed biological father, my third parent, lived in Ecuador. He was a professor at the university, and he had a large family there, five children.

I wrote him a letter saying I wanted nothing whatsoever from him, except maybe to meet him sometime later. I just wanted to know if it was all true. I received no reply. I tried again. *Would you, please, let me know at least if you've gotten my first letter?* I wrote.

He sent back a postcard of a town nestled high in the Andes. You could see from the handwriting that he was an old man now.

"I did receive your letter and I send my regards," said the large, trembling letters.

Years later, I took both the letter and the postcard and threw them away—I didn't pursue it further. I myself don't understand why.

LOVES OF A BLONDE

Of all my movies, *Loves of a Blonde* is the one in which life inspired art, which went on to inspire life again, even though the whole process took years to run its course.

Late one Saturday night, back in the late fifties, after my first marriage had collapsed, I saw a girl in the center of Prague. She was pretty. She dragged a small battered suitcase. She was not in a hurry to get anywhere, not looking for attention, and she certainly wasn't a hooker. She was lost, but she didn't seem to mind very much. I was curious to know her story. I guess I'll always be moved by the sight of a young person with a suitcase seeking a connection in a strange city. I struck up a conversation with her and tried to pick her up. She went to my room with me and told me her story. She was from Varnsdorf, a textile town in northern Bohemia. The industry employs mostly women, so the ratio of men to women was low, nearly ten to one, and the girls there were very panicky about finding a man. They all worried that they would never get married.

The girl with the battered suitcase had met a balding engineer from Prague who had come to Varnsdorf on business. He said he wasn't married. He took her to a bar and kept telling her that she must come and see him in Prague. He wanted to share the city with her, show her a good time there. She let him make love to her. He gave her his address.

Two weeks later she went to Prague to see him. She barely knew the city. It took her all day that Saturday to establish that the address didn't exist. She spent the evening sightseeing. She spent the night talking with me. At five o'clock in the morning, I drove her to the train station and she took the first train out of Prague, but she stayed on my mind for years. Her story touched me for some reason and it would come back to me at odd times, so I kept thinking about it. I finally asked Papoušek and Ivan if they thought there might be a screenplay there.

"Maybe, but it still needs one more thing," said Ivan.

"What's that?"

"A billiards table."

In those days, we played billiards with a passion, and it seemed to us that we could transform even the slimmest idea into a movie if there was a pool table nearby. The Communists regarded billiards as a bourgeois pastime, so there weren't very many good tables around the country, but there was a fine one at the Dobříš Castle, and we wrote the screenplay there. We called it *Lásky jedné plavovlásky* (*Loves of a Blonde*).

We shot the film in the small town of Zruč nad Sázavou, which had shoe factories that employed mostly women who were spooked by the same penis shortage as Varnsdorf. All the locals immediately understood the story, and the place happened to have a decent billiards table, too.

In our film, a kindly factory manager feels sorry for his lonely girls, so he gets the army to promise to station a garrison in their town. The town of women is all atwitter when the big day comes, but the military train discharges only a raggedy troop of balding, beer-bellied reservists. At the welcoming dance for the garrison, the film's blond heroine is picked up by a piano player. He is not a particularly smooth operator, but he is a Prague boy and he gives her his address. A couple of weeks later, the blonde shows up at his apartment and finds only his parents home. She knows no one else in the city, and the parents finally let her sleep on their son's couch in the kitchen. The young man winds up in his parents' bed that night. It's a tight fit. The old man wants to sleep, the son would like to get thrown out so he can join the girl on the couch, but the mother runs the show and won't tolerate any such filthy ideas. Not under her roof. The disappointed blonde returns to her factory dormitory in Zruč and makes up stories about a loving fiancé in Prague, which the whole room of lonely girls dreams on.

I never considered anyone but Vladimír Pucholt for our piano player. This great actor, who had tremendous artistic intuition, completely distrusted his talent. I think this was because he had a very rationalist disposition and could never see, much less measure, the results of his acting.

It took him only a few years to become one of the biggest film stars in Czechoslovakia, until suddenly, in 1967, he defected to England. He had no money and he spoke no English, but he did have a good place to start: he knew Lindsay Anderson. Anderson let Pucholt stay at his house for two years while this star of Czech cinema washed shop windows during the day to support himself and took English classes in the evening. In four years, he graduated from the secondary school and went on to study medicine. Five years later, Dr. Pucholt moved to Canada with a girl he met in England.

Today, Dr. Pucholt runs a thriving pediatric practice in Ottawa. He can see the results of his work every day, and he is happy. I have dinner with him now and then, so I know that he has never looked back. He harbors no regrets, though many people in Czechoslovakia still don't comprehend how he could have thrown away the life and adoration that others would kill for. Pucholt's reasons, however, were simple: ever since he was a kid he wanted to be a doctor. He had applied to the medical school at Charles University in Prague three times, and three times the school turned him down as being of "bourgeois origins" (his father had been a lawyer before the Communist revolution). As Pucholt sees it, his career in the movies was only an accidental detour on the road to his true calling.

Back in *Loves of a Blonde,* as a rising film star, Pucholt seduced my ex-sister-in-law Hana Brejchová, our girl with the suitcase. Another wonderful actor, Láďa Menšík, played one of the reservists. We used nonactors in all the other roles, among them Ivan Kheil and Jiří Hrubý, both of whom who had once done *The Ballad in Rags* with me.

Shooting *Loves of a Blonde,* I learned that mixing professional actors and nonactors actually helped both groups, but you had to have actors who could stand up to the challenge of the unstudied, natural behavior of nonactors. It takes a great actor to blend into a scene with people who are being themselves. A lesser actor, an actor who doesn't fully exist in the situation he creates, who reflexively assumes an attitude and isn't open to the moment, loses hugely by contrast with the nonactor who is always either truthful or stiff. Conversely, when an actor is giving a calculated performance, the lack of spontaneity in his behavior inhibits the nonactor because anything that's false in the scene throws a non-actor off. While nonactors keep the actors honest and real, the actors give the scene the rhythm and shape that the nonactors don't feel. A nonactor inhabits the situation so completely that he or she isn't able to view it from the outside, to perceive it as a rhythmic whole with its punctuation and its larger dramatic purpose. Nonactors are perfectly content to repeat themselves and ramble on, so an actor can pull them through the dramatic arch of the scene and draw out the emotional contours of the situation.

The cast of *Loves of a Blonde* was a perfect balance of actors and nonactors, and I remember those few months in Zruč in 1964 as some of my sunniest days in the movie business. We had all the time we needed. We played billiards. We choked on laughter watching Pucholt fight his "parents" in the narrow marital bed. We delivered the film on schedule and on budget.

The prettiest of the Zruč girls in our cast fell in love with one of the technicians. She was only a teenager, coltish, good-hearted, and blond. The handsome technician neglected to tell her that he had a wife and a kid in Prague, so they conducted a torrid love affair for the few weeks of shooting. The envious girls in the factory started calling her "movie star." She didn't mind. With her role in our film, her looks, and her Barrandov boyfriend, a career in the movies no longer seemed like a delusion of grandeur.

We finished shooting, and the technician went back to Prague. He told the girl that he first had to set up a living situation for her. She was to stay in Zruč and wait till he sent for her. She waited and waited. She had, of course, told all the girls in her dorm about her boyfriend's promise. They began to make fun of their movie star. Defending her boyfriend, she started making up stories, saying that he was coming to carry her off any day now. But the lie became harder and harder to sustain.

One day, she had had enough. She packed her belongings and told her roommates that she'd finally gotten the word. Her boyfriend had a love nest waiting for her. He had the ring, too. He was dying for them finally to be together. In Prague, she found out that the technician wanted no part of her. He had no intention of leaving his family—her experience seemed straight out of our film.

What happened to the girl from Zruč after this point, however, would make for a much more melancholy picture. She couldn't bear to go back home, feeling anything would be better than the derision that awaited her in her old dorm: "Hey, movie star, you got a phone call from Hollywood. Hey, movie star, your fiancé's downstairs with a jeweler, get that finger out of your nose." In Prague, she had no place to go, but she had her looks, so she started living off them. She worked the bars of the Hotels Alcron and Jalta and got paid in foreign currency. She was just waiting for the screen test that would spring her.

One evening when *Loves of a Blonde* was history and I was working on another project, I had a meeting with a Western journalist in the Alcron and ran into her. I bought her a drink. She was flustered and happy to be seen with someone from the movies. It made her somebody in the eyes of the other girls. I was interested in her stories from the demi-monde, so I'd stop in now and again and talk to her.

In those days, the biggest pimp in Prague was the government. All the hookers had to report on their customers to the State Security, which could then use the information to blackmail those foreigners in whom they were interested. The girl from Zruč didn't want to rat on her johns. She didn't like the game, so she was thrown in jail for a few weeks, went back to work the bars, got picked up again. For the hookers, this was life.

After a few stints in jail, the girl from Zruč signed on the dotted line for the State Security, but she never intended to keep her end of the bargain. She didn't produce for the pimp. She went back to jail. The charge was never prostitution because the Communist Party had decreed that in socialist Czechoslovakia, prostitution had ceased to exist after the revolution. The Alcron hookers who didn't respect the State Security pimp were all sentenced as "social parasites," or people who didn't hold jobs.

The girl from Zruč figured that she would beat the system by getting a job. It was all about a stamp. A job would put a stamp in the employer's window of her citizen's passport, so she could never again be thrown in jail as a parasite. The ploy worked, but it was murder on her. She had no education, so she couldn't get decent work. She wound up washing floors in a hospital. Her shift ran from four in the morning until noon. She'd go home, sleep for four or five hours, make herself beautiful, and head to the bar to enchant some Western tourist. I had to admire her character. She was killing herself so that she wouldn't have to become an informant.

One evening I dropped in at the Alcron, but the blonde from Zruč wasn't there. The other night butterflies told me she was doing time again. The government made the rules and the government broke the rules, so the State Security had found something to get her with anyway.

I didn't see her for months. The next time I did, she was happier to
see me than ever before. I noticed that she was hiding her hands from
me. I seized her arm, and she slowly showed me a hideous scar running
across her wrist.

"I didn't know what else to do," she said.

She had been squeezed into investigative detention, which was
tougher than the penal institutions. Her cell was tiny, and she could
only see a patch of sky through the bars on the high window. There was
nothing to do. The only books they gave her were those of Marx and
Lenin. Finally, she came across a novel from the nineteenth century. It
was a quaintly written story about village people, but the girl from Zruč
didn't care. She didn't read the book. She only looked at the illustra-
tions: "They were so beautiful I couldn't keep from bawling every time
I opened the book." She was especially taken by the only picture that
had no people in it. It rendered a meadow sloping down to a shimmer-
ing pond. There were some trees on the brow of the hill, birds were
singing, and the sun was shining. The colors alone were as beautiful as
anything she'd ever seen. In her gray cell, even the patch of sky was
mostly yellow with smog.

The girl from Zruč kept looking at the pastoral scene until she
decided she didn't want to live anymore. But it wasn't easy to take your
life in jail.

"I fooled them though!" she reported to me proudly. She told the jail
matron that she was an actress and had to take care of her skin. If she
wasn't allowed to use her makeup kit, her career would be shot. To her
surprise, the matron agreed and showed up every day in the cell with
the kit. But she didn't leave the blonde from Zruč alone. She stood there
and watched while the girl took good care of the very skin that deep
down she felt like peeling right off her face.

One afternoon, the girl slipped a small glass mirror out of the powder
box and hid it in her ugly prison clothes. The matron locked her up in
the cell again and the girl waited until night descended, then broke the
mirror and opened the book. She looked at the green, luscious meadow
and the bright, warm sun while she drove the shards of glass into her
wrists.

"It hurt so much! The pain was killing me, but I wanted to make sure
that I didn't just black out and have somebody find me and save me,
so I kept cutting and cutting," she told me.

The blood spurted out of both her wrists, and she began to feel
lightheaded, so she shoved both her hands into the stinking, shit-
smeared toilet hole in the corner of her cell.

"I wasn't taking any chances. I wanted all that horrible filth to finish the job. If the blood loss didn't kill me, I was going to die of an infection for sure." She blacked out with her bleeding hands in the toilet. She came to again in the hospital.

She still dreamed of making more movies but now she was beginning to have her doubts. She didn't regret anything though. "You can't begin to imagine how beautiful that picture was," she told me.

In 1968, Czech borders were briefly opened and the girl from Zruč disappeared from the hotel bars for good. The night butterflies told me she'd emigrated to Australia. Australia was the exact opposite of Zruč. There was a woman shortage there, especially among the Czech émigrés.

Years later, she began calling me in New York. She was usually drunk. She had a daughter, a very talented girl, who studied acting. She wanted me to see her. The daughter would accomplish everything her mother had missed out on. I never hung up on her. The girl from Zruč was no longer a girl and I could hear in her voice that life had made her tougher than leather, but I could never forget how she was when we found her standing by a conveyor belt in that shoe factory and cast her in *Loves of a Blonde*. She was like a cherry blossom then.

ALL THE SADNESS OF RUSSIA

Loves of a Blonde sold out in theaters across Czechoslovakia and won me the State Prize of Klement Gottwald. Gottwald had been the first Communist president of the land and a legendary boozer, so the prize was more of an embarrassment than anything else. The only good thing about it was the fat envelope that came with the ribbon. It held 20,000 crowns, nearly a year's salary, and it went a little way to make up for the contempt that Ivan exhibited for all the laureates of the State Prize.

Loves of a Blonde also enlarged the world for me. The film opened the 1966 New York Film Festival, so I was allowed to visit the capital of the world again. I went to Cannes, London, and several other places with it, and the film was nominated for an Oscar in the Best Foreign Film category, but it was beaten out by Claude Lelouch's *A Man and a Woman*.

Czechoslovakia had started moving toward the political openness of the Prague Spring of 1968 and travel to the West no longer seemed like a very big thing. Václav Havel was the most daring and promising playwright in the country, and his absurdist plays vividly mocked the totalitarian bureaucracy and power.

In the Soviet Union, Brezhnev had deposed Khrushchev and the empire was sliding back from the relative liberalism of his era, so Moscow proved to be one of the more memorable places where I showed *Loves of a Blonde*. I went there with another young director, Pavel Juráček, as a guest of the Union of Soviet Film Artists. We stayed in one of their huge hotels and got a young lady translator to show us around the city, but we never felt welcome or at ease there. Everything seemed to be a problem. I wanted to meet Andrei Tarkovsky, the master of the modern Soviet cinema, and it took all the cunning of another fine director and friend, Elem Klimov, to arrange it. In the end, Juráček and I got to shake Tarkovsky's hand in some forsaken park on the outskirts of the city in an awkward, clandestine encounter. We knew by then that our lady translator was a subversive at heart. We had been talking with her openly, and one morning she told us that some of her friends in the Moscow underground were dying to meet me. They'd seen *Loves of a Blonde* at some secret screening and thought the world of it. They were mostly painters and sculptors. She'd organize a get-together for us if Juráček and I were willing to risk giving the slip to the people who watched us. We agreed.

Most of the hotel people where we stayed worked for the KGB, so one evening we faked calling it an early night and then slipped out again through the back entrance. The translator waited for us in a side street. She was very nervous. She made sure that no one had followed us, then quickly hustled us off to a taxi that she had waiting around a corner.

Our destination was a desolate block of cement high rises somewhere on the periphery of Moscow. You could easily lose a shoe in the swamps around the buildings and never pry it out of the mud again. We got out of the taxi and waited for the translator to find the place where we were to meet. It turned out that she'd never been there before. She finally located an iron door, leading into some communal basement and began pounding on it. It took forever before a long-bearded Russian showed up. He was holding a candle and led us down a long, dark corridor, closer and closer to the sounds of a balalaika being strummed and mournful voices singing in the entrails of the cement warren. We reached a small room where the hallway ended. There were five or six bearded men inside, sitting on overturned crates. At the center of the room lay a large box and, on top of it, a few bottles of vodka, a loaf of bread, a chunk of salami. Around the walls towered hunks of abstract sculpture, some wrapped in rags. The room was lit by a bare bulb, and Dostoyevsky probably ran the boiler room beyond.

Our guide blew out the candle and motioned to us to sit down on some crates. The others barely glanced at us and went on singing the slow song that contained all the sadness of Russia. The balalaika player hardly even opened his eyes.

We sat there. The bearded men sang. Now and then they passed a bottle of vodka around and we took a hit. No one said a word. The Russians crooned their endless melody. Half an hour later, our translator got up. "All right. Now we go," she said. Our Russian admirers never stopped singing. We didn't even get to say good-bye.

Memory has a way of betraying you, but I recall this evening very clearly because something about that situation deeply resonated in me. I suppose that it had to do with my being an outsider there, with my hovering again on the periphery of an enclosed world that had promised to have a place for me.

Perhaps that evening stirred up the old feelings of a ten-year-old kid who is never given the time to fit in anywhere, who is kept outside the emotional core of other families. It's the emotion of standing by a glass house and seeing everything that goes on inside, but never touching it, never being touched by it. Maybe this feeling is never quite forgotten, maybe it can't be forgotten, maybe it still reverberates, maybe it always will, because looking back on my films I see outsiders everywhere and I see outsider feelings at their emotional core.

I see the blonde in the piano player's house spending the night on the couch and listening to her hosts argue about her while she has nowhere else to go. I see McMurphy faking a mental illness in the mental ward of *One Flew Over the Cuckoo's Nest*. I see all the misfits of *Hair*, the black man in the white world of *Ragtime*, the genius among the mediocrities of *Amadeus*. They are all repulsed and attracted by an enclosed world, all struggling to belong and never making it, though they all manage to make their mark on that world.

The psychic motor that drives your creativity doesn't change and nearly always runs on the same fuel. You read reams of material and, suddenly, a story grabs you and you feel the excitement stirring in you and you never really know why. It's an unconscious, but palpable process. Something inside you has locked onto the subterranean currents of feeling that course through the particular theme or story. And more likely than not, it's a feeling that has gripped you before because in the end this feeling is your artistic identity, so I suppose that the cement basement of a forsaken high rise on the muddy outskirts of Moscow contained not only all the sadness of Russia that night, but all of mine, too.

SWIMMING POOL CINEMA

The success of *Loves of a Blonde* brought Carlo Ponti into my life. The New Wave of the Czech cinema was then cresting, films by Věra Chytilová, Jiří Menzel, Ján Kadár, Elmar Klos, Jan Němec, and others were getting written up all over Europe, and Ponti wanted to buy into the publicity. He had just made millions on *Doctor Zhivago,* and we were a good deal.

Moris Ergas, Ponti's right-hand man, set up his boss's investment in the development of a script I am still sorry about not having made. The story of *Americans Are Coming* began with the last wild bear in the Tatra Mountains. The bear is very old and probably about to die, so Czech forestry officials decide to sell him to Western hunters. A hit-or-miss shot costs $10,000, and a rich American buys the first go at the last bear of the Carpathians. But before he arrives, the bear wanders off and crosses the border into Poland. Panic sets in—the money's in the bank. The American has landed in Prague and the bear is abroad. The story takes off from there.

Papoušek, Ivan, and I were excited about the situational sketch we had, and we were humming with ideas. Ponti immediately invited us to Italy to work on the script in the countryside outside Rome. He didn't want us to write it without his input. He would provide an English screenwriter who understood the commercial side of the business in the West and who would help us shape our comedy for audiences that paid hard currency. The three of us talked it over and agreed to give this collaboration a shot. Even if nothing came of it, we'd at least get a few weeks in Italy out of the deal.

Ponti put us up in a heavenly hotel by the sea in Torrvaianica, gave us a rented car, some pocket money, and an intimidating English screenwriter who shall remain nameless. This man had recently penned an extremely successful commercial movie, had two secretaries, rented half of a splendid castle with a wonderful swimming pool, and seemed more prolific than locusts. He was dictating both his secretaries to an early grave.

We would drive to the castle and work by the swimming pool with him every afternoon. The place was straight out of an absurdist play. It was owned by an aristocrat from one of Rome's oldest families. He wasn't rich, though he did keep two servants, so he rented out a wing in the castle to interesting tenants to support the household. He spent his time writing abstruse Marxist essays and, as a passionate Communist, rarely asked his servants to do anything for him. The servants sunned themselves by the pool with the rest of us. Whenever the aristocrat got up, they would lift their heads.

"Where you going?" one of them would ask.

"I'm just going to get a Coke," said the castle owner.

"Can you get me one, too?"

"Of course."

And so this Marxist aristocrat waited on his servants all week. But on weekends, when the castle filled up with other aristocrats visiting from Rome, the servants would put on their uniforms and do their jobs. Evidently, they had some affection for their boss and didn't want him to lose face before his peers. On Monday, however, they would be sprawled around the pool again.

Italy was fun, but screenwriting by the swimming pool got scary. Our Englishman had two other projects going at the time. He was dictating a play in verse about Samson and Delilah to one secretary and a learned treatise on Chinese porcelain to the other. He usually devoted his mornings to the couplets, then squeezed us in around his scholarly book in the afternoon.

He would set up his pretty secretary on the far side of the pool from us and dictate to her for an hour. It looked to us as if he were spinning whole chapters off the top of his head while splashing in the pool. Our English wasn't very good, so we couldn't be sure, but he kept talking and the secretary kept nodding and putting away sheets of densely written paper. When he reached a convenient point in his narrative, he would commute to his other job, that is, he would wade across the pool to us. For twenty minutes, we would discuss how best to shoot the last bear of the Carpathians.

The man rarely got out of the water. He would give us something to chew on and then commute back to his secretary with slow breast strokes, giving us an hour to argue about what he meant by what he had just told us.

The screenwriter loved our ideas, but thought they were just a little off. In our broken English, we struggled to understand how we could improve them. We had come with the script already outlined in our minds, but in spite of ourselves we began to adopt his half-understood suggestions. The man was obviously a writing factory, and what did we know about Western audiences?

After a week by the swimming pool, the four of us drove to Rome for a story conference with Ponti. We got to Ponti's production offices on time, but we were made to wait for a couple of hours. As we sat there, our Englishman started getting more and more nervous. Suddenly, he pulled out a pipe and a chunk of hashish and lit it up right there in the waiting room.

"Have a hit, guys! Ponti's going to want us to act out for him what we've got. This will definitely help," he said. We passed the pipe around in silence. The hashish was fine.

When we at last got invited in to see Ponti, his office was slightly cloudy and objects had a way of slipping out of focus. The room was surprisingly small, lined with red-bound books, and crowded with a pack of porcelain dogs. They were life-sized and hideous, the kind you see around dusty railroad stations. Ponti sat behind a human-sized desk on a stair-high platform, overlooking the visitors' chairs in front of it. He peered at us thoughtfully while we acted out for him what we had so far.

"That's fabulous," said Ponti when we finished. "But here's what I thought we were all working on." He proceeded to give us a different story, focusing not on the Czechs with the bear, but on the American hunter. I am not sure whose story was better, but clearly they were never going to converge into one screenplay.

Driving back to the hotel, Papoušek, Ivan, and I sank into depression. Our "screenwriting factory" didn't see the situation nearly as darkly. He was sure we could still iron everything out. It would only take some intestinal fortitude on our part.

"*La vie c'est la guerre,*" he offered.

The following day, by the pool, we tried again. The Englishman swam back and forth, but now he tried to incorporate Ponti's ideas into our script. Most likely, his fee was at stake.

Three days later, we went for another conference with Ponti. We waited again for a long time, smoking hashish and listening to a yelling match in Ponti's office. Three men were hollering in Italian at the top of their lungs, and when the door opened, Vittorio De Sica and Cesare Zavattini staggered out. They weren't bloodied, but they moved as if they'd just taken a beating. I think that De Sica and Zavattini have made some of the best films in the history of motion pictures. I must have seen *Miracle in Milan* at least twenty times by now. I'd have loved to shake their hands, but I didn't dare open my mouth as I watched them drag themselves out the door.

Surrounded by his pack of silent dogs, Ponti seemed very much himself. I really disliked the man by then, though I didn't let on.

"That was Mr. De Sica and Mr. Zavattini, wasn't it?" I asked Ponti.

"Don't even remind me!" growled Ponti, pointing at his stone hounds. "These dogs here could write a better screenplay than those two!"

"So why don't you just write that script yourself, Mr. Ponti?"

"Oh, I'd love to! Do you think I've got the stomach for dealing with people like them! But where am I going to find the time?"

The first to leave Italy was Papoušek.

"This is nuts," he said. "I can't do this."

Ivan and I stayed for a few more days, but it was no use. We parted with Ponti like a couple of old business partners who couldn't agree on a deal.

FIREMAN'S BALL

When you fail at something, the natural tendency is to throw yourself into work and press hard to redeem the failure.

We returned from Italy and Ivan got busy on another project, but Papoušek and I immediately started to write a screenplay about an army deserter living in the bowels of the Lucerna Concert Hall. We headed to the Krkonoše Mountains, where we had a wonderful billiards table, yet the writing was slow and painful, and then it completely bogged down. I think we were trying too hard or perhaps there was some fatal flaw in our story. Ivan came to help us, but even he couldn't push us off the dead spot.

Frustrated and testy, the three of us decided to forget about the script and go to a ball the local fire brigade was throwing. We'd watch people, get drunk, maybe talk to some girls, relax. We had nothing better to do with our Saturday night anyway.

The Vrchlabí Fire Department was staffed by volunteers. The men mostly worked factory jobs. They came to have a great time, and they did. They held a beauty contest for their homely daughters. They ran a raffle. They drank and they argued with their wives and they were utterly themselves.

On Sunday, Papoušek, Ivan, and I just couldn't stop talking about everything that we had seen at the ball. On Monday, we were developing our impressions into what-ifs. On Tuesday, we began writing.

The script nearly wrote itself. When any questions came up, we just headed back to Vrchlabí and checked with the firemen. We found the tavern where they drank beer, played cards, shot pool. They got to know us and talked to us openly. Six weeks later, we had the final draft of *Hoří má panenko*, or *Fireman's Ball*.

Our screenplay was firmly grounded in what we had seen at the ball and built on those situations. An elderly fireman watches over disappearing raffle prizes, a beauty contest for the homely daughters excites mostly the mothers, who put heavy pressure on the judges, a fire starts in town.

Šebor liked the screenplay, and while he got the production process rolling, I went back to Vrchlabí. I checked into the local hotel and made myself a regular at the tavern near the fire house. I closed the place with the volunteer firemen every night for a couple of weeks. I still had the liver you've got to have for that sort of filmmaking. By the time I left town, I had all the roles cast with people whom I liked and who liked me.

When we were ready to go into production, Ergas and Ponti decided to invest in the project. Ponti put down $80,000. On paper, this made him the producer of our film, though he never even laid eyes on the set, and gave us a chance to make our film in color. In those days, most films produced by Barrandov were in black and white. Only the most senior and meritorious directors, who usually also happened to be the biggest party hacks, got the approval for East German color stock. It was called Orwo, and its colors were uneven, soft, and lyrical, which didn't make it particularly suitable for a comedy. With Ponti's money, we were able to buy good color stock in the West. I wanted to shoot *Fireman's Ball* in color simply because it brought the film another step closer to reality. Usually, I don't have any deep feelings about color in my films, though I do insist that black always be truly black and that skin not look embalmed.

We had enough dollars left over to buy Elemac, a dolly with a crane that made our dance scenes much easier to shoot. Our firemen didn't

have to trip over the rails and cables of a standard Barrandov produc-
tion, so all in all the Ponti investment seemed a fine deal to me.

We returned to Vrchlabí and started to shoot. There wasn't a profes-
sional actor in the cast, and all our volunteer firemen had full-time jobs
at the local factory. They got up at five in the morning, punched in at
six, punched out at two, went home, ate, changed clothes, and reported
to the movie set. We started shooting at four in the afternoon and
worked till ten or eleven at night, day in and day out, for seven incred-
ible weeks.

The firemen were enthusiastic and selfless, and the rushes looked just
fine. I used the same working method I did on *Black Peter*. I never
showed the script to anyone in the cast. I acted out each scene for the
firemen and then let them find their own words when the film was
rolling. The structure of our screenplay didn't change much, but the
dialogue, the rhythms, the behavior became much more authentic.

When I locked myself in the editing room with the footage, I realized
that I'd have to keep the final cut fairly short. *Fireman's Ball* was a film
about an event, so it had all the Aristotelian unities in place, but this
worked against its emotional impact. There were no central characters
for the audience to identify with, no one to carry the film.

When I finished editing the movie, it clocked in at seventy-three
minutes, but I was very happy with it. The only thing I worried about
was how it would play to the cultural apparatchiks. Most of them got
promoted for having absolutely no sense of humor, so I knew they
wouldn't like my realistic comedy. But I hoped that Ponti would like it
and that he'd set up a distribution deal in the West. At that time in
Czechoslovakia, hard currency already talked louder than the Party.

We had been in touch with Ponti throughout the production. Ergas
had even visited us on location a couple of times. I liked Ergas because
he wasn't pretentious. He had started out by exporting pasta and the
last I heard of him he was in hotel management, so for him business was
business. He had married a movie star, Sandra Milo, but he remained
folksy and down-to-earth and had a genuine affection for Czech mov-
ies.

Whenever we showed Ergas a scene, he made his standard sugges-
tion: "Needs more love!" By that, he meant naked girls. I have nothing
against love scenes or naked girls, but I just didn't see any way to graft
them onto our story. I'd gone over the subject with Ergas several times
and thought he had finally accepted my point.

As soon as we finished the first rough cut of the film, we invited Ponti
to come to Prague and see it. Ponti showed up with the standard retinue

of a mogul, which was good because I didn't want to show him *Fireman's Ball* in a human vacuum. I was sure that the bigger the audience, the bigger the laughs it would get.

At that first screening there were a few chuckles when the projector began to spin, but they soon died out. A silence descended on the room, spread, deepened, and reigned. The movie ended, the lights came on, and Ponti got up. He nodded to me, looked away, and headed for the exit. He said nothing. His entourage gave a few embarrassed smiles, and then they were all gone.

The next thing I heard was that Ponti wanted his $80,000 back. The official reason he gave was breach of contract. I hadn't even read the contract the Czech Filmexport people had me sign with Ponti because my English wasn't up to it. I was told to sign my name on the dotted line and I did. Now I learned that one of the fine-print clauses specified that Ponti was buying 75 minutes of film product from us. We had only delivered seventy-three minutes; we had cheated him out of two minutes of product, so the contract was null and void.

I was later told what Ponti's real objection was. He felt we were mocking the Common Man, which was not good for business. Within the month, the Communist bureaucrats would level nearly the same charge against *Fireman's Ball*. They said I was mocking the working class, which of course was not good for *their* business. The Italian millionaire and Party apparatchiks shared the same bogus sentimentality about the Common Man, this mythical construct of bad philosophers and statisticians, because neither of them knew anything about how regular folks lived and thought.

BANNED FOR ALL TIME

While there was still the chance that my film might bring the national treasury some hard currency, no one dared attack *Fireman's Ball*, but as soon as I lost my Italian patron, I was in trouble. The Party's cultural department declared open season on the film, and it didn't help that Communist President Antonín Novotný asked for a private screening. I was told that the president "climbed the walls" when he saw it.

In the movie, an elderly deputy chief watches over a table with raffle prizes. He is conscientious, but drowsy, so the gifts start walking. His wife is furious with his incompetence, but when stealing the raffle prizes becomes an epidemic in the hall, she cusses him out for being stupid: why the hell doesn't he at least pocket something for himself, too, before it's all gone?

The table is nearly empty by the time the matter is brought to the attention of the fire chief. The chief, played with genius by the old bandmaster Vostrčil, gives a scolding speech to the partygoers. Too many things have disappeared, too many people are involved, and it's a big stain on the honor of everyone present. Even though he is of a mind to call the police, he magnanimously declares an amnesty: if the thieves return what they have stolen, all will be forgiven.

No one steps forward, so the chief orders that the lights in the ballroom be turned off so that the thieves can return their loot in total anonymity. The lights go down. When they come back on, they catch only the old deputy in their glare. The poor man passes out—he was returning a chunk of headcheese his wife had stolen after their argument. Mortified, the chief calls a council of firemen into the back room. A lively argument ensues. Some of the firemen hold that the deputy did the right thing in returning the headcheese, because it showed that the only honest man in the room was a member of the fire brigade. Others argue that once the deputy had stolen the headcheese, he should never have put it back. He had dishonored the department not by stealing the headcheese, but by returning it and making all the firemen look stupid.

In this story of the looted raffle, the guiding lights of the Czech Communist Party saw a satire of themselves. In the past, they would have simply prohibited the showing of the film, but in that strange era before the Prague Spring, the Communist leadership was losing its nerve and had started to finesse its unpopular decisions. Now they would set up a screening of a film they wanted to ban before an invited audience. They planted a few provocateurs in the crowd to shout that the movie insulted the working people, then ordered the film removed from distribution on the grounds that the "people" had demanded it.

The first public preview of *Fireman's Ball* was scheduled for Vrchlabí. The cultural apparatchiks chose the place because they figured that the Vrchlabí folks would feel ridiculed once they saw the way I portrayed them on the screen. They thought my firemen would be so furious that I was ordered to stay away from Vrchlabí because my personal safety at the screening could not be guaranteed.

In reality, the Vrchlabí crowd laughed uproariously throughout the show. When the discussion started, the first of the Party plants rose and gave his by-the-numbers speech about how the film insulted the working people. He finished and Mr. Novotný, one of the firemen in the film and no relation to the president, raised his hand.

"Yes!" said the comrade running the discussion, clearly licking his chops. "What did you think, comrade?"

The fireman got up. "Well, I don't know, comrades, I just don't know. I am not an educated person and I'm not much of a speaker, but I don't know. You say that this is an insult to us, and maybe it is, but do you people remember when Jíra's goat shed caught fire? And we were all drinking in the tavern? And how by the time we finally staggered out there, we forgot the nozzles? Remember? And then the whole fire truck tipped over on that ice! Remember how Jíra's goat burned up? Hell, we don't even look that bad in this movie!"

The audience of our actors, their families, and neighbors began to applaud. The comrade quickly thanked them and closed the discussion.

The cultural apparatchiks had outsmarted themselves because they forgot to take into their calculations the magic of the movies. When the Vrchlabí folks saw themselves up on the silver screen, suddenly they weren't just firemen, they were actors. They were captured on film forever, they were larger than life, and they wouldn't let anyone take that away from them.

The Vrchlabí preview wound up a total bust for the Party, but the apparatchiks had no problem turning other firemen against the movie. Most of the fire departments in Czechoslovakia were then staffed by volunteers, and the Union of Fire Fighters quickly proclaimed it was not going to volunteer for anything if this vicious mockery was allowed to pollute our cinemas. *Fireman's Ball* was banned by the Party "for all time." The year was 1967.

"All time" is never forever. It denotes a longer or a shorter period, depending on the fortunes of those who lay down the ban.

In January 1968, Alexander Dubček came to power in Prague, and, in the summer of 1968, *Fireman's Ball* was released all over Czechoslovakia, so I finally got to see it with an off-the-street audience in Prague. They greatly enjoyed it, which made me very happy and proud.

In August, the Soviet tanks rolled into Prague, the film was pulled out of distribution once again, and it wouldn't be shown for another twenty years.

CARLO PONTI'S MONEY

In the summer of 1967, I had bigger worries than having my film banned "for all time." Carlo Ponti was squeezing Czech Filmexport for his $80,000, and Barrandov quickly fingered me for breaking the contract. It didn't matter that the seventy-five-minute clause was utter nonsense, that I hadn't read the contract because it was written only in English, or that I'd been told by the Filmexport people to sign it. My name was on the dotted line, so I was liable for the money.

In Czechoslovakia in the sixties, $80,000 was an astronomical sum. The State Bank was so desperate for hard currency that Czech tourists traveling to the West could only buy the maximum of twenty dollars there. If Barrandov was going to pay Ponti back, there was going to be a scapegoat. I would be accused of causing "economic damages to the state, " a criminal offense that carried a mandatory prison sentence of up to ten years.

I was scared; I thought a lot about the girl from Zruč bleeding into the shit-smeared toilet. I flew to London and requested a meeting with Ponti, the man who held the balance of my life in his hands. Ivan was in England at the time, and he came with me for support. This time, we didn't prepare for the meeting by smoking hashish, but my broken English rose to a height of eloquence that I've never attained since. I told Ponti what the Czech prisons were like, what a few years there did to a man, how I'd never last there. Ponti got up before I finished:

"My God, Miloš! I never knew any of this! I just had no idea! Of course! I'll take care of it!"

I felt such a surge of gratitude that I almost kissed his hands. I rushed back to the hotel and called Prague: "Everything's okay. I just saw Ponti, and he doesn't want his money anymore."

The next morning, Prague called me back: "What is this? Why are you pulling our leg? We've just spoken to Mr. Ponti, and he insists on having his contract honored." They ordered me to report back within five days for "urgent consultations." The ax was about to fall. In desperation, I headed to Annecy, France, which was hosting a film festival devoted solely to the New Wave of Czech cinema. I was hoping to sell myself to somebody for $80,000. I'd met Claude Lelouch before and thought that maybe he could put me in touch with some distributors, but he was out of the country. I was grasping at straws, telling anybody and everybody about the fix I was in, when I ran into Claude Berri.

It had to be fate because Berri decided on the spot that he was going to take care of my problem. He grabbed the nearest telephone and started dialing. He himself pledged to invest all the money he could scrounge up, some $11,000, and quickly set up a screening of *Fireman's Ball* for François Truffaut and other producers, directors, and film lovers who could cover the rest of the sum.

I had no print of the film to show them, but crises spur creativity: Ivan had returned to Prague, and he persuaded Jan Němec to somehow steal a print of *Fireman's Ball* from a safe at Barrandov. Pavel Juráček then brought the film to Paris, where he was coming on other business.

The print had no subtitles, of course, so during the screening I used my very rough French to translate for Berri and Truffaut. I don't know how, but they understood everything. Two days later, Berri flew to Prague with $80,000 and bought the foreign rights to my banned film.

In the end, *Fireman's Ball* was chosen to close the New York Film Festival in 1967 and was nominated for an Oscar. Claude Berri wound up distributing it around the world. The film became my boat to America.

PART 6

NEW YORK

PHONE CALLS

I see now that when I came to New York in 1967 with the ambition of making a film in America, I didn't sufficiently respect the difficulties of working in another language, in a different film tradition, and in a world whose messy life I didn't know even superficially, much less intimately.

I had done everything I could in Czechoslovakia, so Hollywood was the logical next step for me. I was a man in a hurry, but I eventually learned that there were no shortcuts. My filmmaking instincts were still very much Czech, and I had never put together an American production. I now think of *Taking Off* as my last Czech film. The only problem is that it was shot in New York—and in English.

With this film, I attempted to skip a developmental stage, as if I tried to write before I could speak. When it was over, I knew if I really wanted to make films in Hollywood, I'd have to change my whole style of working. I'd have to swallow my impatience and acknowledge it would take years to absorb American culture.

To a certain degree, I was a victim of my previous success. There were people who saw my Czech films and, betting on my potential, made it possible for me to overreach myself. They, too, didn't respect the director's need to know intimately the world that his work reflects—a need that was particularly acute for a director whose working style depended on nonactors. But I can't blame them for that; they weren't filmmakers or artists, only businessmen who didn't understand that in art God really is in the details. So they gambled a little money on a risky investment.

My ticket to America was handed to me by an old-fashioned tycoon, the chairman of Gulf and Western, which owned Paramount. Charlie Bluhdorn had come to America as a young teenager and made good, and he remained sentimental about immigrants. He called me when I was in New York at the 1967 film festival and invited me to lunch at a fancy French restaurant. He soon had the attention of the entire dining room. When he wanted to make a point, he summoned such theatrical passion that you didn't dare take your eyes off him. It didn't matter that he was making a commonplace observation.

Bluhdorn told me that immigrants were the fresh blood that America needed to rejuvenate itself, and when I said that for years I'd been secretly dreaming of making a movie in Hollywood, he responded that he'd give me a chance to do just that.

Bluhdorn's whole reasoning was faulty, though I didn't point that out to him. I was not an immigrant and had no intention of becoming an American at that time. In fact, my contract to develop a film for Paramount was eventually negotiated by Czech Filmexport, in accordance with Communist rules, assuring it of a huge cut of any profits.

My first idea for an American film had been an adaptation of Franz Kafka's first, unfinished novel, *Amerika,* but I quickly dropped the notion when, that summer, I had the great fortune to see the first public preview of an extraordinary new musical. I was completely taken with it. I'd just gotten the backing of Paramount, so I decided to pursue the rights. I also enlisted the help of a friend, the French writer Jean-Claude Carrière. We moved into the Chelsea Hotel on Twenty-third Street and began preparing an outline of an adaptation of *Hair.*

I'd met Jean-Claude at a film festival in Sorrento in 1966. After the showing of a wonderful film by Pierre Etaix, I went to congratulate its maker. There was a youthful, bearded guy hovering about and smiling, who turned out to be the author of the screenplay. We started talking, and Carrière asked me to call him if I ever found myself in Paris. Not long after, I was in Paris, and we became friends.

Carrière had written most of Buñuel's recent films, working with the old master in French and Spanish, so he wasn't scared to try to work with me in English. In fact, he helped me get a clear conception of how I wanted to shoot *Hair,* but then, after getting fairly close to making the film in the spring of 1968, a wicked pack of tarot cards put the musical out of my reach—a bizarre story I will recount later.

I was determined not to let the chance to make a Hollywood movie slip through my fingers, so when *Hair* fell through, Carrière and I started looking for other material and I remembered a melancholy newspaper piece that I'd read some time before. It was an interview with the father of a runaway girl. She came from a tolerant, upper-class family in Connecticut, and every Monday she would commute from her suburban life to a street life in New York City. At home she pretended that she was a student, but in reality she was a part-time flower child. On Fridays, she would head back to her affluent family and act like a college student for the weekend. The parents and the daughter would sit down to dinner, but they lived in completely different worlds. Her parents didn't learn about her street life until she was murdered in an East Village crash pad by a drifter—just a random act of urban violence.

This story so intrigued me that Carrière and I set out to learn more about American runaways. We went to New York and talked to kids in the East Village and interviewed their parents. The more I looked into the phenomenon, the more I was drawn to the parents rather than the runaways: in that human equation it was the parents who were the real outsiders. Slowly, Jean-Claude and I began to weave a story.

I had decided earlier that I'd insert a documentary of an audition for singers in my first American film because I felt that I hadn't put this richly dramatic situation fully behind me. In shooting *Audition* back in 1961, we'd been too hampered by the unsynchronized picture and sound, and now I figured I could better disguise my thin knowledge of American life by incorporating a straightforward documentary into my fictional film.

In the spring of 1968, New York was a very distracting place. There were the assassinations of Martin Luther King and Robert Kennedy, race riots, antiwar protests, and huge shifts in cultural values. One wanted either to sit by the television or walk the streets, so as soon as Jean-Claude and I had a rough idea of what we wanted to write, we headed back to France to put it down on paper.

We thought that it would be easier to sit down and work in Paris, but shortly after we got there the students on the Left Bank started a revolution. They torched cars, painted political wisecracks on the walls, and fought pitched battles with the police. Whenever I managed to pull Jean-Claude off the barricades, he was too keyed up to think about movies, so I moved us to Prague.

I thought that we'd finally get to work in peace, but there was more going on in Czechoslovakia than in Paris or New York. The Prague Spring was in full bloom, and the Communist Party had lost control. New parties were being set up, secret files opened, history rewritten, and Soviets taunted, but all the while the Red Army was holding ominous maneuvers in the countryside. Not a single sheet of paper rolled through our typewriter.

In August, Carrière and I went back to Paris. The traditional vacation season had calmed the city, and at last we were able to start writing our screenplay.

One summer day, Jean-Claude and I put in a light shift at the office and then sauntered to Pigalle, to see if another friend, filmmaker Jean-Pierre Rassam, was at his usual haunt, the seedy corner bar. We found him there and spent a pleasant summer evening getting drunk and talking with a shady, beautiful Israeli named Eva. We were young and did nothing in moderation. Jean-Pierre got smashed and offered Eva a thousand franks to spend the night with him, and they were off in a taxi to her place. Jean-Claude and I finished our drinks and returned to his apartment, which seemed more like a hostel at the time. Jean-Claude had friends on every continent, so there were always exotic guests staying there. He also had a wife, a baby daughter, and a mother-in-law. The whole legion was sound asleep.

We tiptoed down the creaking hallway into the kitchen, had a snack, downed a nightcap, and talked some more about our screenplay. It was a while before I got into bed. I had my own room and dozed off instantly.

The next thing I knew a telephone was ringing by my head. All the receivers throughout the house were ringing loudly. Finally, someone answered. The clock showed two-thirty in the morning. I started drifting off to sleep again when the door of my room opened quietly. It was Jean-Claude, bleary-eyed, in his shorts.

"It's for you, Miloš."

I picked up the receiver and heard the slurred voice of Jean-Pierre, a notorious practical joker.

"Miloš, the Russians are invading your country!" The newspapers had been full of Dubček and Brezhnev and the Prague Spring.

"Listen," I said. "You're drunk, and this isn't funny."

"I'm not drunk! The Russian tanks are rolling into your country!"

"Jean-Pierre, I gotta go."

I hung up and waited to see if I'd been sufficiently cold to discourage him from calling again. He was pretty drunk, but so was I, and I could barely keep my eyes open. The moment I surrendered to the sweetness of sleep, however, all the phones in the house started to ring. Jean-Claude appeared at my door again. "For you."

I reached for the phone. "Yes, Jean-Pierre."

"Listen to me, Miloš! I am serious! Turn on the radio, for God's sake! Wait a minute! Wait! Don't hang up! Here's Eva. She'll tell you."

Jean-Pierre heard the news while Eva was giving him a cold shower. She'd been trying to revive him in the bathroom and punched on the radio thinking that some rock 'n' roll might help her with the monumental task. And so I learned that the Soviets had invaded Czechoslovakia and that nothing would ever be the same.

THE ROAD TAKEN

On August 21, 1968, Czechoslovakia was cut off from the world, and my Věra, Petr, and Matěj were in Prague. I thought of my parents and the chance they had missed before the war, when the Koukols had offered them a way out of the country on the brink of German occupation. I decided I wasn't going to make the same mistake.

It turned out that my brother Pavel, a notorious homebody, was sweating the same dark thoughts. That very day, he packed up his family and left the old country for the only place he'd ever seen outside of Czechoslovakia. He had just been to Brisbane, Australia, a few months before, so that's where he wound up and found his happiness. He is there still, painting abstracted views of the sea bottom and presiding over a growing family.

For the first few days after the invasion, Czechoslovakia was in turmoil. Dubček and the other leaders had been spirited off to the Soviet Union. There were rumors that they had been shot and that a new government was being set up by the Soviets, but there was also tremendous popular resistance to the invasion. Crowds of crying people surrounded the Soviet tanks and yelled at the soldiers. Some begged them to go home, some reasoned with them, and some threw rocks at them. Many people were shot. A couple of tanks were set on fire. Radio Prague stayed on the air and directed the passive resistance, urging people to remove street signs in order to further confuse the already disoriented Soviet army. Meanwhile, thousands of Czechs and Slovaks began streaming over the Western border, which was opened for the first time in twenty years.

I quickly sobered up and sat glued to the radio for as long as I could bear. I felt as helpless as when I had tried to move the horn-legged cupboard during the Gestapo's search of our house. The Russians were playing for keeps, and they would surely throw the wet blanket of coarse Stalinism over the newly invigorated society. It would take generations to recover from this trauma.

I had to get my family out of the country. Claude Berri and Jean-Pierre Rassam immediately volunteered to go to Prague and drive Věra and my boys out of Czechoslovakia. I didn't dare go back myself, so I leaped at their offer. There was only one problem. They didn't have a car that would get them there. In 1968, Claude Berri was not yet an internationally acclaimed director and producer. He was still an actor who had just directed his first film and whose old car spent more time in the repair shop than on the road.

I was afraid the border might get sealed again at any moment. Rassam solved the problem by borrowing a Citroën from Truffaut, so I scribbled a few hysterical sentences to Věra, imploring her to grab the kids and come to Paris. Berri and Rassam took off and drove nonstop. They got to the Czech border and discovered crowds of nervous people leaving the country, but no one entering it. They got in very easily, then found themselves in a vast maze the moment they pulled away from the border. There were no road signs, no street signs, no numbers on any doors, and no nameplates anywhere. They didn't have a map, and no one spoke French or English or Spanish. They drove around on bad roads. They saw Russian soldiers and tanks. They began to experience *déjà vu* at every crossroad. At a sprawling small-town gas station, a guy finally spoke back to them in broken French. *Monsieur* wanted to go to Prague? *Pas problem* because this was just where he was headed, too, to check out the situation. *"Suivez-vous!"* he ordered. *Follow yourselves!*

They didn't have time for clarification. The guy jumped into a car, raced around the tiny town to collect a couple of buddies, then zoomed out into the countryside. They followed him, scared, edgy, nervously joking about Franz Kafka. Jean-Pierre suddenly realized his bladder was nearly bursting. He hadn't been conscious enough of his body to sense it before. Claude wouldn't stop for fear of losing their guide, who was flying down twisting roads full of potholes at breakneck speed. They argued. Claude wouldn't relent, so Jean-Pierre finally climbed into the backseat and began to relieve himself out the back window. Just as he did, a convoy of Russian trucks rattled toward them, their hoods looking like mean mastiffs. Jean-Pierre scrambled to get away from the window before he could stop what he was doing. He was afraid that the Russians might see his act of nature as a political statement and shoot him. He wound up pissing all over himself and the car, which took the edge off the tension.

The guide helped my kind French emissaries find our apartment. Věra was home, but she spoke no French, no English, no Spanish. Jean Pierre had a large wet spot on the front of his pants. Claude had a tiny sheet of paper with my handwriting. Věra read it several times, then grabbed our four-year-old twins, packed up as much as she could throw into a couple of suitcases, said a tearful good-bye to her parents, and climbed into the Citroën. She had taken everything except her passport, but luckily the Czech border guards were still letting anyone out with a citizen's ID. Věra and my boys wound up crossing all the borders without any papers.

My French friends helped us find a spacious apartment in the suburbs of Paris, which soon filled up with other Czechs. There were nights when we had nine guests sleeping over, a virtual *Who's Who* of the Czech New Wave bedding down in the hallways. Ivan showed up, and Juráček, Jaromír Jireš, Němec, and Škvorecký, too. We listened to Prague radio announcements and read between the lines of Czech newspapers. We flogged our options to death. Should we go back home? Should we sit tight and wait the situation out? Should we stop kidding ourselves and just apply for political asylum somewhere? We talked into the night and then couldn't sleep. We were at the crossroads of our lives, and everyone saw the future differently, had different fears, talents, and dreams.

For a few months that fall, it seemed the country had weathered the Soviet invasion. Dubček signed a dictate in Moscow because he'd had a gun to his head, but he later returned to Prague and got a hero's welcome. He was back in power, censorship had not been clamped back on the press, and Czech radio went on speaking as openly as it had in the spring.

Some of our guests returned to Prague. Věra was not happy in Paris. She missed her parents, her world, her language. In Prague, she had a blooming career at the Semafor Theater as an actress and singer. She was afraid that she'd wind up an alcoholic housewife if she emigrated. Our marriage was out of its romantic phase by then, too, and she was miserable for a few months. Finally, one evening, she told me she couldn't live outside Czechoslovakia any longer. She was going back. I told her I was going back to my movie, back to America.

We said good-bye. In a way I was glad to travel light on my way across the Atlantic. I was broke and had only a dubious contract. Not a suitably stable situation for a family. I had little besides the determination to conquer Hollywood. The rest was details.

I flew to New York with Ivan, who had decided to emigrate outright. I didn't have to burn my bridges to Czechoslovakia yet because I was still under my official Filmexport contract with Paramount. I entered the country with my Czech passport, on a visa that gave me the right to work in America.

Jiří Voskovec, who had once written *The Ballad in Rags* with Jan Werich, but who had changed his name to George Voskovec and become an actor in New York, where he had been living for the past twenty years, found us a wonderful cheap little house to rent. It stood in the hollow of a block of brownstones off Leroy Street in the Village. You had to stoop down and slink through a narrow entryway between two houses to reach it. We called this short tunnel our "mouse hole"; it led to a small garden, shaded by a few big trees.

Our house looked like an old cake—a tall, faded, pink and vanilla stack of four floors with four rooms, connected by a corkscrew staircase. The bottom floor lay partly underground and housed a kitchen with an ancient table running the length of it. Ivan and I were trying to learn English, so we taped three-by-five cards on the walls and the cabinets and tried to memorize strange idioms like "flipped out" while cooking. The first floor was a living room, the second floor a bedroom, the third floor a studio.

The scraggly garden was enclosed by ivy-covered walls that sheltered it from the exuberant streets of the neighborhood, where life was one endless hippie parade. It offered a quiet, contemplative space that seemed straight out of Alexandria, Barcelona, or some other aging metropolis.

We never turned anyone away, so there was a constant flow of people through the house. Some friends stayed, some left, and some probably only stepped out and are still trying to find their way back. Playwright John Guare described our small house as an Italian villa. Every time he came, he had the sensation of leaving America and entering a colony of refugees and foreign artists, where only books and alcohol mattered: an embassy of avant-garde Bohemia.

I had a wonderful time on Leroy Street. I was in my late thirties and I'd walk down the New York streets, feeling that any day now this cerebral, neurotic city was going to be mine.

My American film was moving forward, the screenplay almost done. *Taking Off* took shape as the story of a middle-class couple desperately looking for their fifteen-year-old daughter who had entered a competition for best original song in the East Village. The parents comb the streets with no luck, then join SPFC, the Society for Parents of Fugitive Children, and find themselves in a well-lit conference room dutifully smoking reefer in order to understand just what it is that has lured their darling away. They come home stoned with another SPFC couple and start playing a giggly game of strip poker. They don't realize that their daughter has had it with the street life and is sleeping in her bedroom upstairs.

I'd met a young filmmaker named John Klein and his dandy friend Vincent Schiavelli, who had just made a student film about a runaway girl, so I asked John to help Carrière and me with our script. Then I rewrote the script with John Guare and finally submitted it to Paramount.

The first reaction to the screenplay came straight from Charlie Bluhdorn: "Nobody likes your script, Miloš," said Bluhdorn.

There followed frantic negotiations, maneuvers, dinners, nightcaps, and offers. Paramount wouldn't produce *Taking Off*, but wanted me to direct other films for them, such as *Galileo* with Rod Steiger. I had complete confidence in my screenplay and couldn't conceive of working on anything else. Luckily, my contract with Paramount had an escape clause. Once Paramount turned down the script, I had the right to buy it back by reimbursing them for their expenses. I had been paid about $10,000 dollars in per diems by then, and then there were some plane tickets and other expenses: I figured I could buy back the screenplay for some $30,000 or $40,000.

I'll never cut it as a Hollywood accountant. The real cost of my script to Paramount had been $140,000. Claude Berri's agent, who represented me, was also the agent of a production manager who had signed a contract to do my film. It was a "play-or-pay" agreement that guaranteed him $50,000 whether or not the film was made. Then there was the matter of overhead . . .

One hundred and forty thousand dollars was a huge amount of money for me. I'd nearly gone to jail for just over half that amount. I was an unproven director, spoke broken English, had an iffy screenplay, and I was already a hundred and forty grand in the hole.

I found that I couldn't get out of bed in the morning. I'd get up and my knees would feel like rubber under me. I barely managed to make it to the bathroom. All my muscles and joints ached if I stayed in an upright position. I'd stagger back to bed, collapse, and an indescribable sweetness would flood my body. I felt that I was dying, that I'd never make it out of bed.

I was incredibly lucky to have a friend like Ivan. He took exemplary care of me, screening all phone calls and visitors. I wasn't up to talking with anybody. After a week of this, I didn't feel like talking to Ivan either.

"Maybe you should see a psychiatrist," he finally gently suggested.

"Maybe *you* should see a psychiatrist," I told him.

"Well, your ego's in working order," said Ivan. "That's something anyway."

In the days that followed, Ivan started to ask me mysterious questions about my feelings, my childhood, my symptoms. Now and then, he'd come with a medical opinion and bring me some pills. He always explained that he'd just talked to his friend, another ambitious, driven man who had never failed in anything before and who'd gone through a similar predicament. He even started to throw out learned terms like "horror mortis."

I was to learn later that Ivan had been going to a psychiatrist for me, and *as* me. The psychiatrist was a film buff, so a Miloš Forman got a discount. Ivan knew me inside out, so it was easy to describe all my symptoms to the shrink, tell him my dreams, try to display my reactions. The good doctor never caught on, though Ivan finally did tell him that he'd been psychoanalyzing me by proxy.

Meanwhile, I started to improve. When I got up to go to the bathroom, I'd notice that I was able to linger in the room. I could even look out the window for a while. I'd venture down the stairs and make it to the sofa in the living room. One morning, I stepped out into the courtyard. I stood in the open space, breathing fresh air, still wearing my pajamas, but the imaginary fever was finally going down. I'd been in bed for two months.

After I slowly found my energy and rejoined the world, I had dinner with Helen Scott, who told me that Universal had just started a new policy. The studio was looking for another *Easy Rider,* which had made a lot of money for them, so they were producing risky films for under one million dollars. She called Ned Tannen and got him interested in my project. I flew to Los Angeles and read the screenplay to Tannen and Danny Selznick, acting out all the roles for them. I gave the performance of my life. I forget why, but for some reason, I had to fly right back to New York. When I got to Leroy Street there was a message from Universal. They wanted to produce *Taking Off*.

TAKING OFF

I refused to get excited about the telegram. If you've just been pummeled by hard times, you're afraid to believe any scrap of good news. I was sure that some insurmountable problem or another would soon crop up, and I was right.

Universal gave the screenplay to several producers to prepare a budget. The lowest, bare-bones numbers came out to $1,200,000 and Universal's company policy was ironclad. It was not going to spend a penny over $1 million. And because I had to pay off Paramount before I could do anything else, my budget had already shrunk to a mere $850,000.

I began searching for madmen who had produced movies on a shoestring and someone told me about Michael Hausman. He rode motorcycles and had some underground films to his credit. If he had to, they said, he'd pick pockets to finish movies.

I had dinner with Mike. He was a young, tall man of action, and indeed a madman. I was just starting to recount the history of *Taking Off* when he cut me off.

"How much have you got for this?"

"I'm getting to that in a second."

"No, no. How much?"

"Well, all right. Eight hundred and fifty thousand, but I . . ."

"So we'll do it for eight fifty." Mike shrugged his shoulders.

He was wrong. I deferred my fee, and he deferred his. All the actors worked for scale. Our transportation was Mike driving his own car to the location. The car was no limousine—it overheated—but it fit Mirek Ondříček and myself in the front seat and our principals Buck Henry and Lynn Carlin with one other actor in the backseat. We shot the film for $810,000.

You'd never know that Michael Hausman was from one of the

richest families in New York. It made more sense when you found out that his parents weren't talking to him. He'd been groomed for taking over the family businesses, but he walked away from it all. As his people saw it, he was wasting his life in a gypsy business. I really owe *Taking Off* to Mike. He's since made good in the movie business and done it his way, which I suppose was the point all along.

By the time we actually got around to shooting *Taking Off* in the summer of 1970, I'd been casting the film for a couple of years. My casting director, though she didn't know it at the time, was Mary Ellen Mark, the great photographer and a great friend. Every weekend, Mary Ellen and I would get together and go watch the perpetual happenings at the Bethesda Fountain in Central Park, where the hard-core hippies mingled with the weekend hippies. It was a street-theater spectacular that never stopped. Mary Ellen took pictures, and I looked for faces for my film. I was also collecting material for my eventual production of *Hair*, but I didn't know that at the time.

One day I saw two young girls in the fountain splashing water at each other. One of them looked as if she could easily be the runaway daughter in my film. She was about fifteen and wanted to belong to the flower generation, but she clearly wasn't living on the street. I decided to try and get her to do a screen test.

In Czechoslovakia, I would have just walked over to her and popped the question, but in New York, with my sputtering English, I was afraid I might come across as some sort of Eurosleaze pedophile, so I sent Mary Ellen to make the initial contact for me. She came back with the girl and took some pictures of her. Her name was Linnea Heacock, and she looked so confident and utterly herself in the screen test that I offered her the role.

Mary Ellen introduced me to her friend Buck Henry, whom I chose to play Linnea's father. I cast Lynn Carlin as his wife because she had made a big impression on me in a film I love, John Cassavetes' *Faces*.

I had cast all these people before our financing fell through at Paramount, so by the time Universal gave me another chance, I was suddenly making a much smaller movie. I tried to put as many friends in the minor parts as I could. Michael Housman did, too—to save money, he even talked his dad, Jack, with whom he had made peace in the meantime, into taking a small role in the film. Many people worked on the film for free, and they wore their own clothes, as did our principals, chosen by our costume designer from their own wardrobes.

I directed *Taking Off* the way I'd shot all my Czech films: I'd explain the basic ideas of the scene to the actors. I'd discuss their characters' motivation and mind-set and then give them the dialogue we'd written. They would then often rephrase our lines in their own words.

I tried to capture as much spontaneity on film as I could. In the strip poker game near the end of the story, I didn't let the actors know who was going to lose each hand. For the first take, I arranged the deck the way I needed the game to come out, but the actors were playing real strip poker.

The atmosphere on the set was wonderful, as indeed it had to be under those circumstances. There were no prima donnas, no barriers, no envy, no hairdressers, no makeup people, no trailers. We were truly a family. I think you can still feel it when you look at the film.

I was amazed at the talent that walked in off the street for our audition, which incidentally, wound up looking very different from my old *Audition*. A guitar-strumming girl who had just come to New York from the South made a big impression with her own composition. Her name was Kathy Bates. Another complete unknown by the name of Carly Simon came in and did a wonderful song for us. Ike and Tina Turner performed in our nightclub scene.

Taking Off ends with a formal dinner. Linnea is introducing a boyfriend whom she had met on the streets to her folks. He's several years older and sports an unkempt beard, long hair, sunken cheeks, and the demeanor of an addict. He doesn't talk. The parents pose their usual leery questions, which Linnea keeps answering for him, disclosing that he's a musician who composes his own loud, modern music on the piano. The parental interrogation continues by proxy until Buck Henry poses a pointed question that Linnea can't answer: "Make any money at it?"

The boyfriend takes a long beat and then nods.

"How much?" asks the father patronizingly.

After another long beat, the hippie speaks up for the first time: "Two hundred and ninety thousand dollars."

The father chokes on his soup.

"Before taxes," adds the boyfriend, to make the old man feel better.

The film ends with the father pounding the ivories and belting out an off-key "Stranger in Paradise" for the boyfriend.

John Klein had found a real musician, David Gittler, for the part of the boyfriend. He fit my concept of the character perfectly. I liked David's deadpan face and expressive eyes. When we got around to shooting his single line, "Two hundred and ninety thousand dollars," I explained what I needed from him and told him what his cue was. I rolled the camera.

"Make any money at it?" asked Buck Henry.

Gittler took his sweet time and nodded. His timing was perfect.

"How much?" said Buck.

Then came a brilliant pause, which dragged on too long and finally became a pause to end all pauses.

"Cut!" I said, "David! That's when you say 'Two hundred and ninety thousand dollars.' When he asks you how much, okay? Yes?"

David was nervously rocking in the chair, his head bopping, which I took for a nod, so we got everything ready again.

"Camera! Action!"

"How much?" asked Buck again.

Silence. David just sat there, eyeing the table.

"Cut! David, this was when you were supposed to say your line! You're answering his question, okay?"

David resumed rocking in his chair, sort of nodding, this time looking as if he understood.

"Please, don't forget now, all right? Okay! Camera! Action!"

The dialogue flowed smoothly again up to David's line, and then came another stretch of deafening silence.

"Cut! David!? Why don't you say your line?!"

"Because I never made two hundred and ninety thousand dollars in a year," mumbled David, staring at his hands.

"But, David! This is a movie! This is not about you!"

"No, this is about me. I *am* playing myself here in this film, and I'm not saying anything that's not true. Because I *am* a musician. I *do* play the piano. I *do* write songs."

"David, you came here to this dinner as the boyfriend of Linnea! And you're *not* her boyfriend!"

"What do you know? In my head, I am."

I tried arguing with David, but he wouldn't even look at me as he stubbornly maintained that our film was about him. Finally, I threw up my hands and John Klein stepped in. He took David aside and whispered to him for two hours while we paced around nervously. Then he walked up to me and said that David was ready to deliver the line as it was written. Now *I* took John aside: "What did you tell him?"

"I asked him what his highest income in a year was, and then I explained the two hundred and ninety grand away. I told him that the government would take half the money right off the bat, and then there were agents and accountants and expenses to pay, and so on. I finally got the three hundred grand down to the money he made last year."

"So he still thinks the movie's about him?" I asked incredulously.

"Do you want him to sound convincing, or not?"

I set the scene in motion and watched with bated breath. It started out smoothly again.

"How much?" said Buck.

"Two hundred and ninety thousand," said David, and he paused. "Before taxes . . ."

I sighed with relief and was about to say "Cut!" when David spoke up again and began to improvise. He sounded in character, so I let him have a go at it.

"It's a very funny thing," he said. "You know, like you see a lot of things the government is doing that makes you kinda angry, so you write some songs about it and you try to reach as many people as you can . . . And then you end up paying for those very same things that made you angry in the first place . . . But you know, I guess I accept contradictions . . ."

It was perfect.

When we wrapped *Taking Off*, I was sure we had a very good film. In fact, I counted on its being a success in America, which would allow me to return to Prague and to my family for good.

The political situation in Czechoslovakia had by then become tragic. Alexander Dubček and the other liberal Communists of the Prague Spring were history, and the old Stalinists were back on top. There had been purges, arrests, books and films banned, but I still didn't want to emigrate from the old country as Ivan had done. I thought that *Taking Off* would be such a hit in America that even the jealous Party people at Barrandov wouldn't be able to touch me anymore. I'd make a lot of money, go back home in four or five months, take a long vacation with my family, and then start looking for something to work on again. Besides, Papoušek and Ondříček were both now back in Prague, so with a little luck I hoped to put most of my old team back together.

HOLLYWOOD COMMIE

Americans are the most generous people I know. They are incredibly open, flexible, helpful, and innovative. They can also be incredibly ignorant of the world. In the eyes of many Americans, being from a

Communist country automatically made you a Red or at least a leftist.

In 1971, *Taking Off* was finally to open in the theater at the Plaza in New York. The first show started at high noon on a Sunday, and Michael Hausman and I had decided to go and case it. That morning, I woke up at four and couldn't go back to sleep. At six o'clock I ran out to get the Sunday *Times*. I rifled through the thick paper and found a pretty favorable review. They even ran my picture.

I read the whole paper and then decided to treat myself to a grand opening of my first American film. At ten o'clock I headed to the garage down the street to get my car. It was an old green Mercedes, now pretty much a beater because it hadn't been driven for over a year. I'd brought it over from Europe, so it still had Czech license plates. I was going to drive to the cinema, get breakfast somewhere, and stretch the coffee till Mike showed up.

I was so jittery that day that I ran a red light as soon as I pulled out of the garage. The moment I saw flashing lights in my rearview mirror, I realized I hadn't grabbed my wallet when I left the house. I had no driver's license on me, no passport, no ID of any kind, and strange license plates.

The cop didn't give me the time of day. He booked me the moment he heard my accent. At the station, I told the desk sergeant I was a Czech film director, which made me not only a car thief but a Commie car thief. I tried to explain that the whole thing was a matter of nerves. My first American movie would be opening at the Plaza in another hour, and I just hadn't been able to think straight.

The more I talked, the more suspicious the cops got. They were about to throw me into the holding cell when I had a brainstorm: "Wait! Do you have a copy of today's *New York Times* here?"

They sneered as they watched me leaf through the paper. They thought they had me cold. I got to my smudgy picture and showed it to them. Their sneers melted away. Suddenly I was Mr. Hollywood. A VIP from the movies. They quickly called the Plaza Theater for me and got hold of Michael Housman.

By the time Mike bailed me out, he was laughing so hard that if someone had canned his laughter we'd still be hearing it on sitcoms. He was still snickering as we stepped into the movie house, but he stopped the moment he entered the auditorium: the premiere of my first American film drew a total of eight people.

Mike and I stayed at the Plaza all day, and we slowly calmed down. By late afternoon, the shows were selling out. The moviegoers were laughing and enjoying themselves during the film, but they seemed puzzled by its open ending. The runaway daughter has come back home, but it's hard to say for how long. Clearly no one in the family has learned anything from the trauma. The New York audiences seemed unsatisfied. Nevertheless, when the last show ended, Mike and I were happy with what we had seen.

The reviews ranged from excellent to a pair of write-ups that said I was slinging mud at America and should go back to spit on the country I came from—perhaps there was some meaning in that both were penned by fellow immigrants from Communist countries. The film later had a nice run in Europe, but it didn't make any money in America. Its quiet ending had a lot to do with this, but the fact that Universal didn't support the film with a single word of advertising didn't help any either. *Taking Off* ran for sixteen weeks. It was never widely distributed, and it still isn't available on video.

Because I had to defer my pay for *Taking Off* until the profits came in, I never saw a penny. I was broke, and my American visa was running out. I had to decide where I was going to live and work. The most important decision was easy: going back to Czechoslovakia was no longer a viable option. For one thing, I was afraid to return because I knew how the Communists mistrusted anyone who had lived abroad and had nothing to show for it. Secondly, I was too vain to go back a loser. My American film hadn't conquered Hollywood, and I had nothing but a few reviews to show for it. But I was resolved to try again. In my heart of hearts I knew I was going to make a successful movie in America—a movie I wouldn't mind taking home to Prague.

Finally, when you're down and out, even tiny things blow up in importance, and I simply didn't have the money for the ticket. So I wrote a polite letter to the Czech authorities requesting their permission to stay abroad longer. They quickly answered that I was to come back to Prague for the proper stamp. It was clear that once I did, I'd never get out again, so I wrote back that I didn't have the money for the airfare and all I was asking for was a stamp that the Czech Embassy in Washington could easily give me.

The next thing I heard was that Barrandov had fired me. The die was cast. I was an émigré, so I applied for a green card. A few months later, I received notification to appear at the Immigration Office.

A dour man with a clip-on tie faced me across an office counter. "Your application for a green card has been denied."

"How come?"

"Because you've lied on your application."

"What did I lie about?"

"You stated that you've never been a member of the Communist Party."

I stared at him in shock. "Look," I said, "I don't know what you know, but personally, I've never been a member of any political party, much less the Communist Party."

"Our sources indicate otherwise," said the bureaucrat. "You are now subject to deportation proceedings."

That shook me up, so I scrambled to find an immigration lawyer. He agreed that the situation was serious, but he appealed the case and was able to delay my deportation.

A year later, I got another notification from the Immigration Office. It summoned me to see the old clip-on tie. He was as dour as ever.

"Mr. Forman, you've never been a member of the Communist Party," he notified me, and handed me a green card.

I don't have a factual explanation for what had happened. I think that the U.S. government had gotten its information from sources that worked both sides of the Iron Curtain. The Americans probably didn't have an independent network of informants in Czechoslovakia, so they didn't have much choice about whom they dealt with. And when the Czech State Security wanted to hurt some émigré, it just passed on information doctored to suit its purposes.

I hadn't particularly minded being in legal limbo for a year. It meant that I couldn't work, which I wasn't eager to do anyway. I'd seen clearly just how much I had to learn about America before I could make films here. I realized that there would always be some things in America I'd never completely catch up on, which was okay as long as I was conscious of this fact and operated within my limitations, but I had to change my whole style of working.

In America, I simply couldn't go after an original story from everyday life and shoot it with nonactors. I could still adapt books or plays to the screen, but I'd have to learn everything about the world in which the story was set in order to make it as true as I could.

The bottom line was that if I walked into a bar in my neighborhood and didn't understand every single word that was said, I had no business trying to make movies like *Loves of a Blonde* or *Fireman's Ball* anymore.

ANOTHER APPRENTICESHIP

Back in Czechoslovakia, I'd broken into the movie business as a screen-writer and, in my first years in America, I had to start out as a screen-writer again—in English and in a very different story-telling tradition. Looking back on that time now, it's as if I am watching a man who is relearning how to use his faculties after a debilitating injury. I was going through my second apprenticeship. I passionately believed in each screenplay, but I also knew how painful writing could be, so I chose wonderful, witty, playful collaborators who made that pain as amusing as possible. First I wrote a script with Buck Henry called *Harry, the King of Comedy,* which was a precursor of Martin Scorsese's *The King of Comedy.* The writing process with Buck was a lot of fun, but we couldn't get the script produced, so Buck introduced me to another excellent writer and a wonderful guy, Eddie Adler, and we worked on another screenplay, *Bulletproof,* which didn't make it any further. Then I began adapting a novel of black humor, *Vital Parts,* with its author, Thomas Berger.

Berger was a tall, striking guy with a shaved head and a big, V-8 imagination constantly firing on all cylinders. We never stopped laughing and amusing one another. We'd conscientiously get together to work, then spend our time arguing the relative merits of film and literature. Nearly all my screenwriters are directors at heart, but Berger was proud of having no directorial ambitions at all. He maintained that literature was the superior art and I disagreed, and we had a ball thrashing it out.

The strange thing about filmmaking is that each phase of it always seems the most important element of the whole enterprise while you're involved in it: when I am writing a screenplay, I'm absolutely convinced that the script is the most important element; I get the very same feeling again when I am casting the film or shooting or editing it.

But screenplays do come first, and they really are the foundations of movies. It would take a lot of effort to ruin the great screenplays, such as those written for Marcel Carné's *Children of Paradise,* Ernst Lubitsch's *To Be or Not to Be,* Billy Wilder's *The Apartment,* or anything Zavattini wrote. You have to be open to anything good that comes out of the

process of shooting a script and you have to be able to revise it again
in the editing room, but there always has to be a good screenplay to fall
back on if nothing better develops in front of the camera.

As far as I can see, screenwriting has only a few general principles.
I believe that every moment in a film, every word and every reaction,
should carry psychological truth. It may be embedded in a very imagi-
native and fanciful frame, but anything that you hear and see on the
screen must be humanly convincing. If you try to cheat with behavioral
and motivational implausibilities, the audience will always see through
it and you will lose them.

But truth alone is not enough. In large doses, truth becomes obvious
and boring, so it's extremely important that a film constantly surprise
its viewers but it's hard to surprise anyone with the truth: no one wants
to hear you prove that two and two is four. But if you say: "Let me show
you that two and two is five," everyone perks up. "Here, I'll prove it."
You can take them on a little mind trip: "First, take two sheets of paper,
one blue, the other red. Now put the red paper in a yellow envelope and
the blue paper in a black envelope. Write two times seventeen on the
yellow envelope in green ink. Write seventeen times two, minus six, on
the black envelope in pink ink. Then switch papers in the envelopes,
folding the red paper vertically twice and the blue paper horizontally
four times. . . ."

Chances are that you will be amused while they follow the instruc-
tions and try to keep up. But of course the whole thing is a con job that
you'll finally have to joke your way out of. The audience will realize that
they've been had, but maybe they'll feel the way many an audience
leaving a theater has felt: "The movie was pretty dumb if you think
about it, but it was kinda fun."

Incidentally, this may explain why some fairly inane movies become
more successful than films that, earnestly and ploddingly, search for
truth. A good screenplay plays with the audience's expectations. It sets
them up and undercuts them or fulfills them in unforeseen ways. It
holds an ironic conversation with the audience. So the second basic
ingredient of film writing is lightness of spirit.

But the process is riddled with theoretical traps. It frequently seems
that two characters should have a scene together or that the plot should
turn in a certain way. It just makes sense, so you sit down to write it and
you find that it doesn't work. The scene that seems so obvious and
logical simply refuses to come alive.

The thing to do in that predicament is to take a nap and forget about
the idea because you have merely fallen into one of those strange traps
that theory often lays.

When I was young and didn't know any of this yet, I thought that perhaps there was a secret to writing, a way of unlocking the craft, a shortcut I could learn from the old masters. Searching for it, I once cornered the great actor and writer Jan Werich: "Mr. Werich, when you and Mr. Voskovec wrote all those wonderful plays, would you start out with some sort of an outline? Some kind of a concept or a design that would bind it all together?"

Werich's face lit up with amusement as his little dark eyes savored my earnest, thieving naiveté. "Hell no!" he said. "For us it was always just 'Who enters the stage?' and 'What does he say?'"

THE CHELSEA HOTEL

I went through most of my cultural rehab at the Chelsea Hotel, which had for years been at the center of New York's Bohemia and was perfect for my purposes.

The house on Leroy Street had been a wonderful place to live, but I let go of it once I realized that *Taking Off* was a bust. Ivan and I couldn't afford to keep it any longer, so we both moved to the Chelsea and I wound up living there until 1973. Back then, this ramshackle hotel was the home of Janis Joplin and a host of writers, painters, musicians, actors, exhibitionists, groupies, junkies, and gurus. The lobby was crammed with canvases that guests had used to pay their bills. The hotel's life was full of gestures in search of meaning. My room was on the eighth floor, and it had a view of sooty brick walls, fire escapes, and the snaking taxi-yellow traffic below. There was a kitchenette, a double bed, and a fake fireplace.

I wonder now how it was that I hadn't lost my self-confidence. Somehow I retained a strong conviction that things would work out in the end. My budget shrank to a dollar a day for weeks on end, which greatly simplified everything. I'd buy a can of chili con carne and a bottle of beer every day and a loaf of bread every other day, and I was all set. I found out that I'd have to try hard to die of hunger in New York. With friends always passing through or a friend of a friend inviting me for dinner, I was never bored and rarely hungry.

It helped immensely that I had the most generous landlord in New York, Stanley Bard. On the first of each month, I'd find an envelope

with my bill in the room. When I started to fall behind on my rent, I'd
go down to the manager's office.

"I can't pay you, Stanley, not yet," I'd say.

"Okay," said Stanley.

"I'll either pay up or die here, but I'm never moving out, you know
that."

Stanley smiled and waved me off. His gesture never changed,
whether I was three months in the red or eight.

One night at the Chelsea, the ringing of a fire alarm jolted me out
of bed at three o'clock in the morning. I raced into the hallway to see
what was happening. I'd just seen a horrible hotel fire in Tokyo on the
news, and all I could think of were the poor Japanese with their hair on
fire diving off the ten-story roof to shatter themselves on the cement
sidewalk below.

There was no sign of fire in the eighth-floor hallway, no smoke, not
even a whiff of anything burning. Then I realized that I was naked from
the waist down. I'd been sleeping only in a short T-shirt. Other doors
in the hallway were starting to open, so I turned around to go inside and
put something on.

As I reached for the doorknob, a sudden draft slammed the door shut
in my face. I couldn't pull the tiny T-shirt down far enough to cover my
balls. I was standing there thinking about what to do when a young
woman peered out of the doorway across the hall. I cupped my hands
over my manhood.

"Miss, could I use your phone? I just got locked out." I asked.

She waited a moment before she agreed, then looked away discreetly
while I made my bare-assed call to reception. I began explaining my
problem, but the guy was hysterical: "We have an emergency here!
There's a fire! Fire! You understand?! Fire! Fire!" And he slammed
down the phone.

Clearly it was going be a while before I'd be able to get into my room.
The young woman seemed sympathetic, but her mind was on more
important things.

"This place is a firetrap, don't you think?" she asked.

"Yes. You wouldn't have a pair of pants here, would you?

"No. So shouldn't we get outta here?"

"Yeah, but I gotta put something on first."

"The only thing I got is a skirt, but that's—"

"I'll take it."

The skirt had an elastic waistband, so it fit fine. With my ass covered,
thoughts of death on cement quickly returned. We opened the door

again. The stench of smoke had made its way up to our floor, and we heard the sounds of people yelling and water splashing a few stories below. We rushed to the stairwell.

The stairwell at the Chelsea runs from the ground floor to the roof, with stairways zigzagging in galleries down the sides. On our floor, a small crowd of people had gathered by the railing and were staring down at a troop of firemen on the fifth floor. Their black rubber smocks were barely visible through the billows of white smoke as twitching hoses blasted water into a room right by the stairwell.

Packs of onlookers were gathered on all the galleries above the fire and people from the lower floors were making their way up the stairs to get a better look. Everyone was dressed in wild combinations of night and street clothes, so I fit right in. A tall man in bare feet and a mink coat stood beside me. It was Clifford Irving, the man who wrote the hoax autobiography of Howard Hughes. Before the flames were put out, bottles of wine and joints started to circulate around the railing. At the Chelsea, even a raging fire made for a breathtaking sort of theater.

Suddenly, everything stopped. A hush fell over the stairwell. Only the sound of water dripping, the drops smacking the floor, could be heard. Two firemen carried out a limp body on a stretcher.

"She's dead," said one of them to all of us onlookers.

She was an older lady with a hot plate in her room. That night, she had put a roast on and fallen asleep. The meat burned until it caught fire. Someone on the street noticed the smoke pouring out the window. The fire never spread beyond the pot inside the room, but when the firemen busted into the smoke-choked space they couldn't see anything, so they let loose with their hoses. They pumped hundreds of gallons of water into the small room. The old lady died of asphyxiation, though whether it was the smoke or the water, no one knew.

The stretcher bobbed down the hallway in silence. But the moment the elevator began its clanking descent, the party came back to life. The bottles resumed their rounds, the firemen started collecting their tools, the show went on. An hour later, I was able to get the reserve key from reception and return the skirt, but the hotel party rolled on until dawn.

My stay at the Chelsea yielded many other memorable nights. One of them came at Christmas, 1971.

I get very sentimental that day, and I had $3 to my name, so I bought a little jar of ersatz caviar and a small bottle of sugary champagne that had nothing to do with grapes, and I climbed into my bed and turned on the television. I flipped the channels until I found a stationary shot of a fireplace crackling with flames. I stretched out, ate three spoons of imitation caviar, had a glass of imitation champagne, watched imitation flames flicker in psychedelic oranges and browns, and listened to Muzak carols. I felt so sorry for myself that I was happy.

That feeling of self-pity was luxurious. I liked myself again. I was in America, and I was going to make great movies.

ROBBY

The very first time I came to America back in the sixties, I found a message in my hotel room one evening that said to call Robert Lantz. I did and learned that he was an agent. He had heard about me from Ruda Dauphin, the wife of actor Claude Dauphin, who was a client of his.

Lantz and I had lunch at the Oak Room of the Plaza Hotel, and I liked him immensely. He was a short, impeccably dressed gentleman with a slight German accent who preferred to be called Robby. He had charm and wit and put me at ease instantly. His father had been a successful filmwriter and producer in Berlin, where Robby had had a career as a young playwright, but now devoted himself to the business end of the arts.

"If you need anything at all, call me," he told me as we said good-bye.

I didn't need a thing, but Robby had made an indelible impression on me. I asked the film festival people if they'd heard of him. They thought I was kidding. Robby represented Tennessee Williams, Elizabeth Taylor, Richard Burton, Mike Nichols, and Leonard Bernstein, among others, so I made sure to call him when I next came to New York.

Every time after that, Robby and I would have a memorable lunch together in New York. When I moved there, I finally began a professional relationship with him.

I'll admit I was wary of the man at first. He represented people with whom America was on a first-name basis—Liz, Richard, Lenny—and yet he made me feel as if *I* were the most important person in the world. I was suspicious; he was so kind and pleasant that it just didn't add up. It took me some time to realize that this was no trap, this simply was how Robby dealt with people. For example, he never asked me to sign anything with him. After all these years and movies, we're still operating under a handshake contract.

Since that first lunch in the dark-paneled Oak Room, I've changed just about everything in my life. I've changed languages, nationalities, my marital status, producers, screenwriters, but I still have the same agent. Robby has been a strange beacon in my life.

Because Robby Lantz was my agent, I got scripts even while I was half a year behind on rent at the Chelsea Hotel. They were not first-rate projects, but the steady stream was a considerable boost to my self-confidence.

While waiting for the right movie project, I realized an old daydream and directed a Broadway play, Jean Claude Carrière's *The Little Black Book*, which had been a great success in Europe.

The play is very witty and beautifully orchestrated. A girl with a suitcase shows up in the apartment of an aging ladies' man. She's looking for someone else, but quickly makes herself at home. All she needs is a place to crash for the day. As she negotiates with the bachelor, offering to clean his apartment in return, she begins to seem very familiar to him, so he tries to find out if she is one of his old amorous conquests. She talks of an abortion she had, and he starts to worry that she is setting up some sort of a revenge. In the end, the girl remains as mysterious as when she first entered and theatergoers have to decide for themselves whether there was a shared past between them.

I loved going to the theater and exploring the text with Delphine Seyrig and Richard Benjamin, the two actors in our production. The process really gripped me, but in the end I had to admit to myself that I was not a theater director.

There are a few directors, most notably Ingmar Bergman, who are able to work comfortably in both film and theater, but I am not one of them. I don't have the kind of abstracting imagination that the theater requires; I wind up feeling as if I am stuck with one lens on one camera that can't be moved for a couple of hours. I am always stifling a shout that's forever sticking in my throat—"Cut!"

VISIONS OF EIGHT

In 1972, David Wolper, producer of *The Hellstrom Chronicle,* a cult film on insects, asked me to shoot a short film for an anthology about the Munich Olympics. I've always been an avid sports fan and would have paid a lot of money to watch the Olympics from the stadium grounds, so I grabbed the opportunity.

The movie was called *Visions of Eight,* and it gave directors from all corners of the world a free hand in choosing any aspect of the Games they fancied. I went to the track and field championship of Germany in Munich to research the project. The most dramatic athletes I saw there were the completely drained decathletes, so I chose the decathlon as my event. Each of the ten disciplines had its own rhythm, which I resolved to bring out by means of a matching piece of music. I also wanted to show the entire context of the event: the organizers, the spectators, the preparations, the dead moments, the bursts of excitement.

The Czech authorities refused to let Mirek Ondříček work with an émigré, so I chose the Swedish cinematographer Jörgen Persson as my eye. I wanted to make my film as different from television as I could and Persson had shot *Elvira Madigan* with Bo Widerberg, so I knew he would have a greater feel for decadent beauty than for naturalism and reportage.

We worked with several crews and had as many as eighteen cameras rolling at one time, which was a completely new thing for me. Ultimately, it was the camera operators who brought back the best images. If you've spent years sitting in the director's chair, you slowly start to believe that nothing worthwhile can be filmed without you. But in Munich, I suddenly learned that my presence wasn't all that necessary, which made for a healthy, humbling experience.

The Olympic Village underwent an astounding transformation during the Games. The night before the Olympics opened, the place was ringing with laughter and buzzing with curiosity, friendship, and fine sportsmanship. The buildings were spotless, everything worked, everybody smiled. The ten thousand athletes living there were all potential winners.

By the end of the two weeks of competition, you had two hundred winners and nine thousand eight hundred losers. The Olympic Village was a melancholy mess. Faces were grim, body language spoke of hangovers. Garbage and empty bottles were everywhere, the toilets stank of vomit, everything that wasn't nailed down had disappeared.

The Games were still in progress when, one morning at seven o'clock, I was awakened by the phone. It was the production secretary.

"Do you know already?"

"Know what?"

"You don't know yet?"

"No, what?"

"Look out your window!"

I lived on the highest floor of the highest building in the village, so I had a grand view of the grounds. I saw ambulances, police cars, trucks, SWAT teams below me: Palestinian terrorists had attacked the Israeli team in their lodgings. They had murdered two people in cold blood, and now they were holding hostages and negotiating a safe passage out of Germany, which, in due time, they would obtain, but not before nine more members of the Israeli team were slaughtered.

I stayed glued to the window and watched the event unfold. And as the day progressed, I witnessed a fascinating thing: the Olympic Village resumed its everyday rhythms. A few yards from the killing grounds, people played miniature golf, Ping-Pong, chess. They warmed up, exercised, read books, argued with coaches, suntanned, sipped soft drinks, watched the girls.

The athletes had trained for this competition for most of their lives, and until the Olympics were called off they weren't about to allow anything to distract them. They didn't permit themselves to think about the tragedy. They could hear and they could even smell the aftermath of the bloodbath, the siege, the helicopters, the bullhorns, but they simply blocked it all out.

Life went on, as it always does.

IVAN PASSER

The life of my dear friend Ivan Passer is the stuff of movies. He is a very talented man, but a few episodes in his life seem to belong to someone caught up in an inner struggle, a man fighting himself.

We were both living at the Chelsea in the early seventies when Ivan got an offer to direct the remake of *Iron Cross* in California. I remember him telling me about the job over some paella in the El Quijote restaurant on the ground floor of our hotel. The offer seemed pretty solid and he was flying to Los Angeles the next morning to negotiate everything.

As we talked, an older Indian in an embroidered shirt was sitting near us by the bar and keeping half an ear on our conversation. He was the spiritual type, sipping green tea, wearing sandals over woolen socks, a sort of a guru. Ivan and I were about to call it a night, because Ivan had an early plane to catch, when the guru stepped up to our table. I'd never seen him before, but he knew both our names.

"Mr. Passer, you see I couldn't help but overhear that you're going to be traveling for a week. So I was wondering, will you be letting your room go? I've met some temporary adversity lately, you see, and . . ." The guru was clearly a good judge of people, because he had Ivan down pat.

"You're absolutely welcome to stay in my room," Ivan told him. "I won't be back for a week."

The guru wound up living in Ivan's room for three years.

Ivan turned down the *Iron Cross* remake, but not before he had gone out on a blind date, where he met a young black woman. She was a wonderful lady and he moved in with her and her children. Then he started making a movie. He never bothered to check out of the room at the Chelsea, so the guru went on making his green tea there. No one was paying the rent, however, and Stanley Bard was getting nervous about Ivan's ballooning debt.

Meanwhile I had also gotten a couple of letters from Czechoslovakia about Ivan's son. The boy's mother had died (she and Ivan had divorced years before) and Little Ivan was living on the edge of poverty in Prague, so I called Big Ivan in Los Angeles and told him that he had to deal with his son.

"What's going on, anyway?" I asked him when I warmed up to the subject. "I mean you're still paying the rent here as far as Stanley's concerned."

"I know. I'm good for it. I'll finally be making some money."

"I know you're good for it, Ivan, but Jesus Christ, who's more important to you, this complete stranger from India or your own son?"

I was getting excited and Ivan was sounding more and more sad. "Miloš, I stopped at the Chelsea a couple of months ago. I was going to tell the guy to move out. But before I got a word out, he started kissing my hands. He had such sad eyes, Miloš, I could never bring myself to tell him. Look, I *will* take care of it. Let's talk about something else."

It was Stanley Bard who finally asked the guru to leave. Ivan never came back from California to get his things, but I think that he covered the bill.

As soon as Ivan made a little money, he got his son out of Czechoslovakia, pulling off a Cold War caper that he directed brilliantly. Little Ivan had for years been applying for trips to the West, but the government suspected that he wanted to defect and join his father, so they wouldn't let him travel anywhere. But in 1981, Ivan's father lay dying, so the Czech government allowed Ivan back into the country on a five-day visa. In that short time, Ivan managed to say good-bye to his dad, be at his side while he passed on, bury him, and set his son's defection in motion.

Little Ivan was living with his maternal aunt, a very capable woman, who promised to get Little Ivan on a factory bus going to a seaside camp in Yugoslavia. Big Ivan was going to take it from there.

As soon as the vacation season began, the aunt delivered on her promise. Little Ivan boarded a bus with a group of people who knew each other intimately. None of them had seen him before, though, so no one would sit next to him—they thought that he had been planted in the group by State Security to keep an eye on them.

Little Ivan didn't complain and minded his own business. He made it to the seaside resort on the Adriatic and checked into his cottage, but he hardly slept that night. In the morning, he headed out of the camp to look for the local post office, where he was to meet his father at ten o'clock in the morning.

Big Ivan was there, waiting. When they embraced, however, the clock started ticking: Passer junior could now be reported missing from the camp at any time.

By then, Big Ivan had been in Europe for a month, on the phone, darting from country to country, setting up contingencies for his son's escape. He'd decided to overengineer everything. He was getting Little Ivan out, period. He had worked out the main plan in detail, and he had five fallback options. The plan was for Little Ivan to fly out of Yugoslavia on a Venezuelan passport. It had been obtained through rich relatives in South America, and was waiting for them at the embassy in Belgrade.

The most promising fallback was an answer to a question Ivan asked himself: "What would I do if I were directing this scene in a movie?" The answer was that he'd call a propman and get a fake passport. Through Claude Berri, Ivan had the the best propman in the French movie business forge a French passport that looked absolutely real, used and well-stamped. The hitch was that the photograph wasn't of Little Ivan but of a generic young man. But French passport pictures were the size of a thumbnail, so that didn't matter all that much. The real problem was that Little Ivan spoke no French, so Big Ivan hired a French lady friend to come and spend the weekend in Belgrade. If necessary, she would lead Little Ivan through customs to a French charter flight.

Big Ivan's other solid fallback was a German trucker who hauled vegetables from the Balkans to Germany. He had a regular route, knew the border people, and thought it would be no sweat to hide Little Ivan in his load of watermelons. The German wanted to see some serious money upfront, however, so Ivan paid him, though he worried that the trucker didn't appreciate how daunting the task was. The guy just seemed too cavalier about the risks involved.

Big Ivan's other contingencies were more iffy. He had hired a skipper of an Italian yacht to stand by on the far side of the Adriatic. If Big Ivan called, the Italian was to sail to Yugoslavia and rescue Little Ivan by sea, but this option was underplanned and navigationally tricky. A contact in Zagreb could help Ivan's son stow away on the train to Vienna; a smuggler near the Italian border walked people across the poorly guarded frontier.

The first thing that Big Ivan did was drive his son to the Venezuelan embassy in Belgrade, but the passport that awaited them was no good— it was a bright red emergency passport with Little Ivan's picture but no entry stamp. The Venezuelan chargé d'affaires proceeded to talk openly about Little Ivan's defection in front of the Yugoslav staff of the embassy, some of whom were sure to inform the Yugoslav secret police. Big Ivan grabbed the red passport, thanked the diplomat, and hurried to meet the German truck driver.

The German never showed up. He had been so casual about the defection because he merely pocketed the money.

Time was of the essence. Big Ivan decided to go with the propman's passport. He put his son on the French charter flight. His French lady friend handled her assignment like a born conwoman. She flirted with the Serbian customs officials and had them in such a tizzy that they barely noticed the pale young man at her side. She took care of everything, coolly addressing Little Ivan in French now and then. He grinned back, having no idea of what she was saying. Big Ivan watched the two of them from a distance, his heart pounding.

They boarded the plane. The flight took off. Little Ivan was free. And Big Ivan was only too happy to go back to directing movies.

MILLION-DOLLAR MINUTE

The biggest paycheck I earned while living at the Chelsea was for directing a television commercial for Royal Crown cola. I was probably offered the project because the idea was a rip-off of the audition sequence of *Taking Off*, which featured a montage of fifty singers, each performing a snippet of one song. The ad agency wanted to give the jingle of its soft drink similar treatment—a number of people would belt out their catchy tune straight at the camera.

I took on the one-minute commercial thinking it would be easy. Cast the singers, teach them the ditty, put them in front of the camera, and edit the results. I didn't realize I was dropping through a rabbit hole into the wonderland of corporate America.

An endless chain of meetings followed as the simple idea ballooned into a nightmare of logistics. The advertising people decided that the spot should be shot in London because a commercial for Royal Crown cola should have the royal symbol that hung in the London theaters in each frame. The reasoning didn't make a milligram of sense. The insignia was going to come across only as a huge pancake in the background of the shots, and, in any case, it could have been cheaply duplicated and hung up on any soundstage in New York.

I didn't mind a trip to London, however, so I stayed out of the absurdist deliberations. I soon found myself flying first-class across the Atlantic with thirty other people. The executives were bringing their wives along. It was a massive junket. "It's only money" was the trip's refrain. I had a day of prep in London, shot the footage the next day, edited it for a few more days, and pocketed $10,000.

I discovered that I didn't have to go back to Prague and its Communist bureaucracy to find myself in a pure *Kafkárna*. I had just spent two years making a feature film for $810,000, whereas a one-minute rip-off of it cost one million dollars to produce. I was starting to catch up to speed in America.

PART 7

AMERICAN MOVIES

ONE FLEW OVER
THE CUCKOO'S NEST

I've come to dread the time of day when the mail arrives. Whole libraries of books and screenplays, actors' résumés, crank letters, requests, appeals, accusations, and solicitations wash up every day.

When I lived at the Chelsea, however, the mail delivery was often the high point of my day. I was waiting for that one offer that was going to change everything, and in the meantime, I grabbed all the invitations that looked like a free meal.

One day, I got a package from California. Inside was a book I'd never heard of, written by an author I'd never heard of, accompanied by a letter from two producers I'd never heard of. When I opened the novel and started to read, it gripped me immediately. I had no idea that the book had been not only a best-seller but a publishing phenomenon, yet I saw right away that this was the best material I'd come across in America.

One Flew Over the Cuckoo's Nest took place in a mental ward. Ken Kesey had written it from firsthand experience, and it was beautifully done. The story was told by the Chief, an Indian inmate of the institution who feigns being a deaf mute. A big man with a shrunken spirit, he watches a charismatic new patient, McMurphy, take on the puritanical Nurse Ratched, who has been ruling the ward with drugs and electroshocks. McMurphy particularly takes Billy Bibbit, a young stutterer traumatized by sexual hang-ups, under his wing. He arranges a date for Billy that makes a man out of him and clears up his problem. Nurse Ratched, furious at losing her hold over Billy, swiftly plays on his massive guilt feelings, but she misjudges her hand and Billy cracks and kills himself. Holding Ratched responsible for Billy's death, McMurphy assaults her, but she is an absolute ruler of the ward. McMurphy is administered a lobotomy, which leaves him in a vegetative state. In an act of mercy, the Chief suffocates him with a pillow and then busts out of the ward— presumably to live the life that McMurphy had inspired in him.

The book vividly dramatized the never-ending conflict between the individual and the institution. We invent institutions to help make the world more just, more rational. Life in society would not be possible without orphanages, schools, courts, government offices, and mental hospitals, yet no sooner do they spring into being than they start to control us, regiment us, run our lives. They encourage dependency to perpetuate themselves and are threatened by strong personalities.

I read the book several times before I set out to meet the two California producers who had sent it to me, and I prepared an outline of a script. I knew what I'd cut, what I'd leave, where I'd add and where I'd take away. I also decided that I'd take the point of view out of the Indian's head.

The first-person mode of narration, in my opinion, is better suited to literature than to film. Literature deals in the abstract realm of words, where every sentence can conjure up a new world. The flow of words beautifully reflects the modulation of thought, and the medium is perfectly suited to rendering the stream of consciousness. Film generally views the world from the outside, from a more objective vantage point. The images are concrete, so they have a greater visceral impact, universality, and conviction, but it's more difficult to portray an inner life.

I presented my ideas to the producers at a Chinese dinner in Los Angeles. They were an odd pair, a handsome young man who knew about movies and a witty grizzled veteran who ran a music production company in San Francisco that had Creedence Clearwater Revival under contract. Their names were Michael Douglas and Saul Zaentz, and, between them, they had yet to put together a single movie. In 1973, the producer's names meant nothing to me. The two men came across as very capable and self-assured. They seemed to know what they wanted to do, and they were sure they could raise the money for the film on their own.

At that time, the average movie cost about $6,500,000 to make, a sum that nowadays might buy the services of one barely bankable star, but Zaentz and Douglas figured they could make *One Flew Over the Cuckoo's Nest* for under $2 million. They calculated that they could keep the budget low by using unknown actors and by having everyone in the production work for scale. They needed a director who was ambitious, but cheap, which was perfect for me, and they offered me a deal that didn't pay a lot up-front, but included points on the profit, a clause that wound up working out in my favor.

Over drinks, I learned that Michael Douglas was the son of the famous Kirk Douglas, whom I had met once in Prague. Sometime in the sixties, Kirk Douglas was traveling around Eastern Europe as an American goodwill ambassador and I was invited to a party the American cultural attaché had thrown for him. Kirk had seen my films, and we talked and seemed to hit it off.

"Listen, I'm working on a project that I'm real excited about," Kirk told me. "I'd like you to look at it."

"I'd love to," I replied.

"It's a book. I'll send it to you."

He mentioned the title, but it didn't mean anything to me, so I promptly forgot it. I gave Kirk my address and waited to see if anything would come in the mail. My English was barely up to reading street signs, so I would have to have someone roughly translate the book into Czech for me. I never received anything from Douglas, which didn't surprise me. He was a big star, and I figured he must have said something on the spur of the moment, and left it right there in the room when he stepped out.

When Michael and Saul Zaentz hired me, I came to California and ran into Kirk again at a party at the Douglases'.

"Mr. Forman, aren't you a real son of a bitch?" was the first thing he said to me. I was shocked. Everyone around us fell silent.

"Why?"

"When I sent you the book, you didn't even have the decency to write 'Kiss off' back to me. But now that you live here, you're all gung-ho to direct it!"

It was only at that moment that I realized the book Kirk Douglas had been talking about all those years before was *One Flew Over the Cuckoo's Nest*, so I said, "You know, Mr. Douglas, the funny thing is that I'd been thinking the exact same thing about you."

Kesey's novel had almost certainly been confiscated by the Czech customs, but neither of us was informed about it. It had, in fact, been Kirk Douglas who'd originally bought the rights to *Cuckoo's Nest*. He had even starred in a theatrical adaptation of it by Dale Wasserman on Broadway in 1963. He then tried for years to produce it through one of the major film studios. No one wanted the project because the Hollywood profit charts said no movie about mental illness had ever made money before, so Kirk finally got tired of constant rejection and gave the rights to his son.

When, some ten years after Kirk's visit to Prague, *One Flew Over the Cuckoo's Nest* finally found me at the Chelsea, it seemed an act of fate.

BOOKS AND MOVIES

One morning in 1974, I took ten minutes and packed up all my earthly possessions. After four years in America, they fit into one bag. I said good-bye to the Chelsea and to New York and drove cross-country to California.

I intended to come back as soon as the movie was done and spend the rest of my life in edgy, driven, cerebral New York. The anemic California confuses me to this day. I love to go there, but its palm trees, its turquoise swimming pools, its parties and screenings and tennis matches put me into a vacation mode. I could never get anything started there, but in 1974 I had my work already cut out for me.

Back in Czechoslovakia, I'd adapted two books to film, and the screenplays for *Black Peter* and *Grandpa Automobile* taught me that the business of adaptation is part common sense and part daring. The scope of a film is clearly much closer to a short story than to a novel, so to adapt a book means to pare down and focus its theme. At the same time, books also engage their readers differently. A brilliant piece of writing can be taken in small doses, pondered on sleepless nights, savored at length, reread. In a movie house, you can't leaf through a film the way you leaf through a book, so films need to sustain simultaneously the interests of many groups of people. The daring that's required is similar to the daring that goes into a good translation. A bad translator merely shoves words from another language into the slots of the words in the original, whereas good translators—and good screenwriters—often let go of the precise words of the original to preserve its tone and feeling.

When an adaptation fails, it's usually a matter of misplaced respect. Most movie versions of great novels remain illustrated literature and don't take wing. Nearly all of Hemingway's books have been turned into movies, but not one of those films is as good as the original work. Any number of wonderful novels by Tolstoy, Mann, Flaubert, Proust, Joyce, and Kafka have been botched by screenwriters who have followed the outline of the books too faithfully instead of pursuing their own response to the emotional core of the material.

I strive to hold on to the strongest emotions that the original has provoked in me, to keep all the elements that have moved or amused me. I believe you can only preserve the spirit of a book on film by using the book as a point of departure for a new, filmic creation, even at the cost of altering the book's story, though this step requires some courage.

Zaentz and Douglas already owned a screenplay of *One Flew Over the Cuckoo's Nest* when they hired me. They didn't like it, even though it had been written by Ken Kesey himself, and I had to agree with them. The script was too faithful a transcription of the novel. I understood perfectly why Kesey had kept his script so close to the book: what need could he have seen to re-create his vision in a different medium? It had been hugely successful as a book and as a play. Why change it for the movies?

I'd later have a similar experience with *Hair* and *Ragtime.* In both cases, the authors of the original piece wrote a screen adaptation. In their screenplay of *Hair,* Gerome Ragni and James Rado merely transcribed their musical into screenplay form, setting it in an incompletely imagined theatrical space. With *Ragtime,* E. L. Doctorow simply rewrote his novel into a different format. The sprawling script crawled with characters and gave off a monotone buzz of unaccentuated emotion because Doctorow failed to make any of the hard focusing choices necessary for a good adaptation. He produced a huge libretto of some three hundred pages, a prettily penned paper brick that I wouldn't have known how to begin to shoot. Again, not their fault.

Nevertheless, I regret that I never got to meet Ken Kesey. He was clearly his own man and he wrote a wonderful book with a lot of heart, but when I started working on *Cuckoo's Nest,* the lines of communication between the producers and Kesey had already been severed. I have no firsthand knowledge of what transpired between them, but I heard that when Kesey finished his screenplay, he wanted to direct and star in the movie, which was the beginning of the end of their relationship.

I worked on the first draft of our screenplay with Larry Hauben and later rewrote it with another very fine screenwriter, Bo Goldman. Hauben and I wrote the first version right in the Oregon state mental hospital in Eugene, Oregon, where we would later shoot it, so I got to know the location and the people there before we went into production. It rained a lot, and when it didn't rain, the place was usually shrouded in gloomy fog.

The setting happened to be appropriate to the story, which was a stroke of luck because we didn't have any alternative locations to work with. The producers had approached a number of mental hospitals to see if they would let a film crew on their premises. They were flatly turned down by every one of them. Kesey's best-seller was seen as a vicious ambush of the mental-health-care industry, and most people in the business didn't want to see *One Flew Over the Cuckoo's Nest* made into a movie.

Zaentz and Douglas finally had the luck of running into Dr. Dean R. Brooks. This superintendent of the state mental hospital in Eugene didn't care what we shot in his wards as long as his patients got hired to perform some of the menial labor of filmmaking. He thought that having a job on a movie production and earning a paycheck right there in the hospital would have a very therapeutic effect on his charges. The producers agreed, but they lined up a backup crew of professionals in case the patients couldn't hack the job.

They needn't have worried. The inmates handled all the hurry-up-and-wait labor of making movies just fine, and Dr. Brooks proved to be absolutely right: the work and the pay greatly increased their self-confidence and self-esteem. I remember one patient in particular, a short, intense man who stammered so badly when we first got started that you couldn't understand a word he was saying. He persisted, but nevertheless you always failed to comprehend him.

The guy loved the job, however. He loved pulling cables, carrying equipment, setting up lights, lugging props. He got mad when the other patients did a sloppy job, and he started telling them so. Gradually, he began to get his points across, and, by the end of our shoot, he not only stopped stuttering, he was barking orders like a boot-camp sergeant.

JACK NICHOLSON AND THE BIGGEST SON OF A GUN OF THEM ALL

When I cast a film, I view the world with different eyes. I can't mail a letter without considering the postal clerk for a part in my film. Watching people and watching actors in movies and plays, I take mental notes on various casting ideas. This compulsion subsides once I move on to a different phase of moviemaking, but it never completely leaves me.

In *Cuckoo's Nest,* for the first time in my career I had professional actors in all the principal and secondary roles. My cast members could no longer just be themselves. I decided to compensate for the actors in the foreground of the film by having as many real people on the edges of the film as possible, and so most of the patients, nurses, and other employees of the hospital who pass through the movie are the locals being themselves.

The more I thought about the story, the more I wanted to get a big name for the role of McMurphy. Our film was taking the audience from their everyday world into a raw, threatening, and completely unfamiliar place, and I thought their journey might be easier if they had a familiar guide. I talked it over with the producers, and they asked me if I had any particular guides in mind.

I thought Jack Nicholson would make a great McMurphy. Nicholson had by then already become a star of the first rank in Hollywood. He had made his mark in *Easy Rider, Carnal Knowledge,* and *Five Easy Pieces.* I admired his performance in *Chinatown* a great deal, though I thought he had turned in an even better one in *The Last Detail,* a subtle, powerful, compassionate film. He would be a great asset to *Cuckoo's Nest,* but there was one huge drawback in casting him: our budget was going to balloon. A star's presence pulls everyone else's salary up with it, so none of the other actors would work for scale anymore, the unions would retract any concessions they were ready to make for a small-time film, and so on.

Saul and Michael carefully considered all the costs and benefits of casting Nicholson as our McMurphy. Then they told me to ask him. I'd met Jack through Buck Henry when we took *Taking Off* to Cannes. Jack and Buck were old friends, so I'd get to see Jack now and then when I came to Los Angeles. I'd even been a guest at Jack's house, but I was never completely comfortable around him. He was always very friendly to me, but he spoke such vivid slang that my English simply couldn't keep up. Half the time I couldn't understand what Jack was saying, so I could never completely relax around him. I'd always wind up with a gnawing feeling that I was boring him. Looking back, I think it was probably a matter of my outsider paranoia, but it certainly never lessened my admiration for Jack's work. I simply couldn't think of anyone better for the role.

"Hell, Miloš, I tried to get the rights to the fucking book, if you know what I mean, but old boy Douglas beat me to the punch," said Jack when I offered him the part.

As we had predicted, casting Nicholson inflated our budget to four million dollars—a pittance by contemporary standards. Our whole budget might have covered the cost of catering *Terminator 2,* but for an independent production at that time it was a lot of money. Zaentz approached the major studios again to try to cover the budget. But even with a star of Nicholson's radiance under contract, no one was interested.

Zaentz finally used his own company, Fantasy Records, to underwrite the production.

Casting Jack was the easy part. I saw over a thousand people for the other roles, which has since become my typical auditioning dosage. I'd say that casting amounts to 70 percent of my work with actors; the rest goes into helping them find themselves in the role. I try to guide them to the feeling and energy that I detected in them when I first cast them.

I bring to my casting sessions a rough idea of how my characters should look, though sometimes an actor will show me an entirely different way to go with the role, which is always intriguing. In *Amadeus,* for example, I assumed that the role of the emperor would be claimed by a British actor. I suppose I just associated the idea of ruling aristocracy with the British upper-class accent, reticence, and imperiousness. But then Jeffrey Jones, a red-blooded American, read for the part, and he exuded more imperial bearing, class, and diplomatic cunning than all the British actors I saw. His conception of the emperor was so compelling that he forced me to abandon my original notion completely. I love to watch his performance in the film.

In a first casting session, I only look at the physical presence of the actor or actress in a quick, intuitive read of how he or she comes across. A first impression is also very important because it tells me how the audience will most likely perceive that person. The second step in the casting process is an interview. I talk with the candidate for a short time, no longer than five or ten minutes, just to hear the speech patterns, assess the basic attitude, and get a sense of the personality. If I can feel the character stirring in them, I ask them to come back and read a scene from the script with me. I read with each actor, playing old grandmas, little boys, shy brides, mass murderers, or anyone else the scenes call for. I like to feel the impact of the actor's personality and get a direct read of his flexibility and intelligence.

I assume there are other directors who read with their actors, though I don't think it's a common procedure. I don't want my actors to feel as if they are being judged from a safe distance, so I put myself right in their shoes. You put your credibility on the line so that you can show the actors what you want from the scene. If you can afford to do that, then your directorial authority only stands to gain. (Reading a script over and over again with many different voices also gives you the benefit of memorizing it and of gaining a corrective perspective on it. Some lines invariably sound off-key again and again, so I make my final revision of the script with these bits of dialogue still ringing in my ears.)

Nothing works all the time, and this casting strategy has a severe drawback that I discovered the hard way. Once I was looking for a virile young man for a seduction scene and thought I'd found the perfect actor. As I read the scene with him, playing the part of the swooning lady, he just radiated animal magnetism and sexual power. I never got the chance to have my actress read with him before the shoot, but I didn't think it was necessary—I was sure he would sweep her right off her feet. But when we started to shoot the scene, I didn't recognize the young man: the swaggering rooster had turned into a timid little tit-mouse, so stiff and nervous that he couldn't even hold the young woman's gaze. I tried to put him at ease and bring back the seductive-ness he had shown me in the reading, but I was never able to coax it out of him.

I don't care whether people are gay or straight, so I am not very good at guessing sexual orientation. The young man, as it turned out, was gay, and he was petrified of the subtext of the scene. He was only able to come across powerfully when he read the scene with another man.

Hence, my final casting consideration is assessing the chemistry be-tween the actors. I may have several actors who could become a single character, so what finally matters is how they look together, react to one another, like or dislike, soothe or unnerve each other.

I had found Brad Dourif in an off-Broadway production of *When You Comin' Back, Red Ryder?* and immediately saw Billy Bibbit in him. He was dripping talent and had the core of vulnerability that was right for the role. The other patients in the ward had to be strikingly individual, so they wouldn't blend together in the group scenes. Michael Douglas brought in a short, stout actor named Danny DeVito who had acted in the stage version of *Cuckoo's Nest.* A casting agency sent us Christopher Lloyd, another hard-to-mistake face. His maniacal mug reminded me of my old friend from New York, Vincent Schiavelli.

It was somewhat harder to cast Nurse Ratched. In the book, she is portrayed as an order-mad, killjoy harpy. At one point Kesey even describes her as having wires coming out of her head, so I searched for a castrating monster. One day, a rather sweet actress named Louise Fletcher came to interview with me. She was good-looking, blond, slim, and polite, and she had an engaging smile. She was all wrong for Nurse

Ratched, but there was something about her. I asked her to read with me, and suddenly, beneath the velvety exterior, I discovered a toughness and willpower that seemed tailored for the role.

Discovering Nurse Ratched in the prim, angelic Louise surprised me, but the more I thought about it, the more it made sense. I'd learned long before that it's better to cast against type in the leading roles and with it in the minor roles. For reasons of economy and clarity, I prefer to give the audience a quick read of secondary characters by casting obvious physical types, but with the principal roles, it's more engaging to uncover a different personality under the obvious type, to peel away the erroneous expectations, to be surprised by a deeper knowledge of the character.

In the case of Nurse Ratched, it would have been far less threatening to cast Medusa herself in the part—one look and you'd brace yourself for evil, whereas true horror resides in the sudden revelation of a warped character that hits you when you're not prepared for it.

As usual, I had the toughest time filling a role that I didn't think I'd have any problems with, but it took me a very long time to find the Chief, whom Kesey described as a giant. I was intent on casting a real bruiser of a man because I wanted the actor's physical type to pay big dramatic dividends when, suddenly and for the first time, the Chief's withdrawn, shrunken spirit expands to match his huge body.

I quickly learned that Indians do not generally get as big as I'd imagined the Chief to be. I refused to believe that there wasn't a single Indian who could play a basketball center, so the production sent scouts across the country who got the word out. I remember even looking into the Canadian construction industry, which employs a large number of Indians. For a long time, the search turned up nothing. I'd started grudgingly reconciling myself to using a smaller man in the part when I got an excited phone call from Salem, Oregon.

"Miloš! I found the biggest son of a gun of them all!" It was Mel Lambert, a friend of Zaentz's who ran a used car dealership in Salem. His father had started the car business, and he knew several Indian languages, so the Indians trusted him and he retained a large Indian clientele. A man from Yakima, Washington, had come in looking for a big used car with miles of leg room.

I arranged to meet with the man and asked Jack Nicholson if he would come and read with my only prospect. I needed to see if I could work with this Indian even if he wasn't particularly gifted as an actor.

Jack understood my concerns perfectly, so one misty morning we found ourselves sitting around a drab airport conference room in Portland, Oregon. Zaentz and Douglas were there as well, all of us waiting for the flight from Yakima to bring our Indian. From there we were to fly on to the mental ward in Salem in Lambert's plane—Mel, a man of many talents, moonlighted as the Oregon governor's personal pilot.

The Indian's flight was delayed, and I was tense. I was eager to finish casting and get on with the project, but when the door opened, my tension eased. The man entering the room was so tall he had to bow his head in the doorway. He introduced himself as Will Sampson. We started to talk, and immediately it became clear that Will was sharp. The first thing that I look for in a nonactor is intelligence.

Sampson had been a rodeo rider in his youth, but his career had been cut short by a spinal injury, so he was now eking out a living by painting nature scenes. I was pretty sure I had my Chief by the time Mel led us across the tarmac to his plane. When I had heard the words "Oregon governor" earlier, I expected to see a corporate jet, but Mel pointed us to a tiny, beat-up little buzzard of a four-seater.

With five men and a giant boarding this ridiculous suicide machine, I had to summon up all the will to get on with the film to beat back a panic attack. The flight was supposed to be very short, a matter of some twenty minutes, so I climbed inside the contraption and took the seat beside the pilot, but my heart was racing.

Saul, Michael, and Jack piled into the two backseats and Will folded his huge body across their laps. His feet were nearly hanging out the window. However, the plane seemed to have plenty of power; it took off with ease and climbed higher and higher, soaring almost too far away from Mother Earth.

We were nearing Salem when Mel had a brainstorm. "Damn! I can show you guys where I live! We're practically flying over my house!" He banked the plane sharply over a pine forest. My stomach acids shot up into my throat. The plane dipped down toward the tall trees.

"See that house! That's my house!" he exclaimed proudly. "Wait a minute! Shit! Where the hell is my horse?! Don't tell me that the son of a bitch ran off again."

For the next twenty minutes, we buzzed the pine forest like the Red Baron, looking for the horse that had escaped its hitching post. We twisted with the trails and the roads below, made sharp U-turns, drew figure eights in the sky. Will bounced on the sore knees of the producers and Jack Nicholson. Mel swore at his horse. I took deep breaths to keep from throwing up and gripped the seat so tightly that my forearms ached. It wasn't until Lambert finally started running out of gas that we headed for Salem.

We never did find the horse among the pines, but I'd found the perfect Chief in Will Sampson. He came to the shoot prepared, and his instincts were sound; he rarely needed my guidance. And he was the darling of all the ladies on the set.

There was only one other man who could compete with Will in this regard. We were still in the prep stage when Dr. Brooks asked the producers and me into his office and closed the door. "Look, one of the patients working for you is a sex offender. I can't imagine him doing anything to anybody now—he's under medication and he's been here for years—but maybe you should let all your actresses and ladies know. Just to be fair."

"My God, who is he?" we asked.

The superintendent pointed out a short, rather handsome guy whom I had noticed before. He was so carefully groomed that he stood out from the rest of the patients. His fingernails were never dirty, his shirt collars were immaculate. What could he have done?

"Well, he did horrible things actually," the superintendent informed us. "He stabbed an eight-year-old girl in the vagina with a screwdriver. A real tragedy. He was here for several years and we thought he was fine, so we let him go. But, then he did something even worse, so he'll probably never get out of here again."

The guy looked pleasant enough and he was quick to smile, but this was serious business, so we discreetly passed the word about him to all the women working on the set. After that, whenever I thought to look, I'd find the sex offender surrounded by our ladies. It never failed. It seemed as if some strange psychosis had seized them and drawn them to the guy.

Sex offenders notwithstanding, I wanted to integrate the actors and the patients in order to help them feel what it was really like to be committed to a mental ward. I had them wander around the wards and observe the patients for hours on end. I insisted that they all get their own bed in the ward where we were shooting and that a standard gown and a shaving kit be issued to them as if they were being admitted for a stay. I also assigned each one a patient to emulate. They weren't supposed to study his sickness or pick apart his medical record, they were merely to observe their man and copy his gestures, his pattern of speech, all the tics of his behavior. I was hoping to help them become whoever they'd be if they were crazy.

One of the nonactors whom I used in the film in order to give my actors a pitch of real behavior on which to tune their performances was the open-minded Dr. Brooks. He played himself, and the scene in which he is admitting McMurphy was one of the last times I allowed my actors to improvise their dialogue. I set up the parameters of the situation, gave the pair a few key phrases, and let Nicholson and Dr. Brooks take it from there. It worked just as well as it had worked for me back in Czechoslovakia.

All the scenes in *Cuckoo's Nest* stood or fell with Jack Nicholson, who was a dream to work with. He had none of the vanity, egomania, or obsessions of a star. He insisted on receiving the same treatment as everyone else. He was always prepared for his scenes and had a clear idea of what he wanted. His sense of humor put everyone at ease, which is always a great asset on a set. He helped the people around him because he knew that the better their performances were, the better he would look in the end.

Toward the end of the shoot, Will Sampson stopped by my trailer for a beer and a talk.

"Miloš, the role I'm playing, is it a big deal?" he asked.

"Oh, yes," I said.

"So what do you think, should I move to Hollywood now? What would you do if you were me?"

"Will, go back to Yakima and to your drawings. Because if Hollywood wants you, it doesn't matter if you're on the North Pole, they'll find you. And if they don't want you, then being in Hollywood is not going to make a bit of difference."

A few weeks after we wrapped I heard that Will Sampson was living in Los Angeles and had an unlisted phone number.

This would be funny, but Will's story has a tragic ending. Hollywood is a tough place for an out-of-work actor. Will appeared in a few television shows, but he never matched the success he had in *Cuckoo's Nest*. He died a few years later, still a young man.

ETERNAL PROBLEM

I'd never shot a film without Mirek Ondříček, my cinematographer, but now the Czechs weren't about to release him to work with a traitor to socialism. The producers suggested Haskell Wexler, who had won an Oscar for his work on *Who's Afraid of Virginia Woolf?* I was familiar with Wexler's work and knew that he was a great cinematographer, but he had also directed a film of his own by then and I was concerned that his directorial ambitions might get in my way.

I had dinner with Wexler to see how we'd get along. He struck me as the gentle, quiet type. He was very enthusiastic about Kesey's book and the screenplay, which Larry Hauben and Bo Goldman had written. I wanted a sort of a raw, realistic look for the film, but not so tawdry that it would pull attention away from the story. Wexler said he knew exactly how to give me this look, so I offered him the job.

In filmmaking, as in life, perfectionism presents an eternal problem. You cannot respect anyone who settles for less than the very best, yet you can't work with anyone who demands it at all times. It's a struggle I never cease to wage, even with myself.

For a cinematographer, the perfect way to shoot a movie would be without actors; every image could be lit so perfectly that it could hang on a wall. For a director, the perfect way to make a movie would be without the camera. Nothing would limit the actors, who could invest their work with all the emotional authenticity and behavioral quirks that make characters come alive. Clearly a certain amount of friction between cinematographer and director is built into the relationship. I'd had conflicts with Ondříček on every film we'd shot together, but we'd usually yell and swear and fight it out, then go to dinner and make up.

Wexler was different and handled this inherent tension differently. He rarely confronted me directly, even while he bristled under some of my decisions. For example, during the group therapy sessions, I insisted on working with two cameras. One was trained on the principal of the shot. The other was wandering over the faces of the other actors. The two cameras helped me to even out the performances. It kept the principal from getting too self-important and punching out his lines while the others, never knowing whether the second camera was on them, had to react and stay in the scene. I'd been afraid of these static, sit-down scenes; the second camera was helping me breathe life into them.

Wexler rightly claimed that if we used the cameras this way, it would be impossible to light the scene so that every face was shown to his satisfaction. In a real hospital getting the results he wanted would have required a massive feat of lighting engineering, for which we had neither the time nor the budget.

I could understand his worries, so I gave him my word that I wouldn't use any second-camera shots that would reflect badly on him. I thought my pledge would put an end to his unhappiness, but it didn't. I began to hear murmurs off the set. Actors approached me, tingling with nervousness. They looked as if they wanted to tell me something, but couldn't bring themselves to do it. Finally, a few broke down and told me that Wexler had been expressing his doubts as to whether I was competent enough to make this particular movie.

Before long, the producers heard the same mutterings. They weren't about to let the situation simmer; they had the most to lose if morale started to suffer.

"If you can't work with him, Miloš, we'll get you someone else," they proposed. I've never fired anyone from any of my films. I'm just too embarrassed to do it. I'd rather work around the less competent than get rid of them. "Look, let me talk to Haskell and see if we can work it out," I told the producers.

They were happy to hear this because it's never easy to change a major cog in a running machine.

At that time my girlfriend was Aurore Clement, the French actress who had played the girl in Louis Malle's *Lacombe, Lucien*. She was a fantastic cook, so I invited Wexler to a fabulous French dinner.

"Listen, Haskell, do you really think I won't be able to cut what we've shot so far?" I asked him.

"I don't think that," said Wexler.

"Well, I've heard that's what you've been telling people."

Wexler looked at me and his eyes started to fill with tears, which touched me greatly. We proceeded to talk out our differences, broke bread together, drained several bottles of wine, and I thought everything was going to be all right. In fact, I said so to the producers.

I was wrong. A week later, I heard that Wexler was questioning my competence again. It was becoming a real problem and was causing a lot of tension on the set, so the producers stepped in. Bill Butler, whose credits included *Jaws* and *The Conversation,* took over.

Later, someone tried to explain to me that Wexler probably saw a foreign director struggling with this very American classic and felt he should have more of a role in shaping the final project. It remains the only time someone was dismissed from one of my productions.

Butler looked over the old dailies and shot the second part of the film the same way.

There was still another change to be made before it was all over. We were running a week behind schedule and Bill had to leave for another job before we finished, so the boat scene was shot by one more old pro, Bill Fraker.

All these changes were quite scary. This much turnover in key positions is fairly unusual, but I never lost my faith in the screenplay and the actors. And, more important, I could see the professionalism of Wexler's replacements every night in the dailies. Both men did so well in matching Wexler's tone that it is impossible to see where one cinematographer left off and the other began.

LONGER FOR SHORTER

I love the process of editing, love to tease currents of feeling out of fragments of film, and weave them into a coherent whole. In Berkeley that year, for the first time I was working with two teams of editors. They edited different scenes in separate cutting rooms and I shuffled between them so that, on a good day, I'd have the whole floor stinking of my cigars. We made four rough cuts of *Cuckoo's Nest* in the process.

When I first started making films in Czechoslovakia, it would have been folly to have two sets of editors. The job required high mastery and didn't take very long because there was little room for trial-and-error experimentation in the cutting room. With every cut, you lost a frame of film, so you had to know precisely where to slice the film, which greatly speeded up the whole process.

I was very lucky in those days to be working with a master. Míla Hájek could tell at a glance exactly where each cut had to be made. We had edited *Loves of a Blonde* in a couple of weeks. These days, I work with two teams of editors and we play with each shot. We add three frames on one side of the splice, take away one frame on the other, then go back and add four more until the cut looks and feels on-the-money right. The process of completing a film takes months and months of detail work. This is the paradox of progress.

My memory is an autonomous organ that stores a lot of odd and irrelevant information, so I happen to remember the exact lengths of all four of the rough cuts of *Cuckoo's Nest.* The first ran two hours and fifty minutes. I cleaned up and tightened the scenes, pruned away the inessential moments, and by the time I had the second version I had the film down to two hours and thirty-two minutes. But the film still felt too long, though the cut seemed polished and I didn't see what else I could get rid of, so I stalled at this point.

It took me a while to reconcile myself emotionally to the idea of doing more radical surgery, but in the end I worked myself up into a ruthless enough mood. In the third cut, I pared away everything that didn't clearly advance the action. This meant throwing away a scene in which the Chief was shaved against his will, a scene I liked and thought interesting, though I finally had to admit that it didn't add anything to the picture of the world we were drawing and perhaps slowed down the story. My third cut came out to two hours and four minutes, and everyone was happy. But when we screened it, we were shocked: the film felt much longer to us than it had before. I'd just shortened it by twenty-eight minutes, yet, suddenly, it seemed to drag on and on. What went wrong?

I finally realized that when I'd taken out all the shots that didn't directly advance the plot, I'd also gotten rid of the shots that worked on my feelings and drew me into the story, so I went and put back seven minutes of screen time. A lot of these shots were the early therapy sessions, which sketched the personalities of the minor characters and made them more real, more sympathetic. The restoration also gave the audience more time to get used to the ways of the mental hospital. I screened this fourth cut of two hours and eleven minutes and something amazing happened: adding the seven minutes greatly shortened the film.

There is a peculiar sort of excitement that overtakes you when you near the completion of a movie, a mixture of cockiness and suicidal urges. At one moment you think you've just made your best film, but then you blink and everything on the cutting table suddenly seems so boring, trite, so empty that you hear the shark-infested waters under the Golden Gate Bridge calling you.

I was wired with this emotion when Jack came up to San Francisco to look at the film. He had the right to review the final cut, so I screened it for him and asked when he'd have some time to sit down in the editing room with me.

"I don't see why," he said. "I don't know what I would change in it."

SUITCASE ORCHESTRA

The final step in making a film is the music. I love music, but I have no musical education and need a lot of help to find out exactly what I want for my film. I only know it when I hear it.

The claim can be made that music has greater power than any other element in a film. It sometimes strikes me as an altogether higher form of communication, a pure flow of feeling, so sudden and immediate that at times it's as if a character ripped his heart out and handed it to the audience. At the same time, music is so abstract that I never know how to talk about it. And I have found out that most composers don't really know how to talk about their art either, at least not to a layman like me.

John Klein had taken the job of a stand-in in *Cuckoo's Nest* so he could hang out with me in Salem and San Francisco. John knows about music. One day he brought me a record he liked. The LP was recorded by the London Symphony Orchestra, even though its composer, Jack Nitzsche, was now working mostly in pop music. He had scored the film *Performance,* and John knew him personally.

I liked Nitzsche's music a lot, so in the editing room I played sections of his record with our scenes—they seemed to fit wonderfully. In fact, I even cut a few sequences to the strains of Nitzsche's record.

When I had the rough cut, I asked John to invite the composer to a screening. I proudly played my selections from his record, expecting him to be flattered, but Nitzsche got so furious that he nearly stopped talking to me.

"What is this! This is all wrong! This is nonsense!" he screamed.

I was close to panic. We had deadlines and delivery schedules to meet. We were running out of time and now I was afraid I had mortally offended Nitzsche and would wind up with some by-the-numbers hack composing the score. Mercifully, John Klein was able to smooth things over. Jack agreed to have new music by the deadline.

He went away and worked, but he didn't bother to give me any progress reports. Our recording date was fast approaching, so I collected my courage, called Nitzsche, and gingerly asked him what he would require in the way of studio musicians for the upcoming session.

"I don't know yet," he snarled.

"Okay, fine, sure, sorry," I said and hung up.

We never got an answer about his musician requirements, so to be safe we ordered a complete orchestra for our recording date. The session was to take place at Fantasy Records, where we were still polishing the final cut, so on the appointed day, from an upstairs window, I watched Nitzsche arrive. He came in a cab, accompanied by an old man lugging a huge suitcase.

We got to the recording studio at the same time. Jack strolled in, took one glance at the army of musicians waiting for him there, shook his head, and sent the entire orchestra home.

"Jack, listen, are you sure you don't need *anybody*?" I asked.

"Yes, I am," he said.

"You want *all* these people to go home?"

"They can stay here, but I don't need them."

"Not even a drummer, or, I don't know, a piano player?"

"No."

"Okay, Jack."

While we talked, the old man opened his suitcase and started pulling out glasses of different height, thickness, and size and spreading them around the table in the recording studio.

"Oh, I do need something after all, Miloš," Nietzsche said suddenly. "We'll need some water."

We got a pail of water, and the old man poured it into his glasses, carefully creating columns of different heights. He then wiped off the table and was ready to go to work. He rubbed his fingers around the rims of his glasses, coaxing strange, mournful sounds out of the tap water and glass.

The effect made your hair stand on end. Jack later added some more traditional passages as well as some music of buzz saws and other imaginative instruments, but he recorded most of the soundtrack that morning with only the old man and his suitcase orchestra. I loved the music.

THE BARBED-WIRED HEART

One Flew Over the Cuckoo's Nest opened in November. The reviewers didn't particularly swoon over it, but they also didn't pelt it with the kind of sarcastic one-liners that show their attention has drifted during the film.

The distributor was quite pleased with the first week's box office. United Artists projected that the picture might gross a total of $15 million. This meant a net profit of $3 million, so everyone was quite happy.

After the movie had been out for two weeks, the revenue forecast was revised. It went up to $20 million. Everyone was happier.

A week later, United Artists reported that it now looked as if the picture might make as much as $30 million. Mild delirium set in.

In the end, *Cuckoo's Nest* grossed some $140 million in America, and $280 million total worldwide box office.

As the film got bigger and bigger, the talk of Oscars started. When the nominations were announced, we'd snared nine of them amid stiff competition—*Dog Day Afternoon, Barry Lyndon, Nashville,* and *Jaws.* The bookies in Las Vegas gave us long odds at first. But as our film kept making money, *Cuckoo's Nest* forced the odds-makers to revise their estimates.

At this time I sat down and wrote a polite letter to the Czech government asking that my boys, whom I hadn't seen in six years, be allowed to visit me and share my joy. The old rule that nothing impressed the Communists as much as success among the imperialists kicked in, and my boys were allowed to come, under one condition. Their grandfather would have to accompany them to keep me from kidnapping them. I quickly agreed. I was happy that I'd get to see Mr. Křesadlo again. My three Czechs were to arrive the day before the Oscars. I'd barely have enough time to rent them tuxedos.

Meanwhile, as the Oscars drew nearer, a peculiar psychosis had begun to seize all of us who had been nominated. The previous year, Jack had gone for the prize as J. J. Gittes in *Chinatown.* Polanski's great film received a bevy of nominations, but finally lost in all but one category.

"Don't take out any loans against your Oscar," I was told by many old hands in the business. "When the chips are down, the Academy can get pretty chauvinistic."

To get away from it all, Jack and I went to his house in Aspen and skied.

Finally, at the end of March, my boys and Grandpa Křesadlo were to arrive in Los Angeles. I hired the largest limousine in the city of large limousines and went to the airport to get them. I was very nervous. I hadn't lived with my kids in eight years. They'd been six-year-old first-graders when I'd seen them last, very briefly, and now a couple of twelve-year-olds would get off the plane.

Their flight landed, and the first passengers began to exit customs. I scanned the crowd, watched families embrace, saw tired travelers in the arms of their relatives, and wished that my boys would hurry up.

An hour passed, then another, and another, when Grandpa Křesadlo suddenly appeared with my Petr and Matěj. They were twice the size that I had remembered and they looked fabulous. I grabbed them to me, but they drew away. I could see they were uncomfortable in a stranger's embrace, so I let go of them. I would have to start over and establish a relationship with my own kids. At least now that I finally had them here, I had a shot.

"This is the biggest limousine I could find, guys!" The beautiful car I'd hired to impress them gleamed in the Los Angeles sunshine, but they barely glanced at it. They got in and made themselves comfortable, as if they'd been driven to school in limousines all their lives. It was taking us to the heavenly Beverly Hills Hotel, which also meant nothing to them.

I was so excited to have them that I couldn't stop talking and pointing things out: "Those are the palms, guys! And that's the largest body of water on the planet! The Pacific Ocean! Here are the skyscrapers, see! And lookit here! This is a banana tree! And how about this huge pool! You ever seen a pool that big before?"

"Nope."

"Okay!"

I gushed on, and they obediently looked at everything I pointed out, but they weren't saying much. They looked bored, so I decided to shut up and see if anything at all caught their fancy. I noticed that they eyeballed the cars.

"Ooo, see that thing over there? That's a Porsche! And look at that gray one here! That's a Rolls! A Rolls-Royce, the Silver Shadow, the most expensive car in the world!"

The boys barely glanced at the Rolls, then focused on an old Chevy, yellow and unwashed.

"Dad?" one of them finally said.

"Yes?!"

"Dad, they got women driving cars here?!" they screamed, bug-eyed with astonishment.

It was the only thing about Los Angeles that impressed my boys, and it drove home to me what a world apart they had just left.

The next morning, I rented them tuxedos. The clothes intimidated them. They were scared to take a step, but by evening they plugged right into the excited mood in the crowded, glittering hall. They called my film "Couscous Next" and strained to pick out any mention of it from the stream of words they didn't understand. They applauded wildly every time they heard it.

The first of our nominations was Brad Dourif's Best Supporting Actor.

"And the winner is George Burns for *The Sunshine Boys*," said the presenter, and both my boys jumped up and clapped frenetically.

"It's nice of you to applaud, guys, but we didn't win. That was someone else."

"No?"

"No."

"Oh," they said, and sat down.

The next Oscar and the one after that were not our nominations, and then we missed out in a couple of categories, so the boys became quite cautious and I realized that if we didn't win any Oscars they'd never understand why I'd dressed them up so uncomfortably and dragged them there.

Meanwhile, an across-the-board blowout of our film was becoming a distinct possibility. I could feel the nerves of the *Cuckoo's Nest* family stretching. We all sat in the same section of the orchestra, so I could see Saul, Michael, and Jack, who all wore very serious, very composed expressions. I knew they were thinking what I was thinking: *Chinatown*.

When I looked at Matěj and Petr, I saw they were both sound asleep. I didn't wake them up until "Couscous Next" started its winning streak. Suddenly, Bo Goldman and Larry Hauben took Best Screenplay, Louise Fletcher Best Actress, Jack Best Actor. My boys and I were applauding like there was no tomorrow.

By the time my name was called, I was numb. I ran up and grasped the little statue in my hand. I'd prepared a speech and said something, but the world was a goulash of impressions and feelings. I stood before

the cheering audience of my peers, before the hundreds of millions of
eyes beyond. I had reached the top of my profession, I was in Holly-
wood, I was in America, and I was happy and overwhelmed. I didn't
know what to think about first, the money, the smiles of the world's
most glamorous women, the doors that had been closed to me suddenly
opening. In the glare of lights, I could just make out my two boys in
tuxedos clapping away and beaming. They were my blood, which was
the blood of people who had died behind barbed wire and the blood of
the old man in Ecuador who was now, perhaps, also dead, and, if I took
my eyes off them, they were still only six years old in my head. There
was a strangeness between us, the strangeness that's between all the
people, the concertina wire separating me from the cheering crowd, the
deep strangeness of it all, the barbed-wired heart.

I don't recall much of that evening. The world was coming at me
from all sides. There were the journalists backstage, photographers,
champagne, kisses, congratulations, and two sleepy boys.

The next morning, there was the pile of telegrams. The most moving
one came from Frank Capra, whose *It Happened One Night* was the only
other picture ever to win all five major Oscars.

WELCOME TO THE CLUB, it said.

GLIMPSE OF A FAMILY

My boys had never known anyone who had a pool. When they had
gone swimming, they had gone to the river. Czechoslovakia had re-
cently added a second television channel, but it only broadcast in the
evening. There was a total of four radio stations, and the daily newspa-
pers had eight densely printed pages. The news was mostly about
workers and farmers surpassing their production quotas under the latest
five-year plan, but now and again there were a few stories from the
capitalist, imperialist, militarist, decadent, and polluted United States of
America, which nearly always described grotesque murders, gangsters,
serial killers, armed robbers, crazed drug addicts, or the conspicuous
extravagance of some mean millionaires.

But now, in Beverly Hills, not far from our hotel, Grandpa Křesadlo
discovered an intersection that had gas stations on all four corners,

which simply blew his mind. Every day, he went for a long walk and wound up staring at this marvel. "How can all four of them possibly manage to stay in business? How can they possibly all sell the same thing for different prices?" he wondered.

I took my Czechs to all the studio lots and tourist sights. The boys loved everything they saw, but they dozed off everywhere. They would be okay while we were on the move, but the moment we stopped for coffee, they'd close their eyes and be out like a light. I ascribed it to a severe case of jet lag, and I'd wake them up when the waiters brought their food. But Matěj and Petr didn't seem to be getting over their jet lag. One afternoon in a Chinese restaurant, the boys stretched out on the floor and went into a deep sleep right under the table.

Only three years later, my sons confessed to me why they'd been so sleepless during those three weeks in Los Angeles. I would say good night to them and shut the door. Immediately they would climb into one bed and spend the night eyeing the door and the windows—they were certain some coke fiend or a gangster was about to break into their room and shoot them. Chalk one up for Communist propaganda.

I took the boys and Grandpa to Las Vegas. I was still showing off, so I booked the largest suite at Caesars Palace, with bedrooms for everyone. A big jacuzzi whispered in the living room.

"Go ahead, jump in while I go unpack," I told the boys, and went into my bedroom.

When I came back, Petr and Matěj were splashing happily around the jacuzzi, but I noticed they had put their swimsuits on.

"What're you guys doing? Why the swimsuits?"

"Come on, Dad, what if somebody came in?"

"Who, room service? They knock."

"Well, don't the other guests in this hotel go swimming?" The boys thought our jacuzzi was the hotel pool.

They loved Circus Circus, the kids' playground in the casino. For Czech boys who'd grown up on shooting galleries with plastic roses, slow merry-go-rounds, and basic Ferris wheels, it was a new idea of heaven.

The high point of Grandpa's visit came during his flight over the Grand Canyon. I'd sent him there alone, on a sightseeing plane. He came back beaming. He just couldn't stop talking about what he had seen.

"But you're going to be mad at me, Miloš," he said suddenly, his face clouding with apprehension.

"Why, Grandpa?"

"Well, there was this family there, and they spoke German and they knew you. And they asked me what I did. And I lied. I didn't want to disgrace your name, so I said I was an engineer . . ."

All his life, the sweet man had been fixing radios and TV sets for friends. The people around him thought that he was a wizard of electronics, but, like everyone else in Central Europe, Grandpa Křesadlo believed that you're only as good as your title.

When it was time for my boys and Grandpa to leave, I was in tears, but my kids couldn't wait to get back home. They had all sorts of gifts for their buddies, mostly amazing American objects like skateboards, and they couldn't wait to hand them out in Prague.

I never lost touch with them again. While the Communists were still in power in Czechoslovakia, I couldn't freely go and see them in Prague, but I tried to get back to the periphery of their lives anyway. I would talk to them on the phone, exchange letters, and see them a few weeks every year, in Europe or in America. We'd go skiing or bicycling around Europe, and I was able to show them the Paris and New York I love.

They later attended the Art Academy, where Matěj studied painting and Petr puppeteering, and now they run a puppet theater together and make animated films in Prague.

In 1976, before they left Los Angeles, Jennings Lang, an executive from Universal whom I was very fond of, had offered me the use of the projection room in his villa.

"Is there any movie you guys would like to see?" I asked my boys.

I was secretly hoping they'd say, "Yeah, Dad, 'Couscous Next.' " Neither they nor Grandpa had seen it.

"Oh, yeah, Dad!" they said. "Yeah! Let's see a movie!"

They really loved *Jaws*.

SCRATCHY RECORD

After *One Flew Over the Cuckoo's Nest,* everything in my life turned around. I'd directed a Hollywood movie that had made a lot of money, so I'd shed the reputation of an artsy European director who liked to work with nonactors and whose sense of humor was too cutting for apparatchiks, sentimental producers, and corporate lifers. The best scripts were sent to me, and all my phone calls were answered. I'd made a lot of money and was ready to see what Jean Paul Getty meant when he said that the world is mean to millionaires.

When all the promotional work on *Cuckoo's Nest* wound down, I headed to New York. I missed the intensity and stimulation of that taut, fast-talking city after two years in California, so I moved back to the Chelsea Hotel.

Stanley Bard had my old room ready for me. Some of the old tenants were still there and I could look out the window and see the same Twenty-third Street view, but it wasn't the same. I found that it was easier to live at the Chelsea on a dollar a day than with money. If you had money, you bought books, records, tennis rackets, suits, good booze, even though you didn't have a bookshelf, a big enough closet, or a bar. Things just piled up around you. Pretty soon the room looked like the deck of an immigrant ship.

I'd lived out of a suitcase nearly all my life, and I'd grown comfortable with my gypsy existence. I couldn't afford to think about houses and possessions. If you can't afford the life-style to which your ego aspires, hotel rooms offer a fine alternative. But now I had the means to create a home, so I started to cast about for an apartment or a house in the city.

I was getting a lot of movie offers. One of them had a long history behind it, a creative flirtation that reached all the way back to 1967. That year, I'd had the fortune of coming from Europe and walking in on the very first public performance of *Hair*. I owed this incredible stroke of luck to Rick Edelstein, a soap opera writer of immense curiosity who had an encyclopedic knowledge of the New York cultural scene. No offbeat exhibit or opening escaped him. We had met in 1964, just as I was getting my first write-ups in the New York press, so I suppose that he had originally collected me as an exotic cultural specimen, too, but I was glad to draw on his knowledge. He helped me orient myself in the seething mass of culture that threatens to overwhelm you in New York, and when I landed there with *Fireman's Ball,* I called Rick. "So what's going on? What's new?"

"Well, I'm just off to see a preview of this new musical. Do you want to come?"

Rick took me to the off-Broadway Public Theater to see *Hair*. Only once or twice before in my life had I seen a musical in which every single song was a gem. I was buoyant with excitement when the show ended and raced backstage to compliment the people behind it.

Ragni, Rado, and MacDermot were all there, peering at me suspiciously. This was their very first performance of the work before an audience, and they themselves didn't yet know what they had created. I kept gushing in broken English, asking for the score so that I could get their masterpiece produced in Prague. They nodded politely and scratched their heads. I added that if they ever wanted to make a movie out of *Hair,* they should please keep me in mind.

It turned out they had seen my films and liked them, so when I had Paramount behind me for a moment in 1968, I decided to go after *Hair.* The authors endorsed the idea, and, that spring, Jean-Claude Carrière helped me put together an outline of a screenplay. Claude Berri was going to be one of the film's producers, so once I had a firm idea of the musical's structure, Berri and I flew to Los Angeles to talk to the authors.

The cab discharged us at a lovely bungalow set in a tropical garden. Ragni and Rado were still performing in the touring version of *Hair,* so they lived by night. We'd been told to come at noon, but they still looked underslept when we showed up. An enormous, muscular black man was with them.

"This is Earl," they said.

For the next half hour, I went over my ideas for the film version of *Hair.* Ragni and Rado nodded their heads and ooohed and aaahed. I finished, and, without a word, the two authors turned to Earl, who pulled out a pack of shiny tarot cards and spread them on the table. No one spoke. As he gazed at the pictures, Ragni and Rado studied his face. Claude and I didn't dare say a word. Earl worked the cards for some twenty or thirty minutes, an eternity if you don't understand what is going on. Finally, he looked up. He stared at Ragni and Rado for a minute and then shook his head. No. They immediately got up and shook our hands.

"Sorry, guys," they said matter-of-factly. "The constellations just aren't in our favor. Not yet. We've gotta wait."

It would take another ten years before the Lady of Situations smiled on the project, but in every intervening year, someone would call, claim he had the rights to *Hair,* and ask if I were still interested in directing it. For the first four or five years, I would run to my record bin and pull out the old cast recording. It always rekindled the old charge of feeling, so I'd tell the would-be producers, "Yes, I'd love to work on the project."

I never heard back from any of them. No one could untie the knot of rights that was entangling the show. As years went by and people continued to call, I stopped taking them seriously. "Sure, I'd love to do *Hair*," I'd say without missing a beat. "Why not?"

I said the same thing to Lester Persky when he called me in 1977, but as it turned out, he really did have the rights to the musical *and* the backing of United Artists.

Suddenly, I got cold feet. I knew that *Hair* would be a bigger and more visible production than any I'd ever directed. I had had no experience with a musical before, had never worked with a choreographer, had never had the silk tie of a big Hollywood budget strangulating me.

I didn't mind these challenges, but there were other things I had to think through before I could commit to the project. I knew that if I were to take on *Hair* now, I'd be shooting something utterly different from the musical I first fell in love with in the sixties. I had become someone else over the ten years that had elapsed. I couldn't use the old script anymore. I'd lost the arrogant innocence that I exuded as a fresh-off-the-boat tourist in America. I no longer had Czech license plates on my car.

Another thing I had to consider was the fact that in 1967 Lyndon Johnson was president, the San Francisco summer of love still lay in the future, and the musical rode the charging bronco of a social revolution. It preached sexual liberation, war resistance, pacifism, gentleness, flower power, and ecology, and its music captured the energy that these concepts were releasing in society. Long hair was still a big statement.

In 1977, even lawyers and bankers wore their hair long. The American attitude toward sex and ecology had changed markedly. But the Vietnam War and flower power were history, marijuana and LSD remained illegal, and no one cared enough to question the old power of wealth and its distribution anymore. Some of the values of the counterculture had been co-opted by the American mainstream, some discarded, some forgotten, but none of the notions raised blood pressure anymore, so *Hair* had become a period piece.

I'd never directed a period movie before, though I'd worked on Radok's *Grandpa Automobile*. I didn't mind the idea that I'd have to stretch as a director, and, anyway, period movies were just movies. They simply cost a lot more money. The real problem was that *Hair* would be coming out at an awkward time commercially. By the late seventies the "sixties" were over and hadn't yet begun to provoke nostalgia. Nostalgia implies distance. It's the joy of recognizing and remembering the details of a bygone era and recognizing the behavior that had once seemed so dashing and significant and that now seemed merely trivial. Nostalgia happens only when the era stops threatening you with its messiness, contradictions, anarchy, and choices.

Hair would be nostalgic when lawyers and bankers cut their hair short again. In 1977, this seemed a long way off, but in the end I told myself it wasn't really my problem. The nostalgia deficiency was something for the salesmen and marketing people at United Artists to worry about.

While I pondered all this, I kept playing my scratchy record. Directing is an emotional business, and if I were to make the film, I needed that old enchantment to carry me through. I couldn't help it, I still loved the songs, and that was finally the deciding factor. The thrill was still there.

At the same time, I decided I wasn't clever enough to comment on, judge, satirize, or lionize the sixties. I'd simply try to find a story for the songs and then film them in a way that excited me and was true to what I myself had seen and remembered from that time. I had spent many days watching the be-ins, the love-ins, the smoke-ins, and the war protests in Central Park. I had seen draft cards and bras burned there, so I thought that it was natural to set the film there.

When I told Lester Persky that I would like to work on *Hair* with him, I also mentioned that my first order of business was to make a real home in New York. Persky was living in a fancy building on Central Park South and suggested that I move there, too.

I bought a small apartment with a sweeping panorama of the park that I didn't at all mind calling home.

"Hell," I told Persky, "now I'll be able to direct our movie from my window."

MICHAEL WELLER

In the sixties, Jean-Claude Carrière and I had wanted to shoot *Hair* as an audition for the musical, a backstage story, a semidocumentary, an idea I'd used in *Taking Off*. The concept now seemed to me a gimmick, a distraction designed to hide the thinness of the play's book.

In 1977, it was the very paucity of the story that attracted me to *Hair*. I decided that instead of concealing it behind a slice of backstage life,

I'd lock myself away with a screenwriter and invent a new narrative for the musical. I'd keep the songs, the energy, the attitudes, the youth of the play, but I'd shape this material with a story that would fit them into a new whole. My first order of business was to find a very good screenwriter.

Persky helped me with this search, putting together a list of young writers, most of whom had probably been shaped by the sixties. I called every name on the list, asking my candidates if they'd be interested in working on *Hair*. Mostly they were, so I told them to listen to the recording before we got together. They all said they'd give it a listen and some thought, but I should have known better than to believe them.

I'm not sure if the writers I saw simply didn't give a damn or if they were afraid of having their ideas stolen, but all I got from them was a lot of dense theories about the expanding universal consciousness, the immorality of war, the morality of protest, and so on. I could hardly follow their abstractions, and I was starting to lose faith.

One afternoon, a short, dark, and intelligent-looking young man named Michael Weller came to interview with me. He was a playwright who had already penned *Moonchildren*, a very successful play, and who had been recommended to Persky by Peter Shaffer.

"So," I asked him, "did you have a chance to think about how to do *Hair*?"

"Yes," he replied.

"And?"

"Mr. Forman, I don't have a fucking clue," he said, looking me straight in the eye.

"I don't have a fucking clue either," I said with an immense sense of relief. "Call me Miloš."

Michael was a wonderful collaborator who ended up writing both *Hair* and *Ragtime* for me. I don't look for a screenwriter who merely executes my ideas. I often don't know what I want until I have it, so I need a strong personality who can engage me in creative dialogue. Michael has always had his own sensibility, and he didn't mind going toe to toe with me.

Our most difficult task came right at the beginning: we had to find a natural way to introduce the first musical number. I love old musicals where hard reality suddenly goes opera, where the music swells and strangers riding on a bus inhale deeply and break into three-part harmony, but I accept that freedom as a part of the old charm of the genre. I didn't want any operas erupting in *Hair,* so I thought that the first transition from words to music was what mattered most: if we could slip

27 *Top* Learning how to
stage a true blue American
slugfest on the set of *One Flew
Over the Cuckoo's Nest*, with
Nathan George and Jack
Nicholson.

28 Will Sampson in the
bastketball scene of *Cuckoo's
Nest*, making Jack Nicholson
as tall as "the biggest son of a
gun of them all."

29 *Top* The therapy of laughter in the grim mental ward of Salem, Oregon,
with Danny De Vito, Jack Nicholson, Will Sampson, Vincent Schiavelli,
and Louise Fletcher.

30 Five Oscar winners for *Cuckoo's Nest*, 1976 (*from right*): Saul Zaentz,
producer; Jack Nicholson, Best Actor; Louise Fletcher, Best Actress; myself; and
Michael Douglas, producer. Missing from the picture are Bo Goldman and
Larry Hauben, winners for Best Screenplay Adaptation.

31   With sons Petr and Matěj after the 48th Academy Awards ceremony.

32 *Top* "Looking For My Donna" on the set of *Hair* in Central Park, 1977 (*from left*): Donnie Dacus, Dorsey Wright, and Treat Williams.

33 Showing Twyla Tharp my idea of how you sing and dance in jail, for the title song from *Hair*.

34 *Top* The cast of *Hair*
(*from left*): John Savage,
Dorsey Wright, Annie Golden,
Donnie Dacus, and Treat
Williams.

35 With President Johnson in
the "be-in" scene from *Hair*.

36 *Top* With James Cagney on *Ragtime*, 1980.

37 The gentle persuasion of Mandy Patinkin on the set of *Ragtime*.

38 Showing Elizabeth McGovern how to avert a blushing face on *Ragtime*.

39 *Top* Seeing Uncle
Boleslav after ten years of
exile, in Náchod, 1979.
Looking on is his daughter
Jana.

40 A few minutes later,
embracing Boleslav's wife
Anna.

41 *Top* With my boys in Prague in 1979.

42 Visiting Jan Werich, the legendary Czech actor and writer, with Jean-Claude Carrière and Cheryl Barnes, "the maid from a motel in Maine."

43 *Top* Having a beer with Debelka of *Fireman's Ball*, who in 1979 was still a volunteer fireman in Vrchlabí.

44 A husband and his wives. Jana is on the left, Věra on the right.

45   *Top* With Hana Brejchová of *Loves of a Blonde* in Prague, 1979.

46   Returning to the spot on the shore of Mácha's Lake where I lost
my virginity.

47 With F. Murray Abraham as the court composer Salieri on the
set of *Amadeus*.

48 The splendid castle in Kromeriz, Czech Republic, which we transformed into a piece of Imperial Vienna for *Amadeus*.

49   Twyla Tharp holding up just fine, in the Stavovske Theater where Mozart's
Don Giovanni had its premiere in 1787 and which we almost set on fire in 1982.

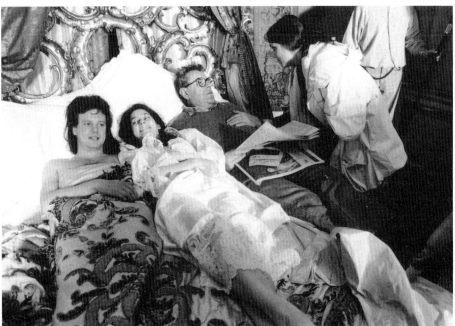

50   *Top* Tom Hulce as Mozart conducting *The Abduction from the Seraglio* for the
Emperor of Austria, Jeffrey Jones (*on his left*).

51   Nap time on the set of *Valmont*, with Meg Tilly and Colin Firth, 1988.

52 Many a tough task rests on a director's shoulders.

the first song into the story organically, we'd set the tone for the whole film and be free to weave in the other songs as we saw fit.

The solution that Michael and I came up with has the draftee Claude at the beginning of his journey to Vietnam. He says good-bye to his father on a road that cuts through the farmlands of Oklahoma and gets on a bus that will take him to New York City. He has a window seat, and, squinting into the blinding sun, staring at the roadside, he rides it straight into the draft-card-burning, hallucinatory Age of Aquarius.

Some of the best ideas that Michael and I came up with grew out of fierce arguments. For example, for a long time we couldn't find an ending. In my memories now, it feels as if it took weeks, but perhaps it was only a few days. We had taken the story of the Oklahoma draftee, played by John Savage, through his culture shock in New York, his friendship with the band of hippies led by Treat Williams, his LSD initiation, and his separation from his new friends when he decides to report to the army after all. We had his character in the boot camp in Arizona and we had his New York friends on the way there to try, for one last time, to save him from the army and from Vietnam, when we stalled.

We wrote several scenes, but none of them gave the proper sense of closure to the screenplay. Michael had his idea for the ending, which I didn't like, and I had mine, which he didn't like, and as we argued about the two notions, our respective positions hardened.

I impose only a few rules on writing collaborations. One is that you can't waste time talking generalities. Another is that you can't feel ashamed of your own stupidity. You need to feel the freedom to blurt out any dumb idea that pops into your mind—it often takes ten inane ideas to come up with a good one.

Still another rule: if you have a new idea, you've got to show precisely how it ties into the existing script and how it then builds step by step. My last rule is that all the writers involved in a screenplay must sign off on the final version. We work until we have a script that everyone can put his name on, which can sometimes get to be as bruising as a tough jury deliberation.

During our search for an ending, Michael and I were hopelessly locked. We kept talking at each other, agreeing on less and less, getting more and more sarcastic, raising our voices. I'd never gone through such a battle of wills. There didn't seem to be any way out of the stalemate when suddenly, somehow, during another stream of stupidities, we got the idea that enabled us to get the rest of the screenplay down on paper in half an hour: what if the hippie leader Berger and his troop arrive at the army base just as it's going on an alert and being closed off? Then Berger would have to sneak into the barracks and switch places with the Oklahoma draftee in order to spring him from the base so that his old buddy can, for one last time, make love to Sheila. While the New York flower child plays soldier on the base, the whole unit is suddenly ordered to pack up and move out, destination: body-bag Vietnam.

TWYLA THARP

My second order of business on *Hair* was to find a choreographer. I don't know much about ballet, and this was another make-or-break decision for the film, so I went to see every dance company appearing in New York. I sat in auditoriums of all sizes and waited for the moment when I'd suddenly know that what I was watching was what I wanted.

It finally happened when I saw Mikhail Baryshnikov in *Push Comes to Shove* by Twyla Tharp. The piece gripped me immediately with its humor and its thoroughly original movement. Once I'd seen it, I couldn't think of any other choreographer to work with. I asked if I could meet with Ms. Tharp, and one afternoon some weeks later, a tall and severe lady in blue jeans showed up at my apartment. She didn't bother with small talk.

"So what is this about?" she asked me in the doorway, sounding as if I'd just made her walk up thirty floors to meet me.

"Listen, Twyla, do you know the musical *Hair*?"

"That piece of shit?"

My heart sank. I didn't know what to say. "Oh . . . Well, I don't know, I kind of like it . . . I'm going to be making a movie out of it, so I wanted to ask you if you'd want to work on it with me . . ."

"On *Hair*? Never!"

"That's really too bad . . ."

"And how come you like it anyway? What's good about it?"

I started to tell her why *Hair* was going to make a fine movie musical, about how wonderful all the songs were and how differently I'd frame them, how far away from the author's original musical adaptation I intended to go in order to capture its spirit on film, and so on. As I described the screenplay in detail, I could just see the movie roll in front of my eyes, which got me excited, and I talked for hours.

"All right," Twyla sighed when I finished. "I'll do it."

I am not sure if she was doing it consciously or unconsciously, but Twyla had completely turned the tables on me. She hadn't worked in the movies before and I was probably "Hollywood" to her, so she was suspicious of me and wound up auditioning me more than I auditioned her. I suppose that she wanted to make sure that I was absolutely taken by the material before she committed herself to it.

Soon after that, we sat down with the script and I told her where in the film I saw dancers and what mood they were to convey. I certainly didn't know her business, so I didn't try to tell her how to produce that mood. She went away and did her work alone, then called me to come and see what she had.

I came to the palatial space in Phoenix House where her troupe rehearsed. She showed me the rough choreography. I watched it carefully, then listed my opinions: "This was wonderful, this was gorgeous, this I liked, this was fine, this I wasn't so sure about."

"Well, there's a lot of stuff I still want to change myself," said Twyla.

She went back to her work and I went back to mine.

The next time she showed me the revised choreography, everything that I'd praised was out and all the dances that I wasn't sure about were in. Then it all changed again, but by then I trusted Twyla completely and left her alone. And when we started shooting and I saw her work on location, it seemed pure poetry.

Twyla had taken the movements right out of the dramatic context of each scene. In the episode where the Lipizzaner horses dance, Twyla's choreography echoes the odd, jerky jumps of the horses; on the military base, her dancers move in tight blocks of old drill routines; the hippies in the park dance with the shaggy anarchy that perfectly captures their aversion to all forms of conformity. In each case Twyla's dancers greatly enlarged the scene.

Twyla herself dances in the LSD wedding sequence, and to me, she was the real star of the film. She was the most difficult collaborator I've ever had, but I'd work with her again any time. She is a perpetual seeker, suspicious, driven, never happy, a workaholic, and full of genius.

DEGREES OF DESIRE

Before I started casting *Hair,* I'd made a decision that greatly complicated the job. I was resolved to cast only people who could act, sing, and dance so well that we wouldn't have to resort to any cinematic sleights of hand. It's not uncommon in musicals for an actor to have two voices, his own for talking and someone else's for singing, but I've always found that jarring, as jarring as if the actor had two heads, so I wanted to avoid all dubbing in *Hair.*

We didn't want to miss any possible talent, so we decided to hold open auditions for all the singing parts. These auditions would get under way at ten o'clock in the morning, but the most ambitious kids began to sign up on our casting sheets as early as seven. The first name on our very first casting sheet read Madonna Ciccone. Somehow I overlooked her among the hundreds of people I saw.

I managed to get a cast of fine actors, including Beverly D'Angelo, John Savage, Annie Golden, Dorsey Wright, Miles Chapin, and Don Dacus. They all had the youth and the fresh look I wanted, and they could all act and sing so well that I wound up having to dub only a single bar of music in the entire film.

The only casting choice I regret making was Nicholas Ray, the director of such great films as *Rebel Without a Cause* and *Johnny Guitar,* who played a general in our last scene.

"I know someone who'd be perfect for a general and who could use the money," Michael Weller told me when I was casting the role. He had been playing cards with Nicholas Ray and Nick did have the right look for the character, so I asked him to don a uniform and give a stern speech to the troops going over to Vietnam. In my mind, I saw the general's face drifting in and out of smoke, so while we shot the scene I had the smoke machines churning out billows of black fumes around him. Nick understood immediately what I was looking for and worked hard to give me the right effect. His performance in the film is excellent, but the scene was fairly complicated and he wound up inhaling that heavy smoke for days on end.

He never once complained, so it wasn't until a few weeks later that

I found out he was dying. Cancer was shutting down his lungs. I only wish I'd known about his condition earlier.

The one actor who would have been virtually impossible to miss was Treat Williams. I first saw him in a Broadway production of *Grease*. He flung himself into the part with a rare abandon, so I invited him for an audition. He seemed right for the role of Berger. He had the daring, the presence, the natural leadership the part required, and he could certainly sing. The only catch was that Berger had been owned by Jim Ragni, who originated the role and stayed with it even after *Hair* had gone on the road. So of course he wanted to play it on film as well. I understood Ragni's feelings completely. He would have probably gotten the part in 1967, but now, ten years later, he had simply grown too old for the character I imagined, and you can't lie to a movie camera, certainly not about your age.

Treat projected the vigor and naïveté of a youth who still believes anything is possible and therefore achieves it. I think Treat was asked back to audition a dozen times. The more I called him back, the more I saw his name on the part, but he still had to convince those who saw only Ragni in the role.

The part was going to be a big career move for Treat and he wanted it badly, so he kept coming back and singing for us. One day, in the rehearsal space, Galt MacDermot sat at the piano and the authors, the producers, and the casting crew stood around and watched Treat sing. When he finished, they asked him to do it again. Treat suddenly exploded.

"Oh, Christ! You know, I don't give a *fuck* about this anymore! Fuck *this* and fuck *you*, I've had it!" He grabbed Ragni and wrestled him down on the floor. It didn't look as if he were trying to hurt him. It seemed as if he had simply decided he had to wrestle the role away from Ragni, and so he did. People jumped in and separated them, and Treat stormed out of the room.

As soon as things calmed down, I went out, took Treat aside, and told him he had the part. His emotional explosion drove home to everyone that he had the courage, the conviction, and the hustle to become our Berger.

The most impressive audition for *Hair* was done by Cheryl Barnes, a young black singer who showed up at our open auditions. As she started to sing the tune she had prepared, a hush came over the room. She had a voice like a bell, flawless musicality, and great presence. I could see how excited MacDermot was getting just listening to her. She finished and I told her that she had given a wonderful audition and we were sure to be in touch with her agent.

"I don't have an agent," Cheryl told me.

"Oh, well, do you have a number where we can reach you here in New York?"

"Yes, but not in New York, I live in Maine."

"Okay. So where do you sing in Maine?" I asked.

"I don't."

"What do you do?"

"I'm a maid. I work in a motel."

Cheryl had taken a day off, gotten on a bus, come to our open auditions, and walked away with the role of the young black mother with a baby boy. She was dripping with talent. When she came to record her song "Easy to Be Hard," she sat down, listened to the recording of her musical accompaniment, took the microphone, and did a perfect take. This first attempt is in the film in its entirety. Later, when we shot this number, she didn't make a single mistake in the lip sync. I've never seen anyone else do that.

Cheryl's last scenes were shot in Barstow, in the California desert, where we were going to wrap the whole production. One night, when there were only a few days left on the shooting schedule and the mood around the set was becoming tender and nostalgic, as it always does, I asked her about her plans for the future.

"So, Cheryl, is it back to New York or off to Los Angeles?"

"No, I found a nice apartment here, so I'm gonna stay in Barstow."

I thought she was joking, so I began to laugh. Even the T-shirts in this desert hamlet said, WHERE THE HELL IS BARSTOW?

"Why are you laughing?" said Cheryl. "I'm getting a piano here."

Now I was sure this was her deadpan humor, and I laughed even more.

Cheryl stayed in Barstow.

I couldn't believe it. I've always admired her sort of blazing talent, so I called her up and said she had to sing, that she owed it to other people, that she could give the world a lot of pleasure. I promised that I'd help her if she came to New York, that I'd do what I could to get her into the business, that she could *own* the town.

Cheryl let me talk her into giving it shot. She came to New York and stayed for a few months. She saw agents and tried to go through the motions of a career, but her heart was never in it. Even with all her raw talent, she suffered from some odd anxiety, a mistrust that bordered on reclusiveness. She was never willing to stretch an inch, and before long she left New York again.

Some of the people who auditioned for *Hair* wouldn't stretch an inch for either the musical or me. Out of laziness, I did many of the New York callbacks in my apartment, and one day a wiry young man with long hair showed up at my door.

"Do you know the musical *Hair*?" I asked him.

"Yes," he said.

"Do you like it?"

"No."

"I see . . . Well, but you'd like to be in it, right?"

"No."

"Well, why are you here?"

"My agent told me to come," said the guy, shrugging his shoulders.

"Okay, well, as long as you're here, would you like to do something for me anyway?"

"No."

We said good-bye. His name was Bruce Springsteen.

WHO'S THE BOSS THIS WEEK?

Shooting *Hair* was a massive undertaking, and it yielded a number of war stories. The one consistently smooth aspect of filming was the cinematography because now that I owned an Oscar, the Czech authorities relented and allowed Mirek Ondříček to work with me again. I didn't fully realize how much I'd missed him till I had him back.

Mirek hadn't been allowed to work in Neo-Stalinist Czechoslovakia, so in the early seventies he had signed up for a job that took him to the Soviet Union. He shot a war epic for Otakar Vávra, whose prewar films I'd once shown on my television show and who was still going strong. Mirek was filming a Second World War battle somewhere in the Ukraine when the pyrotechnicians miscalculated the force of an explosion and he ended up with a face full of shrapnel. The wounds healed, leaving interesting scars, but he lost his hearing in one ear, so when he came to New York and we started going to dinner again, he always made me sit by his good ear.

There weren't any explosions in *Hair*'s script, but we did need an army base, barracks, tanks, and transport planes for the final scenes, so our production people asked the Pentagon for help, hoping we could rent what we needed from the U.S. Army. We started principal shooting before the Pentagon gave us its decision, so I let the producers worry about the base. I had my hands full on the set.

One morning we were setting up a shot in Greenwich Village when the production manager handed me a stack of Polaroids that showed a litter-strewn meadow in New Jersey.

"What is this?" I asked.

"That's where we're thinking about building our army barracks. What do you think?" said the production manager.

"What?! Why?"

"Well, the Pentagon turned us down."

The Pentagon public-relations corps had decided our film portrayed their army in a bad light. They didn't agree with *Hair*'s philosophy and wouldn't let us use any of their facilities.

To build a mock base would bleed our budget and the construction would never look as authentic as real barracks, so I walked to the nearest pay phone, which happened to be in front of the Waverly Theater, and called Arthur Krim. Arthur was the president of United Artists and a big wheeler-dealer for the Democratic Party. I was hoping he could pull some strings for us with the commander in chief.

"Listen, Arthur, is the U.S. Army a public or a private entity?" I shouted over the noises of the street.

"Why do you ask?"

I explained how the army had gotten philosophical on us: "If they are a private entity, then I absolutely respect their opinion and we'll just have to spend millions of dollars to build our own barracks in New Jersey. But, Arthur, if the army is a public entity, then it's a different matter. Listen, I pay my taxes to them, too, and I don't ask them about *their* philosophy, do I?" As it happened, at that time I was paying heartbreaking taxes on my earnings from *One Flew Over the Cuckoo's Nest*. Krim knew just how much I was feeding Uncle Sam. There was a brief silence on the other end of the line.

"Miloš, I think you've got a point there," Arthur said.

A week later, we had our army base in Barstow. Once we got past the Pentagon's desk admirals the army proved very easy to deal with. Our production was the most exciting thing that had ever happened to Barstow, and real U.S. Army soldiers and sergeants were only too happy to take part in a Hollywood movie.

Long before we could move to Barstow to finish up the production, we had to overcome the massive "be-in" scene in Central Park. Our production had scheduled this antiwar, rock 'n' roll rally for December

6, 1977. I was worried about pulling off a summer scene in near winter, but Persky and everyone else assured me that in early December New York would still be warm enough.

On December 6, I woke up and looked out my window. The city was white, the park covered with snow. On Sheep Meadow, about a hundred extras huddled around rusty barrels and warmed their hands in the flames blazing out of them. I climbed back into bed and waited for the phone call from the production manager to tell me that shooting had been officially canceled. No one called, so I threw on some winter clothes and headed to the location.

Seeing me arrive, the production manager galloped toward me like a young colt. He didn't have a coat on and his lips were purple from the cold, but he managed a dazzling smile.

"So where do you want the camera, Miloš? I've got airplane engines on the way here, and they'll melt all the snow! Everything's under control! Just tell me where to put the camera!"

"Wait a minute. Listen, don't you think this is going to look funny? Just look at me, look at my breath!" I was incredulous. With the temperature clearly below the freezing point, every syllable was accompanied by a head-sized cloud of vapor.

"We have that covered too, Miloš! I've made the calls, and I've got ice cubes coming in! Just before we shoot, the dancers pop some ice in their mouths, you say, 'Action!' and they spit it out. For seven seconds you won't see a trace of vapor!"

The idea of shooting the summer be-in on a cold winter day clearly excited him. I've often observed this strange ambition in production people. They think that the true art of moviemaking rests in shooting summer scenes in winter, or jungle scenes in a greenhouse, or in making Toronto look like Paris. Working on authentic locations often strikes them as too boring, too crude, and too easy.

I am not imaginative enough for such cinematic sleights of eye, however, so on that freezing morning in New York I trotted off to another pay phone and rang my big boss in Hollywood. Arthur Krim wasn't very happy to hear that we couldn't possibly shoot the be-in on that day, not in the snow, not with the puny crowd of freezing extras that we had, not with the dancers sucking ice cubes, not without severely compromising the whole film, but somehow he saw my point and agreed with me.

The vastly optimistic shooting schedule that had us shooting winter for summer wound up costing United Artists a lot of money. The wintry weather never broke in December of 1977, so in the end our production spilled over into the spring of 1978. I didn't mind the break at all—it ended up being for the best. Everyone took six weeks off around Christmas, and I used the time to look beyond *Hair*. I had been flirting with the idea of a film about chess, so during our production break I met Bobby Fischer in Los Angeles, but that story deserves its own chapter.

Toward the end of January, the *Hair* family reassembled at Barstow to shoot the army-base scenes, and, when we finally finished them, we returned to New York to wrap up the grueling production with the be-in.

On a warm Sunday in May, some five thousand people showed up in Central Park in response to a few small ads in the *Village Voice* and the *Soho News*. They wore their old torn jeans, beads, and bandanas. Some even brought old antiwar signs they had kept as souvenirs. Many openly lit up joints. Our production provided balding rockers, Lyndon Johnson balloons, and Vietcong flags, so the day was like a short trip in a time machine, just some eight or nine years back, when America was young and high.

The be-in ended our shoot on a high note, and I immediately threw myself into the editing of *Hair*, which proved to be an unusually cut-and-dried task. I am used to trying anything that I can think of in the cutting room, but in a musical each cut has to match the music, so *Hair* couldn't be "rewritten" on the cutting-room table.

Hair only broke even at the box office; it didn't do as well as everyone had hoped. I still think that it came out both too late and too soon after the sixties for commercial success, but I don't judge my films on the basis of how they do at the box office. In fact, I don't judge them at all. I truly feel about them the way I feel about my children: I don't love any of them less or more than the others. Still, I find myself showing *Hair* to people more often than my other films. Partly it's because more guests have seen my Oscar-winning films and fewer of them know *Hair*, and partly it's because musicals are almost always a pleasure to watch.

Perhaps I am getting sentimental in my old age, but I usually wind up sitting through the whole movie with my guests. *Hair* had been such a massive undertaking that every shot reminds me of some feat of movie logistics. Even more important, *Hair* carries a double load of memories. It takes me back not only to the late seventies when we shot the picture but also to the late sixties, to the days when I used to hang out by Central Park's Bethesda Fountain with Mary Ellen Mark and when my English still scared people off.

Treat and Beverly and John and Cheryl and all the other actors who had been so young when we worked on *Hair* are now reaching middle age. They are as old now as I was in the late sixties when I first gathered all those images, insights, and impressions I drew on in the film, and before long, they will be as old as I was when we shot it together, but when I look at the film and see them dancing and singing and beaming, they are forever young.

BOBBY FISCHER

While I was still shooting *Hair,* Peter Falk came to me with an intriguing project. He wanted to produce a film based on the championship chess match between Bobby Fischer and Boris Spassky. This highly dramatic battle took place in 1972 in Reykjavík, Iceland, and it became a minor chapter in the cold war. Falk knew that I loved chess and asked me if I'd be interested in pursuing the story.

Bobby Fischer is a genius, perhaps the best player in the history of the game, but he is a very complex personality. The Soviets had owned the chess championship for decades and regarded it as proof of the superiority of their political system. Fischer had just demolished several of their top players in the qualifying rounds, but they desperately wanted to keep the title, so they were putting all kinds of psychological pressure on him. They hoped to unhinge him completely and, in fact, came close to scaring him away from Reykjavík. I never could get enough chess, and this story was fascinating.

"I'll make the film in a minute," I told Falk, "but under one condition: Spassky and Fischer must play themselves."

Fischer was such an extreme personality that he was actor-proof: I knew I'd never find an actor who could make the chess champion look nearly as captivating as Fischer himself could be just sitting across the table from you.

Falk, who knows a thing or two about acting, agreed with me, and, through an old friend, Lubomír Kaválek, who happens to be a grand master and a force in international chess, I got Spassky to agree to act in our film. That, of course, was the easy part; Spassky is a very sociable and warm person.

By the late seventies Bobby Fischer had become a recluse. He had won the battle of Reykjavík, donated most of his seven-figure purse to the Church of God in Pasadena, and quit organized chess. He was now living near the church, cared for by an older couple who were followers of the faith. He agreed to meet with Falk and me in a hotel in Los Angeles.

Peter and I sat in the hotel room we rented for the meeting when a skittish big man showed up wearing sunglasses and a cap. Bobby was accompanied by a lady in her fifties, Claudia, his rather harried, maternal caretaker. We shook hands, and Bobby pulled a small transistor radio out of his pocket, set it on the table, and turned it on so that no one could bug our conversation.

I fully respect the right of a genius to have his eccentricities, so I didn't say a word and the conversation flowed freely. Bobby was friendly and very inquisitive. He wanted to know all about how movies are made, and I wound up mostly answering his questions.

"Listen," I finally told him. "I'm about to go to Barstow to finish shooting my movie. It's a two-hour drive from here, but maybe you'd like to come and see what it's like for yourself."

"Well, okay," said Bobby. "I'll call you first though." He wasn't going to set any dates ahead of time. He had been burned by duplicitous journalists before, so he wanted to make sure that absolutely nobody knew when he was coming.

At three o'clock one night in Barstow, my phone rang. It was Claudia.

"We're here," she said.

"Oh my God! Okay. Okay." I stammered.

I tumbled out of bed and went downstairs to help Claudia book a room under a pair of assumed names. Bobby was hiding in the car, and all I saw of him that night was a fleeting glimpse of his tall frame slinking down the deserted hallway.

I hurried back to bed and tried to get a little more sleep—the following morning, we were shooting the musical number in which Treat Williams marches into the plane that will take him to Vietnam. Half of the army base boards the plane with him, so I had a thousand soldiers as well as planes, helicopters, personnel carriers, and jeeps reporting to the set.

I awoke at seven o'clock and threw myself into being Patton. I had the soldiers marching, the military vehicles throwing up clouds of dust, the playback blasting. I was so caught up in commanding my movie army that I completely forgot about Fischer.

At about three o'clock, I heard a soft voice behind me.

"We're here!" It was Claudia, alone.

"Oh, good, so . . . Well, so . . . So . . . Let me think now . . ." It took me a moment to realize that the most secluded spot from which Bobby could eyeball the shoot was my trailer. It was parked not far from the camera, so I told Claudia to pull up to the camper in her car, get in, and watch us through the draperies.

"Nobody ever dares go in there," I reassured her.

I went back to marshaling my armies, but shortly after that our generator blew up, a disaster. The cameras had their own power generators, but I needed the electricity for the playback. With less than two hours of daylight remaining, we still had two shots to do. Fixing the generator would take an hour, and the soldiers wouldn't be coming back. Now what? Panic was about to set in when Chris Newman, my longtime sound man, saved the day.

"Why don't I run the juice for the playback out of your camper?" he offered.

"Great idea, Chris!"

I prepared my planes and carriers for the next shot, and the sound crew moved toward my camper.

My camper! Bobby! Oh, Jesus!

By the time I realized the implications of Newman's solution, the door of my camper was yawning open and people were scurrying in and out. I dropped everything and made for the trailer, but when I saw the frantic traffic around it, I lost my nerve and merely crept to the door and glanced inside.

Bobby Fischer looked like a small boy pretending not to be where he was, even while he sat sprawled on a chair at the center of the narrow space. His long body completely blocked the aisle, but he hid his face behind a magazine and a cap so that only his fearful eyes peered over the top. They darted from side to side, following the technicians who hurdled over his long legs with their power cables.

I stole back to my command post. I wasn't sure if I'd ever see Bobby again, but he and Claudia were waiting for me back at the hotel. He didn't look particularly traumatized, so I invited him to dinner at a nearby Mexican restaurant. With dark lighting and secluded booths, the place seemed made for extramarital dates, but Bobby chose the only conspicuous chair in the room. But no one recognized him. He had a million questions about what he had seen at the military airport. I found his curiosity endearing, but, suddenly, a camera flash popped off in the room and Bobby threw himself down on the bench. He thought the paparazzi had tracked him down again, but it was only some patrons who were feeling no pain fooling around with a Polaroid in the back of the room. I might be wrong, but I have a feeling that Bobby was disappointed.

We met a few more times, but I finally realized that Bobby's personality wasn't compatible with the rigors of movie-making, and I abandoned the project.

RAGTIME

Dino De Laurentiis had the biggest desk I'd ever seen, though his office in Hollywood didn't have the acreage of his old office in Rome, where you crossed from the door to the visitor's chair and were glad to sit down. Dino is not very tall and has a small man's energy. He's a real dynamo. He mangles English grammar even worse than I do, but while I do so with a sense of shame, he does it with relish.

You never get bored around Dino.

Dino had called me right after *One Flew Over the Cuckoo's Nest* to ask if I'd be interested in adapting a novel by E. L. Doctorow to film. *Ragtime* had just been dropped by Robert Altman, a director whom I greatly respect, but I knew that the book was beautifully written and I was drawn to the scope of choices it presented. The novel was crawling with characters, yet its stories felt sketched in and not developed to the dramatic fullness film requires. There could have been several completely different movies made of the book, which was a challenge that excited me, so I took Dino up on his offer.

The one narrative strand of the novel that gripped me immediately was the story of a piano player. Coalhouse Walker Jr. is gifted and black, and he drives a gleaming Model T until an envious group of white firemen defile it. They shit on its backseat, so the pianist can either humiliate himself by cleaning their shit with his own hands, or he can stand up to them and risk getting badly hurt in the process.

I had a gut knowledge of Walker's dilemma from the old country: in the everyday life of Communist Czechoslovakia, you constantly found yourself before ignorant, powerful people who didn't mind casually humiliating you, and you risked your livelihood and maybe your life by defying them. Squeezed between the Hitlers and the Stalins in Central Europe, the Czechs had to laugh a lot to keep their sanity, so theirs is an ironic, nothing-is-sacred sense of self-preservational humor. In Walker's predicament, a Czech would probably clean up the backseat himself, complaining how insultingly tiny this shit was, how flat the stink of it was, how it wasn't even worth dirtying a rag over, what an abominable diet the people whose job it was to shit on the backseats of private cars followed, how even human shit had shrunk under socialism, how shit in general wasn't what it had once been anymore, and what a steep decline Western civilization was in.

Coalhouse Walker Jr., however, is an American. He not only refuses to clean his car, he demands satisfaction. The tale snowballs monstrously as Walker's fiancée dies as a direct result of the incident and the pianist winds up barricaded in the Morgan Library, threatening to blow it up, Gutenberg Bible and all.

I suppose that what drew me to the story more than anything else was this wildly romantic American gesture. I had just become an American citizen, and maybe, in some way, I was trying the righteous and violent American psyche on for size.

Michael Weller had just finished a fine play, *Loose Ends,* and we wrote our second screenplay together, trying to keep the feel of Doctorow's sprawling, overpopulated novel, his Breughelian canvas in which fictional characters teem around historical personages. We used the story of the black pianist as our main plot line.

A number of the characters in *Ragtime* were based on real people. Studying their portraits in old magazines and books, I noticed that one of them, the famous architect Stanford White, looked remarkably like Norman Mailer. There was additional symmetry to their lives because both men had unleashed famous tabloid furors, so I asked Mailer, whom I'd met socially, if he'd be interested in reading for the small role. Mailer did a fine audition, and I cast him as Stanford White.

When it came time for him to act, I was as jittery at the prospect of directing the great and notorious author as he was about acting, though he didn't react the way a nervous actor typically does. He didn't snarl at me or launch into an abrupt monologue about some long-winded abstraction as my actors sometimes do when they're at a loss over something in the scene. He struggled bravely with the role. I like him a lot in the film.

No other part in *Ragtime* proved as easy to cast as the infamous architect. I saw at least a thousand candidates, reading with anyone who gave me a glimpse of one of the characters. At last I wound up with a wonderful cast. I had Brad Dourif back to play the Younger Brother, Howard Rollins as Coalhouse Walker Jr., Mary Steenburgen as the repressed Victorian Mother, Elizabeth McGovern as Evelyn Nesbit, Mandy Patinkin as Tateh. All these talented actors have made their impact on the business since the film, but none of them was a bankable star in the late seventies, which presented a huge problem for Dino.

Our budget was high, and Dino had to raise money by preselling the film in Europe. He needed a big Hollywood name to bait the European distributors. Dino knew that I don't like to use film stars, that I'd much rather put in the legwork that it takes to give my characters an unfamiliar countenance. From the start he worried that my casting might make his financing job more difficult.

I'd never used a real star in any of my films with the exception of Jack Nicholson in *Cuckoo's Nest.* But while Jack may currently be one of Hollywood's brightest stars, he has none of the mannerisms that go with that position. When he works, he is simply one of the actors.

I have reasons both fancy and mundane for avoiding stars. My mundane reason is that not having them makes it easier on the budget and on everyone else in the production. It's also easier on me because I don't have to worry about any "star behavior" on the set. My fancy reason is that unfamiliar faces on the screen help the viewers suspend their disbelief. They don't view one or two characters in the film differently, through the filter of stardom. They are not distracted by gossip or by memories of other roles the star has made his or her own. Actors new to the audience add to the authenticity of a story. They have to be good, of course, but I believe that the pool of unrecognized acting talent is very deep. Finally, if an actor or an actress is good, it's always more interesting to watch them for the first time.

The downside of this approach is that sometimes you won't get financing without a bankable actor. With *Ragtime,* I wanted to help Dino pull in the European investors, so I called Jack Nicholson and asked if he'd take a look at the role of Harry K. Thaw.

"Well, what do I do?" asked Jack.

"It's only a cameo, Jack, but you kill an architect." I explained.

"Miloš, I've always wanted to kill an architect," Jack said, and promised to do the part.

Dino was delighted. I told him to be sure to put everything down on paper and get the contract to Jack quickly. Then I put it out of my mind.

The next thing I know, Jack's agent is on the phone, telling me that Jack has three films coming out and he is getting badly overexposed, so he won't be doing *Ragtime.* Dino was crestfallen. It was all his fault for not consummating the deal, but his problem was my problem, too, because now the whole budget for *Ragtime* was in jeopardy.

BARYSHNIKOV AND CAGNEY

I met James Cagney through a twisted chain of events that started with Mikhail Baryshnikov. I'd met Misha through our mutual friend Marina Vlady, the French actress, shortly after his dramatic defection from the Kirov Ballet. I liked him immediately, and we quickly became friends. We ate a lot cholesterol-bomb dinners together, downed barrels of fermented grapes, and even double-dated, so when Misha bought a manor house in the country, he would often invite me there for a weekend, and I discovered Connecticut. Its rolling hills, leafy forests, and lakes reminded me of the Czech-Moravian Highlands of my youth, and, to my surprise, I found myself looking forward to my days in the country.

Ever since I had come to Prague as a teenager I'd been a city dweller. I loved the crowds, the lights, the streets, the bars, the ideas, the women, the conversations, the newspapers, the energy, the encounters of city life. I loved the possibilities and the scale and the economies of scale that made things like theater and music and movies viable. I never went on vacations by the seaside. When I had some time off, I stayed in Prague or New York. But now I could hardly wait to leave the city and get to Connecticut. I started thinking about buying a place of my own in the country.

Misha was very happy when I told him this. He was working hard to surround himself with friends, so he took me to some old property not far from his house. Its barn had been turned into a painter's studio by its last owner, Eric Sloane, and Misha himself had come very close to buying the place before he settled on a larger, more stately house nearby. The farm was still for sale.

I fell in love with it at first sight—the large space in the old barn and the window looking out on a pond with turtles, geese, and herons. I didn't yet know that on summer evenings deer came to graze, and I hadn't yet seen the beaver dam below.

As soon as I bought the farm, Misha sold his house, so we were not neighbors after all.

In Connecticut I met Marge and Don Zimmerman, the caretakers for a couple of distant neighbors, James Cagney and his wife, Willie. Marge asked for my help in finding someone who could play Cagney in an upcoming Broadway musical about his life.

Cagney had a rare personality, but I knew of two men with his range of dramatic and dancing talent, though Treat Williams was a good head taller and Misha Baryshnikov had an accent. They were never going to be Cagney. Still, I brought Treat and Misha to dinner with the old gentleman, figuring I'd let Cagney decide for himself if there was anything to my unorthodox casting notions.

When we all gathered at a local restaurant, it was the first time I met James face to face. Cagney's health had been failing rapidly. He had a bad case of sciatica and could barely walk. He didn't remember a lot of things, and his hearing was shot. He had closed the acting chapter of his life some twenty years before and didn't care to talk about it or even remember it anymore. I got the feeling that he was just waiting to die.

He hadn't been in a movie for twenty years. I knew that Francis Ford Coppola had badly wanted him to be in *The Godfather,* that he'd flown in on a Learjet with a fat contract, and that Cagney had rebuffed him. Nevertheless, at the end of the dinner, I made a joke that I felt was almost obligatory: "I've got a role for you, James, if you ever get bored with your life here."

Cagney laughed and I laughed and nobody took it seriously.

James never did say whether he thought Treat or Misha could portray him, but the musical never materialized anyway. The only thing that came out of the dinner was that I got an invitation to James's farm.

Three weeks after the dinner, I went to visit James. It was purely a social call, but it did come after Jack Nicholson had declined to kill an architect after all, so in a fit of insomnia it occurred to me that if Cagney could somehow be persuaded to act in our film, Dino's financing problems would vanish. I'd sensed that Cagney was firm in his decision to put movies behind him, so I wasn't even going to bring up this dead-of-night notion. I'd resolved merely to get to know my illustrious neighbor.

I knew from our dinner that Cagney didn't care to talk about old movie memories, and when I got to his farm I saw that he didn't have a single photograph, poster, or any other memorabilia on the walls. James was not only through with his glorious past, he had cleaned up behind it. He seemed an old man beyond all earthly matters when Marge took me to see him. He peered at me without recognition or interest.

"So who are you?" he asked.

"Well, I'm a film director," I said tentatively.

"You made any movies that I might've heard of?"

"I don't know. My last movie was called *Hair.* It was a musical."

James' face came alive, and he stared at me for a beat in consternation.

"So now I know, now I see why," he muttered. "I never saw the thing . . . I never wanted to see the thing . . . It didn't interest me in the least, so I could never figure out why the dickens it's here . . ."

He got up, shuffled to a wardrobe, groped behind it for a long minute, then pulled out what had to be the only poster in the house.

"Here," he said, handing me a poster from the first off-Broadway run of *Hair,* a poster for the very performance that I'd seen in 1967 in New York.

James had for some mysterious reason kept this poster from a show he'd never seen. And Marge, who stood there watching, immediately picked up on the implications:

"James! That's an omen! You know what the doctors told you, James! They said if you don't get up off this chair and do something with yourself that you'll die before the year is out! This is an omen! Miloš here is a director, and he asked you to be in his picture!"

Cagney peered at her a moment, then gave a little laugh. "Well, what would I play?"

"James," I said, "I'll send you the script and you can pick any part you want. You want Evelyn Nesbit, you got it!" James gave a big laugh and changed the subject.

I sent him the script. It had a role for a grandfather, which was very small, but James would have been perfect for it. I was a little worried that he might ask for the role of the father, which he was indeed too old for; I know how uncritical some actors can be about their age.

I shouldn't have worried. The next time I visited Cagney, he had found the perfect role for himself.

"Well, I could play the police inspector, I suppose . . ." he said.

"James, you got it!"

"Wait a minute now! I'm not signing anything," he said.

I didn't think that Dino could live without a contract, so it took me a few seconds to answer him: "Okay, James."

"Wait a minute! I'm not saying that I'll do it for sure either," he said.

"James, you have until two days before we shoot your scenes to change your mind," I assured him. That calmed Cagney down and had Marge Zimmerman smiling.

I called Dino that evening. "Dino, we've got the biggest star we could ever possibly have!"

"Yeah! Who? Who?"

"James Cagney, Dino!"

There was a long pause on the line.

"Okay, okay, I'm busy right now! Call me tomorrow," Dino said and hung up.

The next morning, my phone rang early. It was Dino.

"Miloš, guess what! We've got just what we need! We've got our superstar!"

I got scared that Dino had given away one of the roles to some aging European has-been.

"Who, Dino?" I said, bracing myself.

"*James Cagney,* Miloš! You can't ask for a bigger name than that!" Apparently Dino had never heard of James Cagney, and he'd taken the time between our two conversations to find out. But he was speaking in earnest now, and he immediately launched into his spiel for the European distributors, which I found touching.

The next thing I had to do was convince Dino that James didn't have to sign anything if he didn't want to sign anything. Dino finally agreed, but I never dared tell him that I had given my word to James that he had until two days before his first appearance on the set to withdraw from the project.

After that, problems began to pile up. No insurance company would insure Cagney. His scenes were scheduled to be shot on a soundstage in London, and then I found out that James wouldn't go near a plane.

Luckily, I had a sage ally in Marge.

"Miloš," she told me, "I don't know what other roles you've got in that picture, but if you were to cast one of James's old pals and they had to go to London with him . . ."

I immediately cast Pat O'Brien, a great actor himself, as Harry K. Thaw's lawyer. I even gave the role of Mrs. Thaw to Mrs. O'Brien.

When James arrived in London, the first thing he asked me was, "You didn't forget our agreement, did you, Miloš?"

"No, James, you've got until two days before."

"Just checking."

I had to have a double for James anyway because he wasn't able to march the way I needed the police chief to march in one scene, and I'd made sure that the double was also a good actor, so I knew I could use him if James got cold feet.

He didn't, and when the camera started rolling, this sick old man whose body was raked with pain and whose memory had been failing suddenly became a tough police chief. James would finish his takes and I'd try to send him off to his dressing room for some rest because now the camera was to be trained on Kenneth McMillan, the other actor in the scene.

"I'll read your lines for him, James, go lie down."

He wouldn't hear of it. "I think it will help my pal here if I stay," he said, nodding to Kenneth.

His performance was out of all proportion to his infirmities, and Marge had been absolutely right. Working again made James years younger. When I first met him, he was a man who had put this vale of tears behind him and wasn't looking back at anything. Now he started to tell stories again. He came to my farm for Thanksgiving dinners and Misha came, too, because James liked his dancing and felt good around him. James even watched his old films with us, something he hadn't done in decades, and he reminisced about the making of them, and everyone was moved, but we all tried to hide the emotion.

James lived for another five years. When he died, I was one of the pallbearers, along with Misha, Ralph Bellamy, and Floyd Patterson. I never did look at the great man when he lay in his coffin. Again, I just couldn't. But I will never forget the power and simplicity of his genius, of which I'd caught the last gleaming, and I'll always remember how Mandy Patinkin tried picking James's brain one day, asking him what he had learned about acting by making all those wonderful films.

Cagney squinted at him with amusement, then shrugged his shoulders: "Acting? Nothing to it. You just plant your feet on the ground, look the other actor in the eye, and tell the truth."

DINO AND RANDY

Dino milked a lot of publicity out of Cagney's return to the movies, but *Ragtime* was a very expensive film and Dino needed all the help he could get.

We had to build a replica of the Morgan Library on a London soundstage because the real library in New York would not let us shoot there. Its directors were afraid that Coalhouse Walker Jr. and his band might put dangerous ideas into the heads of our impressionable audiences, but of course they couldn't stop the film from being made.

Dino and I had a smooth working relationship until late in the production. We were finished in New York and had begun to shoot in London when he began to ask me to cut some scenes. He said he would send me the pages in the script that he figured our movie could do without. At the time, I was only four days behind schedule, two of which had been lost to inclement weather, but I tried to accommodate him. I left out what I could, which came to several pages of the screenplay, but it wasn't enough. Dino demanded more. We had a meeting in his office to thrash it out, and I told him that to make any additional deletions amounted to cutting our baby to the quick.

"What about you being four days behind!" Dino roared suddenly.

Out of the blue he was staring at me across his oceanic desk as if I'd just spat on his mother. I couldn't believe the change in him. On a production of that size, a four-day delay was nothing. In fact, I'd been rather proud of staying so close to our plan.

"Dino, listen to me: there's nothing extraneous anymore. I went over everything and I can't cut anything anymore," I reasoned.

"Sure you can! I worked with Fellini, I worked with De Sica, and they always cut!"

"Damnit, Dino, don't tell me how to make movies! You just shot a movie about a goddamn ape!"

We yelled at each other for a few minutes, but the argument was cut short when Michael Weller noticed that Dino had an extra week of contingency shooting time right on the production plan that lay in front of him.

"I don't understand what the problem is when we have this cushion," Michael told him.

When Dino regained his composure, he told Michael that if he ever decided to direct, he should talk to De Laurentiis productions first, and the meeting was over.

We finished shooting well within Dino's contingency limits, without either of us raising our voices again.

I locked myself into the cutting room with a new editor, a young man who had been an assistant on *Hair*. I thought he was ready for bigger things, so I asked him to work on *Ragtime* with me as head editor.

During the cutting of every film, there comes a time when I summon the devil and propose a deal to him: my soul for a fresh pair of eyes. After a year of living with the film everything looks overly familiar and bland. You forget your first reactions and become bored with even the most powerful scenes. Any changes start looking good, simply because anything that's different seems fresh and better, even though frequently it isn't. And if you don't recognize this dangerous psychological mechanism, you'll throw away good ideas or good material. I sorely need my editors to become my new eyes.

On *Ragtime,* the young editor didn't question any of my judgments or disagree with my solutions. He never became my working partner. He merely awaited his instructions. I tried to put him at ease, to help him open up, but I never succeeded. Perhaps he sensed some tension in me, perhaps my working style had intimidated him, but he was afraid to stick his neck out.

Without a creative adversary in the cutting room, editing becomes exhausting drudgery. The work itself is repetitive and full of details and minutiae. You count frames of film, switch shots around, and watch the same things over and over again. On *Ragtime* the editing was the hardest part of my job.

Dino and I had chosen Randy Newman to compose the music for the film. I had known and liked Randy's songs and Dino wanted a pop-chart album to go with the film, so it had been an easy choice to make. Once I had a rough cut of the film, I sent it to Randy in Los Angeles.

Some time passed without a word from Randy, and Dino kept pressing for the music, so I called Randy to ask how it was coming. He said he had something, and I asked him to come to New York. I don't own a piano, so we met in a rented studio. I was all ears as I sat down by the huge concert piano. Randy banged out a few ragtime bars and started howling. I can't describe his vocal expression any other way. He sounded like a starving werewolf under a full moon in the most forsaken corner of the Carpathians. I listened to him for five minutes and tried to form some sort of an idea about the score from the sounds. It was hopeless.

"Okay, Randy, that's great. Let's go to dinner," I said.

To this day, I am not sure if he was leading me on or if he was really giving me some interpretation of the score that I, in my ignorance of matters musical, didn't catch.

"So how's the music?" Dino asked me the next day.

"Quite impressive," I told him.

I left Randy alone. I had complete confidence in him and knew he'd compose a fine score, and when it finally came, it really was quite impressive.

By that time, however, I had bigger problems.

My final cut of *Ragtime* came out to slightly under three hours, which made for a very long movie, but the film had an epic scope and I've always believed that if a film grabs the audience, it doesn't really matter how long it is. And if it doesn't engage the viewers, then it will seem interminable even at seventy minutes.

I knew what Dino would say even before I showed it to him, and he didn't disappoint me.

"Way, way too much," he said.

I told him my theory of the paradox of movie time that I'd developed while editing *Cuckoo's Nest*. I tried to explain that film had its own pace and narrative rhythm and there was a danger that making it arbitrarily shorter might cause it to seem even longer, but Dino started getting clock-crazy on me and insisted that we get rid of a sizable chunk of it. I was exhausted from the editing drudgery, tense, and irritable.

"I don't know, but okay, Dino, so what would you cut out?" I sighed.

"Emma Goldman's got to go. All of it. Everything."

Emma's story was fairly self-contained, yet it was important as motivation for the erotic obsession that one of the characters, the Younger Brother, develops for Evelyn Nesbit in another strand of the narrative. Dino was talking about twenty minutes of the film.

I didn't want to slug it out with Dino. I must also say that neither of us ever stooped to fanning each other with contracts or bringing lawyers into the fray. In that regard, unlike Carlo Ponti, who had almost managed to put me in jail in Czechoslovakia on account of a nonsensical, fine-print clause in a contract, Dino had class. Still, I badly wanted to keep Emma Goldman in the film and I thought I could outfox Dino, so I proposed a compromise: "What if we let the author of our novel decide this for us?"

I was sure that as a fellow artist, Doctorow was going to decide in my favor. I also thought he'd want to see more rather than less of his novel on the screen. I was so sure of my proposal that I didn't think Dino would accept it, but he thought it over and, to my astonishment, agreed.

"Listen, Dino, whatever Doctorow decides, that's it! That's our final decision, that's how long our film is when it comes out!" Dino agreed, and we shook hands on it.

Doctorow had already seen my 176-minute cut, so I edited out the twenty minutes that Dino so badly wanted to get rid of and invited the author to be our judge. Doctorow came to a special screening with his agent, Sam Cohn, and I sat through it feeling very smart. I had memorized every shot and every cut, and I felt a huge, gaping hole in this truncated *Ragtime.* Without the twenty minutes, my baby seemed a hobbling cripple to me. It was so obvious.

The movie ended, and the lights in the screening room came up. Doctorow and his agent rose.

"Well, *I* don't miss it," said Doctorow.

Just like that. A crushing uppercut to the solar plexus. I don't think I managed to get a word out. And it had been my own stupid suggestion to appoint Doctorow our referee.

I cut the twenty minutes, of course, but it took away all the pleasure that finishing a movie usually gives me. And I firmly believe to this day that shortening *Ragtime* for no internal reason was a mistake. The film is now an amputee, a perfect example of the paradox of movie time where shorter often stands for longer.

A few days later, a press announcement in *Variety* jumped off the page at me. It said that Sam Cohen had just signed a deal with Dino De Laurentiis to buy the rights to E. L. Doctorow's new novel, *Loon Lake.*

I am sure that it was just a matter of an amazing coincidence and serendipity.

PETER SHAFFER

Back in 1980, when I was in preproduction on *Ragtime,* I came to London for a casting session. My agent, Robby Lantz, happened to have some business there, too, so one night he called me and asked if I'd care to go to the theater with him. I said I'd love to and I didn't even ask what we were going to see. Robby came by in a car to pick me up. On the way to the theater, I finally thought to ask about the play.

"It's a new piece by Peter Shaffer," Robby said.

"Oh, good."

"It's called *Amadeus,* and it's about Mozart and Salieri."

"Oh, shit," I said. I'd seen a number of biographies of composers back in Czechoslovakia. They were a safe subject under Zhdanov and the Stalinists because classical music was too abstract to be politically dangerous. I'd sat through films about Mussorgsky, Glinka, Smetana. They had all bored me profoundly, and here I was, going to a play about not one, but two composers.

If I could have bolted from the car, I'd have made a run for it, but it was too late, so I prepared myself to watch a man in a powdered wig strut about with his head in the clouds where, in these biographies, music always seems to reside.

When the curtain went up, I couldn't have been more surprised. The play could have been about any pair of people connected by a vocation and separated by the deep injustice of supreme talent. I watched Salieri, the king of mediocrity, wrestle with his feelings about a genius. Shaffer's treatment of his envy and admiration, awe and betrayal, had me riveted. Mozart's wonderful music was merely a bonus to a gripping story. When the play ended, I knew that I wanted to film it.

That very evening, Robby took me to see Shaffer, whom I'd never met before, even though we shared the same clever agent. I was crackling with enthusiasm and made a pitch for our collaboration in transferring the play to the screen.

Four weeks later, in New York, Peter and I sat down to talk. I didn't know much about him other than that he was a successful dramatist and that he didn't need me. I explained to Peter that I believed film has its own laws and that to transfer a work from stage to screen, you have to take it apart and reassemble it. Would he be ready to open up his play that way with me? Was he prepared to make that leap of blind faith? He'd used a lot of historical material when he wrote the play, but it was only the point of departure for his story. Now we had to make the play the point of departure for our screenplay.

Peter is a brave man. He said he'd try it.

I think I was lucky, in that Peter had had most of his plays transferred to the screen and had been disappointed with every one of the movies. He had even written the screenplay for *Equus* himself and he still wasn't pleased with the result, so he was ready to be as ruthless with his darling as he had to be.

We didn't actually sit down to write the screenplay for another year and a half because I still had to shoot and finish *Ragtime,* which turned out to be fortuitous because although the play had been a huge success on the stage, when my lawyer and friend Bruce Ramer shopped it around Hollywood, no one showed any interest in it. The project had four strikes against it: it was a costume movie; it was about classical music; it dealt with the past in a remote corner of Europe that no one gave a damn about; and it was an expensive proposition. The only producer who even considered the project was Ray Stark. And even he was merely talking about recording a stage production of the play on film. Peter and I finally wound up sitting down to work under the auspices of an independent producer—my old collaborator Saul Zaentz.

When we started to pick the play apart for the screenplay, Peter's courage never wavered. We took four months, and turned the play inside out. One of the challenges was to find a satisfying narrative frame for the story. We wound up with the simple conceit of Salieri's confession, which sets up the dramatic action of the film in flashbacks. We came up with the idea through a simple chain of deductions: an old composer had attempted suicide, which nowadays would bring a psychiatrist into the picture, but what would have happened in the eighteenth century? They would have rushed a priest to the old man, which was perfect for our story because a man of God made a fitting foil to the blasphemous Salieri, who is railing at the Creator for his whimsical distribution of talent.

Once we had the structure, everything else quickly fell into place: we made the priest a young man mouthing platitudes, a fellow mediocrity and a musical layman who had never heard of the old composer because Salieri had been forgotten even while he was alive, another reason for his self-annihilating rage. In screenwriting, it's the simplicity that usually takes all the sweat.

I'd never worked with flashbacks before and never really cared for them, but I didn't mind using this narrative strategy in *Amadeus* since we had Mozart's music to whisk us through the transitions. And in purely technical terms, the flashback structure lets you pack the story with more detail and incident than linear narration.

Peter approached the work with gut-wrenching humility. He wrote many different versions of scenes that had worked splendidly in the theater but which would not have withstood the sharper scrutiny of the cinema. He added wonderful new moments, and, in the end he produced a superb screenplay.

I wanted to shoot *Amadeus* in Prague. The idea of coming back to the old country after ten years abroad to shoot a big American movie strongly appealed to my vanity, but it also made a lot of sense. Prague had always adored Mozart. In 1791, only a handful of people attended his funeral in Vienna, whereas the requiem mass for him at St. Nicholas Church under the Hradčany Castle drew six thousand mourners. Only half could fit into the ornate church. The others stood outside in the driving sleet to pay tribute to the genius whose *Don Giovanni* had premiered in the city in 1787.

Prague also made a perfect backdrop for a film set in the eighteenth century. This old city of a "hundred towers," an epithet from the days when three digits denoted a stupefying amount, stands on hills that overlook a bend in a wide river. It's spanned by the Charles Bridge, a massive stone structure erected in 1357 and decorated with dramatic Baroque statuary, which connects Prague's Staré Město—Old Town— with its ancient ghetto and the famous clock of seasons to the Malá Strana—Lesser Town—whose oxblood roofs rise up in waves to the stunning Hradčany Castle.

Many of the city's streets had been built in the eighteenth century and are still paved with cobblestones. Things are changing now, but in the early eighties, these streets ran for blocks on end in moving shabbiness, untouched by wars, unspoiled by commercialism.

Being a smart and tough businessman, our producer, Saul Zaentz, scouted beyond Prague for other eighteenth century shooting locations. We checked Vienna and found a lot of neon in its old streets. Besides, production costs doubled and tripled the moment "Hollywood" was uttered there, so we quickly ruled it out.

We also asked the Mozart archive in the Mozarteum's Bibliotheca Mozartiana in Salzburg for permission to shoot there. They asked to see our screenplay. After they read it, they flatly refused to let us shoot there and immediately cut off all access to their archives. We moved on to Budapest, but whole sections of that city had been rebuilt in the nineteenth century. We couldn't find a single street that had been completely preserved.

Prague was by far our best choice. The only problem was that the Czech government had refused to let me into the country—even for a brief visit—since 1977, when I became an American citizen and could start applying for a visa. I wanted to go to Čáslav and Prague to rummage through my memories, to see how my sons lived, have a beer with old friends, speak a language that comes effortlessly and in which I can express myself so much more precisely. I was repeatedly turned down without a word of explanation. The tough, neo-Stalinist government that had "normalized" the country after the Soviet invasion had just thrown my old schoolmate Václav Havel in jail for four and a half years; but everyone cuts deals and I figured that the Czech government might let me come back if there were something in it for them. In a way, shooting *Amadeus* in Prague was my only chance to see Czechoslovakia again.

I called Jiří Purš, the director of Czechoslovak Film, and told him I was working on a big-budget film about Mozart and that Prague was the perfect place to shoot in. I told him I knew that arranging such a thing was a long shot, but there was a lot of money to be made, so I wanted to come to Prague to talk about it.

"Apply for a visa," Purš told me, "and we'll see."

I received the Czech visa so fast I got cold feet. I'd been staying away from all politics abroad, but I was still an émigré, a traitor in the eyes of the Communist government. The State Security comrades were capable of anything—all they had to do was plant some drugs in my luggage and I'd never get out of the old country again. I decided not to go back in alone.

I asked three close friends, Jean Claude Carrière, Cheryl Barnes, and Mary Ellen Mark to come with me. It was to be a tour of the most sentimental places of my life, more important than any business I had in the country. I'd never have dared go in without them. They were my shield; the only drawback was that I never was able to be alone with my emotions.

On April 22, 1979, we landed at the Prague airport. After my long absence, one of the more striking things about Prague was how little had changed. All the old addresses and phone numbers were the same. None of the stores, bars, or theaters had moved, and they still sold the same merchandise. Even the language remained static, because it didn't have to name any new realities.

Věra and my boys lived in our old apartment in Dejvice. Věra still sang and acted at the Semafor Theater, and she was happy. We never divorced, but we'd been separated for many years and she was now living with the son of Miloš Kratochvíl, my old and dear professor at the film academy. They had a small boy, Matěj and Petr's half brother, so there was something new in the old world after all.

I had a long sentimental dinner with Jana, my first wife, and got drunk with old friends. After ten years, the brutal damage done by the passage of time showed in their faces, their walk, their energy, and through their eyes it reflected just as mercilessly back on me. Looking at them, I felt how much I had aged. I'd left the country a young man; I was dragging back a huge weight of expectations, experiences, possessions, and new friendships.

I visited an old buddy from my years of apprenticeship in show business. We opened a bottle of chilled vodka, and the feeling was as if I'd just come back from a long vacation. Life is to be lived and talked about, so we talked into the wee hours of the morning when, suddenly, he turned on me.

"You know, we looked up to you while you were out there. You were like a symbol of what we might have accomplished, too, if we'd had the same breaks. But you sure pissed all that respect away by showing up here now."

To him, I was an American big shot—a millionaire show-off who'd come back to rub in their misery, Mr. Oscar himself feeding on other people's envy, a son of a bitch who only thought of himself. In the morning, he was all smiles. He slept it off, and perhaps he didn't even remember what he'd said.

I piled Cheryl, Mary Ellen, and Jean Claude in the car. I was going to show them the places that had formed me, the landscape of my heart.

The family house in Čáslav, the old school, and the church seemed shockingly small and drab until I realized that, in my memory, I saw them all from the point of view of a four- or five-year-old child, whose impressions lent the world a different size and power.

Náchod hadn't shrunk nearly as much as Čáslav in my mind's eye and I made it back in time to see Uncle Boleslav, who was living in the same house where I'd once tried to sneak a chess move past him. He would die not long after my visit, so I'm very happy that I got to embrace him.

In Poděbrady the cardiac patients still sipped iron-rich mineral water and dozed off during the afternoon concerts. Only the river had grown smaller. You could easily throw a rock across the stream of icy water that had once taken the fins of love to cross.

Dear Hotel Rut now housed a workers' recreational center for a factory, which had made crude additions to the old building. I barely recognized the place, yet the walk I took around Mácha's Lake moved me more that anything else I saw in the old country. I was probably conceived there, lost my own virginity on its shore, was stoned on the road that still lay strewn with pine cones, and spent the best summers of my life there. I only wished I could have a little of that time back.

The people with whom I'd shared life in those places had moved to Prague or left the country or died, but when I got to Vrchlabí, I found nearly all the firemen of *Fireman's Ball* in the same tavern where I used to drink with them. They still worked the same factory jobs and still volunteered for the fire brigade. They shot billiards on the same pool table, which had gotten worse even as the players themselves hadn't gotten any better. They welcomed me like a lost friend, and I got drunk with them again. They told me that *Fireman's Ball* had been the biggest thing ever to happen to them.

"At least this way we'll leave something behind when we die," they said.

From Vrchlabí, we returned to Prague and I prepared to go back to work. Once I set my mind on the negotiations with the Czechoslovak Film functionaries, I saw the city more clearly, from a greater distance, through my American eyes, and now its people seemed sad, weary, worn out from the endless lines, the petty humiliations, the general impotence of their lives. Only the Baroque beauty of Prague was as breathtaking as ever.

ANATOMY OF A DEAL

In my days at the *Laterna Magica,* Jiří Purš was a minor functionary at the Ministry of Culture. Now this tall man with a prominent nose ruled over the Czech cinema and had done so for the past ten years.

Purš had become a member of the Central Committee of the Communist Party and was a drinking buddy of Politbureau members and ministers. He'd been made by the Soviets. He was one of only a few dozen Czechs who'd assisted the KGB in preparing for the Soviet invasion in 1968. Soon after he was awarded the general directorship of Czechoslovak Film, a plum job that came with trips abroad, hard-currency deals, bribes, and actresses.

As the head of Barrandov Studios, in charge of all movie production and distribution, Purš had no blood on his hands; he had protected most of the filmmakers from the rabid Stalinists. But while he had kept many of them on the payroll for years, he had, at the same time, completely snuffed out the promise of the Czech New Wave. The country's cinema stagnated under his directorship, and even when he finally allowed directors like Chytilová and Menzel to work again, they never had the nourishing freedom they had enjoyed in the sixties.

In 1980, Purš invited me to his imperial office, furnished in the people's democratic style with a big desk, sturdy leather sofas and chairs, and stale cigarette air. He had acquired a paunch and a great deal of self-confidence since his days as a minor cog in the Ministry of Culture. I was curious as to how he would behave toward me, but he acted the old buddy. I almost got the feeling that he saw *Amadeus* as a chance to redeem himself a bit, to undo some of the damage he had done to Czech cinema. At our meeting he got to the point quickly. He said that he personally wanted to see me working in Prague again, but there were a lot of people who didn't.

"Look, your old director buddies at Barrandov are hollering the loudest that we shouldn't let an émigré and a traitor like you back in," he told me. He was talking about the Communist Party cell of the film studio and the old-guard directors like Sequens, Čech, and Kachlík. These comrades had always had it in for me, ever since *Black Peter*.

"But here's the deal," Purš went on. "I assume that politically there is nothing in the script that they could hang their hats on, correct?"

"Look, it's about Mozart . . ."

"Right. And as far as I know, you haven't been signing any petitions abroad?"

"I've got my sons living here, don't I?"

"Okay, your production dollars are the trump card for me. We can really use the money. The old boys' only argument is that you're coming here to stir up our dissidents, like your old buddy Václav Havel. So if you give me your word that you won't seek out any of our dissidents while you're here, then I think I can push it through." He extended his hand to me.

"Look, Jiří, I'll shake hands on that if you promise me something in return," I told him. "If some dissident approaches me of his own volition, then you won't do anything either to that person or to our production."

"Deal," said Purš, but the final okay on the Czech side went through only after Gustav Husák, the president and chairman of the Communist Party, approved our handshake.

MOZART IN HOLLYWOOD

Peter Shaffer had once worked for the music publisher Boosey and Hawkes, so he had a knowledge of music, but he was unable to draw on it in his play. Music interferes with the spoken word onstage. This is a matter of simple practicality—they both compete for the attention of the ear. In film, however, the image has a far greater weight than the word, and music mates with images with the greatest of ease, multiplying the power of both, so we were able to restore the genius of Mozart that was left out of the play. In fact, we thought of the music as the third character in our film.

In hindsight, this was our shrewdest decision. I discovered in the cutting room that Mozart's music not only worked magic on the audience, it even had the power to narrate parts of our story. Mozart's notes became as important as the words of our script or the images of our story. I didn't know enough about classical music to choose my musical collaborators, so I asked Czech piano virtuoso Ivan Moravec whom he would recommend as having the greatest practical knowledge and feel for the eighteenth century. He suggested Sir Neville Marriner or Sir Colin Davis.

Neville Marriner happened to be a friend of Peter Shaffer's, so Saul Zaentz arranged for us to meet with him first. Neville had a layover in New York on his way to Minnesota, where he was conductor and musical director of the Minnesota Symphony Orchestra, so Saul, Peter, and I met him in a conference room at Kennedy Airport. The knighted conductor had an hour between flights and seemed leery of us. We made our pitch, and he considered it warily. Perhaps he saw us as Hollywood corruptors of his art.

"I would do it under one condition," he finally said.

"Which is?"

"Not a single note of Mozart's music can be altered in the film."

We shook hands on it, and, in the end, not a single bar of Mozart's music in the film had been touched.

Next I hired Twyla Tharp to choreograph our opera sequences. It never crossed my mind to use anyone else, and Twyla soon left on a casting mission to Prague. She was going to bring the nucleus of her troupe from New York for *Amadeus,* but she needed to find more dancers. Part of her mission was to look for opera singers to act in our operatic excerpts. We didn't need them to sing because Marriner was going to record the sound with different voices in London beforehand, but I wanted real opera singers onstage.

In most movies, the musical score is the last thing added to the film, but for *Amadeus,* where the music was as important as it is in musicals, we had to have it on tape beforehand. We would then play it on location and choreograph our action to this score.

Twyla left for Prague while I was still casting the film in New York. A few days later, her angry phone call woke me up at three o'clock in the morning.

"Miloš, I'm quitting this project! I've had enough of Prague and all these maestros here! I'm leaving!" She got me at the right time. I was too sleepy and disoriented to yell back at her or get insulted or do anything else I might have done if I had my normal working energy, so luckily I didn't shoot myself in the foot. As I lay on the bed with the receiver by my ear, I was overcome by a deep sadness.

"*Say something,* damnit, Miloš!" she said. I didn't know what to tell her. I was feeling so depressed that I didn't want to utter another word in my life.

"Why aren't you saying anything? Hello? Miloš? Are you there?"

"What do you want me to tell you, Twyla? If you're leaving us, what can I do?" Now Twyla was nearly in tears, and somehow, tenderly, she talked her frustration out of her system.

What happened was that when she arrived in Prague, she was taken to the National Theater to see the best dancers and opera singers in the country. They were all dismissive of her. They acted as if they were doing her a favor by talking to her. She had never come across a bigger crowd of prima donnas in her life. In Czechoslovakia, once you get into the National Theater, you have a sinecure for life. People begin to call you "maestro," and anything you do for the mere mortals after that is a huge favor. You certainly never take another artistic risk.

Twyla hadn't come to Prague looking for favors. She was used to working hard and living for her work. She wasn't about to massage egos of second-rate artists whom she couldn't respect.

When she told me the problem, I called a friend in Prague, Jan Schmidt, and asked him to take Twyla to the city operetta, where the dancers were still used to working hard and the heads had yet to swell. We needed professionals, not "artists." Twyla ended up being very happy with her Czech dancers. And she did an absolutely outstanding job on the film.

Mirek Ondříček was, of course, my cinematographer again, and it was his suggestion to consider a Prague costume designer. He thought that a local artist would have a greater feeling for the time and place of our story and that Dóda Pištěk, one of the best painters of his generation, was my best bet. I vaguely knew this bald, athletic man, but when I went to dinner with him, I discovered his rapid-fire wit and unusual sensibility. Dóda was humming with nervous energy and had an immense, almost childlike, playfulness that made for a wonderful asset on a film location, so I offered him the job.

Dóda had designed the costumes for over a hundred Czech movies, but he was very excited to have the resources of an American production behind him. For the first time in a long career, he was able to use craftsmen and materials that would have been too costly for any of his Barrandov budgets. The downside was that this meant he'd have no excuses to fall back on if something went wrong. But Dóda relished the chance to show what he could do. He bought his fabrics in London and had his costumes sewn in Italy. They looked absolutely splendid.

I never considered anyone but Josef Svoboda to design the opera sets. This old collaborator of mine from *Laterna Magica* had become one of the top set designers of Europe. He jetted from one opera house to another, but he managed to squeeze us into his crowded schedule and gave me witty and imaginative sets.

Once again, I saw over a thousand actors during the casting process. *Amadeus* had been a huge stage success and the parts of Mozart and Salieri were rightly considered plum roles in Hollywood, so Robby received a lot of feelers and offers from agents of famous actors.

One night he called me from Los Angeles.

"Something totally unbelievable has just happened, Miloš," he said. He had just had lunch with a high-level executive of a major Hollywood studio. The studio would underwrite our film, he proposed, if we cast Walter Matthau as Mozart.

"Walter is a Mozart freak. He knows every last note Mozart ever scribbled," said the executive.

"Yes, well," Robby replied evenly. "But do you realize that Mozart was this blond young man who died at thirty-five?"

There was a short silence.

"Yes, *I* know!" the executive quickly recovered. "But Robby! Who knows that in America?!"

I later learned that Matthau had in fact wanted to play Salieri, a very legitimate notion; but his request got scrambled in the brain of the executive, who couldn't imagine that, in a movie called *Amadeus,* a star of Matthau's stature could possibly want to play some never-heard-of character named Salieri.

I'd already made up my mind, however, not to be moved by the entreaties of powerful agents or friends or by any pressure from the studios. I'd stubbornly follow my instincts and fill the principal parts with unfamiliar actors.

Mozart's face isn't commonly known, which was good for our film. It gave me a blank spot in the audience's consciousness to draw on, so I had a chance to make them believe from the very first shot that they'd just discovered the man. If I were to cast a star in the part I'd throw that chance away. And if the famous Mozart was played by an unknown actor, then the forgotten Salieri certainly couldn't be portrayed by a film star because that would pull the initial attention toward the wrong character and undercut the delicate transfer of emotion between the screen and the audience.

In the end, I found my Mozart in Tom Hulce, my Salieri in F. Murray Abraham, my Constanze, Mozart's wife, in Meg Tilly, and my emperor in Jeffrey Jones. And so in the winter of 1981, I moved from New York to Prague and started preproduction.

Tom Hulce had to learn to play the piano for the role. He had never played before, but he put in several hours a day at the keyboard for weeks on end, and, according to Neville Marriner, his fingers never hit a wrong note in the film. He also had to invent Mozart's shrill giggle, which Peter had employed to great dramatic effect in the play and which had its genesis in a tiny aside in a letter by an aristocratic gossip who wrote of her shock upon hearing the harsh squawking that issued from the lips of Mozart. When this man who had composed such divine music laughed, she said, he seemed more animal than human. I'd seen six or seven productions of the play and every actor who played Mozart invented his own laugh, so I left Hulce alone. He tried out all sorts of sounds until he struck on a wild, high-pitched giggle that was perfectly pitched to his personality.

Our two principals also had to learn how to conduct an eighteenth-century orchestra, which was a problem because no one knows how this was done two hundred years ago. I asked my old friend Zdeněk Mahler, who has an intimate knowledge of music, to comb the historical record for clues, and he found that no one used batons in the eighteenth century. Finally, though, it was Marriner who gave us the look of period conducting. He videotaped himself conducting all the bits of motivated music in *Amadeus* the way he thought it had been done in Mozart's time. Hulce and Abraham prepared by copying his movements.

Prague and its surroundings provided us with nearly all the locations we needed, except for the interiors of our imperial palace. Only the Hradčany Castle's halls shone with the splendor I was looking for, but it was the domicile of the president, and Communist Party chairman Husák certainly wasn't about to rent out his abode to an American movie company. I'd begun to reconcile myself to someplace in Vienna when someone told me to check out the residency of the Prague arch-bishop, which still belonged to the Catholic Church.

In this wonderfully preserved palace I found precisely what I had been looking for, so our Barrandov go-betweens approached its occupant, the aged Cardinal František Tomášek, and asked if he'd be willing to loan it to us. They brought back a depressing reply: "The cardinal considers all film to be the instrument of the devil."

The quote rang with such medieval pathos that I became suspicious. I'd been away from Prague for ten years, but I still had a lot of friends there and this effective network soon brought me a more plausible explanation of why the cardinal had turned us down: the Catholic Church was closely watched by the Communists, and State Security had an agent serving as the cardinal's secretary. It was this man who had turned Tomášek against our film. He told the old churchman that we were atheists, that we wanted to film naked women in his palace, that we were out to mock him and to desecrate his residency.

Once I understood more clearly what had happened, I searched for a way to approach the cardinal directly. We didn't move in the same circles, but a friend of another friend knew a carpenter who was just then fixing Tomášek's study, so he saw him every day.

The cardinal became furious when the carpenter repeated his puta-tive quote about the devil. He had never said any such thing; he recognized it as the voice of our go-betweens throwing a little extra Marxist creativity into the message, so he immediately invited me to come see him.

"See what I've had to deal with here for the last thirty years?" he complained.

Tomášek, as it turned out, loved Mozart's music, and was very friendly. I described our film to him, and he granted us permission to use his palace on the spot.

We began shooting on schedule, and everything went smoothly until Meg Tilly got into a pickup game of soccer on a Prague street and tore the ligaments in one of her ankles. We hadn't shot any of her scenes yet, but I had to recast the role of Constanze while the production was rolling.

A few day's after Tilly's injury, on a Friday evening, Saul and I flew to Paris and then took the Concorde to New York. We saw fifty actresses on Saturday, did callbacks on Sunday, and narrowed the choice down to two women. We just couldn't make up our minds, so we flew both of them back to Prague for more screen tests.

I was back on the set on Monday, so we didn't miss a day of production. That evening, we looked at the screen tests and I made a gut decision to go with Elizabeth Berridge. She only had a couple of days to prepare for the role between her costume-fitting sessions, but it was all she needed. Mozart's wife had been the daughter of a concierge, and Elizabeth gave us a tart, earthy, wonderful Constanze. And, in the end, she fell in love in Prague and married one of our Czech technicians.

NOBLEWOMEN AND PLAINCLOTHESMEN

When I shoot a film, I try to ignore the gossip, the melodramas, and the feuds that swirl around every production. It's not that I don't want to know who is having an affair, what the crew is bitching about, who got drunk out of his mind, or who said I was a slave driver. I am very curious about all the discoveries and new connections that a group of bright and energetic people away from home invariably makes on an exotic location, but I can't afford the distraction.

This was particularly true of *Amadeus*. The Czech emotional landscape was too rich, the background too charged. I found it harder to concentrate than at any other time in my life.

The distractions started as soon as we arrived in the cold and snowy January of 1982. My Czech liaisons had found me a nice private room right off the Old Castle Stairway, which rises up to Hradčany Castle. The palaces there had once belonged to the families of ancient Czech nobility, but after the revolution they were nationalized, sold to various countries, and turned into embassies. Only one of the servant houses there had been left to its old owner, an ancient Czech noblewoman named Annetka Velflíková.

Annetka became my landlady. She was in her eighties and lived with her sister-in-law in heartbreaking poverty. The two old ladies, with some of the bluest blood in the country, had only a minimal government pension, so they wore tattered old housecoats and torn slippers at home. They were glad to have me as a tenant, and I was grateful to be under their roof.

I was coming home very late one night, shortly after I'd moved in with the two ladies. It was a freezing January evening, but there was snow on the ground to reflect the moonlight, so you could see clearly across the street. I had some boxes of booze and cartons of cigarettes that I used to pay off people—standard operating procedure in Prague—and my driver, Pavel, was helping me carry them into the house. I had just unlocked the gate, entered the garden, and started past the main building to the old servant house when I noticed someone crouched down in the bushes. Against a white wall and through the bare branches, the body was plainly visible.

"Is that you, Mrs. Velflíková?" I asked. I'd seen the old lady look for a cat in the garden the night before and thought maybe something had happened to this frail grandma.

"Carry on! Carry on!" the voice of a young woman ordered me.

I carried on, and, slipping between the warm sheets on that polar night, I wondered if the FBI or the CIA were quite such equal opportunity employers as the Czech State Security. I already knew that Pavel was working for State Security. I'd assumed as much right from the start and didn't expect him to confirm it, but he was surprisingly open with me.

"You probably have to tell them everything I do, don't you?" I tested him as soon as we became familiar with each other. "But you don't have to answer that."

"Miloš, come on! Do you think they'd let me drive you around otherwise?"

As time went on and we trusted each other more, I'd look into the rearview mirror and see a car tailing us.

"That Škoda, right?" I'd ask.

"What else do you see there?" he said.

I started paying attention to the car that followed the State Security Škoda, and it seemed to be staying with us as well.

"Two cars, Pavel? Am I that important?"

"That's regulation stuff."

"Why?"

"Watch what happens when I enter this one-way street."

I saw the second car stop at the beginning of the one-way street. A couple of minutes later, it reappeared in the mirror.

"What are they doing?" I asked.

"Suppose you told me to stop in a one-way street. You could then get out and walk against the grain of the traffic. And suppose the tailing car gets boxed in by the cars behind it. Now what? You're gone! So that second car's a backup. It always waits for us to clear the one-way streets."

"How do they know that?"

"They all talk on the radio."

The entire time in Prague I acted as if State Security was listening to everything I said. This was a necessary precaution because when I first checked into my room, Annetka welcomed me with a very informative bit of news: "Mr. Forman, these people in Prague love you so much! Our telephone was out of order for two years and we couldn't get anyone to look at it for the life of us, but as soon as they heard that you'd be living here, they gave us a brand-new phone! Come and look at it!" She was telling me the phone was bugged. I knew right then that the two old ladies and I would make a fine household.

I eat a big breakfast instead of lunch, so the two ladies got up early every day and served me hearty chicken paprika. They conscientiously took down all my messages during the day. When I came home before ten o'clock, Annetka brought me a sheet of paper with all the callers neatly listed on it, and when I came home late, I found the list on the kitchen table.

One evening, I didn't get home till after midnight. I looked for the sheet of paper and didn't find it anywhere, so I went to bed. As soon as I lay down, there came a soft knock on my door.

"Come in!" I called. Annetka opened the door and strolled into my room, wearing what may have been her wedding dress. It was lacy and fluffy and stunning. Her hair was freshly permed. She moved as if she were made out of fine china.

"You had a phone call, Mr. Forman," she said.

"Oh, okay, who was it?"

"Prince Schwarzenberg called from Vienna."

"Oh, all right. What did he say?"

"There was no message."

"Okay . . ."

"Good night, Mr. Forman." And she turned around and waltzed away.

It took me a moment to work out the implications, but then I realized that if Czechoslovakia had still been a kingdom, Prince Schwarzenberg would have been its ruler and Annetka couldn't simply tell me that her king had called while wearing her old housecoat.

INFORMERS AND VEGETABLE

It was hard to explain the realities of everyday life in a Communist country to the American and British members of our crew. Either they saw spooks everywhere or they didn't notice that they were tailed and that their hotel rooms were bugged. The notions that the day-to-day business of living has to go on even under surveillance, that you block it out and keep working, that you get used to it, and that it, too, can become boring are not easy to understand.

Only the heads of the production departments came over with us, so the majority of the people on our set were Czechs. We realized that some of them were informers, though their job wasn't to report on us as much as it was to report on the Barrandov employees on our production. I had too many other things to worry about and didn't even try to spot them, but there came a moment of eerie clarity when they suddenly stood out of the mass of people they were keeping under watch. It was as if a slash of strobe light revealed them.

On the Fourth of July 1983, a work day for us, we were shooting a big opera scene from *The Marriage of Figaro* in the Stavovské Divadlo. The theater was full of extras in period costumes, an orchestra fidgeted in the pit, the stage crawled with dancers and singers. We rehearsed the first shot of the day with the playback, and everything went smoothly, as it always did in Prague, because our Czechs were thrilled to be working on an American film, so I ordered the candles on the heavy chandeliers to be lit. I then asked the dancers and the extras to take their places.

"Camera!" I yelled.

"Rolling," said the operator.

"Playback!" I called for the Mozart aria to begin.

Suddenly, the deafening strains of the American national anthem shook the old theater and a huge American flag unfurled from the rafters and billowed over the orchestra. Our homesick crew had decided to throw a surprise birthday bash for America.

The whole theater froze for a couple of seconds, but then the extras caught on to what was happening and went wild. At that moment, the informers in the crowd were in plain sight. The extras applauded frenetically, but here and there among them, dressed in the same wigs and costumes, stood men with sour expressions. There was roughly one killjoy per ten beaming Czechs. As the ovation continued, the confused informers began to exchange nervous looks: Do we step in? What do we do? Help! In the end, they did nothing about what, for them, was a shocking political provocation.

I have an immigrant's uncritical love for America, so I was intensely moved by the flag and the enthusiasm. At the same time, I was terrified that the State Security people would somehow make the production bleed for this gesture. We were easy targets. Our generators could have blown up, our sets could have been damaged, anything could have happened. As it turned out, nothing happened. We took the flag down and worked for the rest of the day, and the Czech liaisons never mentioned this "provocation."

There had been friction between our production and the Barrandov management from the start. It began when we moved to provide lunches for all the employees working on our movie. This is customary practice in the West, but in the workers' state of Czechoslovakia, the Barrandov hands had to bag their own lunches.

At first, Barrandov refused even to provide a room where we could serve our meals. When we found a makeup room that wasn't used and seemed adequate for our purposes, the Barrandov liaisons finally consented. We were allowed to feed all foreigners, but we couldn't serve free lunches to the Czech crew. Barrandov didn't need a precedent set. It didn't want its employees getting spoiled.

Saul, however, put his foot down on this point. He wasn't about to allow the Barrandov honchos to split our crew into haves and have-nots and to destroy the fine working morale on our set. It took an ultimatum or two, but in the end, the Barrandov bosses gritted their teeth and allowed us to feed all the people working on *Amadeus*. It was a smart move on Saul's part. Our production van drove to West Germany twice a week for fresh fruit and vegetables. In a country where in winter you could only buy some moldy tomatoes and wrinkled apples in the shops, the smell of a tangerine reserved only for the Americans or the crunch of a pineapple that couldn't be touched probably would have been enough to launch a wildcat strike.

The most dramatic incident of our shoot occurred in the Tyl Theater, a very old and historical establishment that showed every year of its age. I wanted to film the excerpt from *Don Giovanni* there, as that was where it premiered, but the Czechs were reluctant to rent it to us, even though it was still a working institution. I understood their scruples once I inspected the backstage. It was in catastrophic condition, full of cobwebs and dust, old junk and rotted wood. The place was a powder keg and we were lighting our scenes with candles and torches as period authenticity dictated, so we told the Czechs we would pay for as many firemen as, in their judgment, it would take to safeguard the building.

We wound up with firemen crouching behind every stick of decoration on the stage, in every section of box seat, in every hallway. I think we had some hundred fire fighters on the set, but we almost managed to send the historical landmark up in flames anyway.

It was not for lack of caution. We wouldn't light the thousands of candles in the period chandeliers and candlesticks during rehearsals. Replacing all the candles took too long anyway, so we planned to ignite them only when we got ready to roll the camera.

Our first run-through of the dramatic master shot in which Don Giovanni confronts the black-masked ghost went very smoothly. The singer portraying the Don mimicked the words to the majestic sounds of our prerecorded music, and he looked splendid in his hat, adorned with peacock feathers. He was supposed to encounter the ghost, stagger, steady himself by leaning against a table on which stood a beautiful candelabra, and launch into his music.

I sat by the camera in the orchestra and watched. Everything looked fine to me, so I gave the order to light the candles.

With the playback booming, Don Giovanni saw the ghost, staggered, and caught himself from falling backward by grasping the table. He had done everything precisely the way we had rehearsed it, but now the candles were burning up and the long feathers of his hat hung directly over the flickering candelabra. I froze as the peacock feathers began to smoke. A moment passed, then another, then another, as in a bad dream. The theater was crawling with firemen, so I waited for them to spring into action. The feathers were now sprouting tiny flames and I watched and waited, but nothing happened. Don Giovanni went on mimicking the words with grand passion, not realizing that his plumes burned with big bright flames.

Where the hell were all the firemen?

It took another eternity of waiting before one fireman peeked out of the scenery. He was young and shy, and he flashed me an apologetic smile.

"Mr. Forman?" he said timidly. "I am sorry, sir, but could you please stop the cameras? Your actor here is on fire." And he quickly popped back behind the set, so that he wouldn't ruin the shot.

I've never seen a greater tribute to the magic of movies. A couple of steps away from this fireman a man was on fire in a powder keg, but the camera was rolling so he didn't dare interrupt the movie.

"Cut!" I shouted when I realized the fire fighting was up to me. "Cut! Cut! Cut!"

At that moment, a swarm of hollering fire fighters leaped out of the set decorations and threw themselves on the poor, unsuspecting Don Giovanni, knocked the elegant hat off his head, and proceeded to stomp on it furiously. It looked as if a Mel Brooks movie had suddenly erupted on our set.

As it had to be in socialist Prague, the spirit of Franz Kafka presided over our production. *Amadeus* was a big deal in Czechoslovakia, the biggest movie production ever to take place in the country. We touched a lot of lives in Prague, closed down a lot of streets, attracted a lot of onlookers, wreaked havoc with the traffic. Everyone in the city knew about our production, but not one word about the film or about any of us got printed in the newspapers or uttered on radio or television. The Communist government had a rule stating that no émigrés were ever to be mentioned by name. I was an émigré; therefore we occupied a massive blind spot in the Czech media.

The only publicity *Amadeus* ever received came out in the local newspaper of the small town where our hats had been made. Just two lines of text reported that the shop making historical hats for the movie *Amadeus* had fulfilled its plan. The newspaper's editor got fired for letting this piece of subversive news slip out.

Despite the ceaseless surveillance, shooting the invisible, unmentionable film in Prague was a moving experience for me. People kept pulling me aside to tell me apocryphal stories about Mozart that had been passed down for generations. And not a day went by that some Czech extra, or technician, or delivery person didn't grab my hand when no one was looking and squeeze it hard.

"Thank you," they said. "Thank you!"

They were wired with tribal emotion, and so was I. They were reaching through me to the larger world, of which they had many illusions, and I felt honored to be their imperfect medium.

ENTER MOZART

In the fall of 1982, I moved back to Fantasy Records in Berkeley, a place of wonderful memories. I edited *Amadeus* there in that strange and familiar mood in which you hope for the best and prepare for the worst.

One of the hardest things in filmmaking is cutting scenes that are otherwise good but retard the flow of emotion or throw off the film's rhythm. When I edited *Amadeus,* I had to drop three scenes—two big and one small—with the late Kenneth McMillan, an actor whom I liked enormously. He had played the fire chief in *Ragtime,* and in *Amadeus,* he was a rich man whose daughter took piano lessons from our irresponsible genius. Kenneth had great comedic timing and I loved watching him work these light scenes, but when I saw the rough cut of the entire film, these episodes caused the story to drag. It was painful, but I had to admit that McMillan's character had no dramatic purpose.

The editing process always reveals things that slipped by during the film's shooting. I had come to know and love Mozart when I wrote the screenplay with Shaffer. Still, I somehow managed to underestimate the sheer magic of his art. In the editing room, every time I focused on Mozart, he grew bigger. For example, one of the most memorable moments in Shaffer's play occurs at the end of the first act: Constanze comes to Salieri to ask for his help. Wolfgang Amadeus is monumentally impractical, and the Mozarts are broke again. Perhaps the court composer, such an influential person, would be kind enough to pass on some commissions to Mozart.

"He really works hard," says Constanze, showing Salieri a thick stack of Mozart's compositions to prove it. Salieri realizes that she has brought the originals of Mozart's work, and he is eager to have a look at these transcriptions of the volcanic stream of Mozart's creativity. What he sees nearly flattens him: Mozart's first drafts look as neat as other composers' polished presentations. There are hardly any corrections. Even the note sheets reveal the vigor of Mozart's genius, and this realization stabs straight into the heart of Salieri's inferiority. Now he desperately wants to cuckold Mozart, to better him in something, to strike back at him in any way he can.

As the curtain is about to fall, Salieri tells Constanze that he will help her husband, but only if she comes to see him, alone, at night. Constanze seems desperate enough to do anything to save her family from financial ruin, so in the theater I couldn't wait for the second act to begin. Would Constanze go to Salieri? Would she submit to him? Does she have something up her sleeve? Would she stop herself in time?

The curtain goes up and Constanze accepts Salieri's terms. She goes to his room and offers herself to him, but Salieri doesn't take her. He is content to humiliate her and throw her out.

I wanted to retain the juicy drama of this episode. Both F. Murray Abraham and Elizabeth Berridge relished the drama of Salieri's exploitation of Constanze and acted it beautifully. I edited the footage and it looked just fine, but when I added the music, I realized that its power completely changed the scene. As I watched the close-up of Salieri's face while he rifled through Mozart's drafts and heard the four or five celestial motifs from the very compositions that Salieri is examining, as I heard the range of instrumentation, heard the richness of emotion and mood and invention, I was as overwhelmed by Mozart's genius as Salieri was. And once I felt the grand power of that music, I didn't need to see anything more because no sexual betrayal, no mundane humiliation could ever touch this greatness. I would never have believed it, but the music suddenly flattened the fine, titillating scene of high drama into a petty, anticlimactic redundancy.

In the final cut, Salieri skims the drafts, hears the corresponding cadenzas, and is overwhelmed. He has no thoughts of seduction, revenge, cuckolding, humiliation. He has just received the final proof of his own mediocrity. He drops the sheets on the floor, stepping on them as he flees the room, the woman, the music, the spirit of Mozart. And there the scene ends.

When the reviews came out, not a few music critics got violently upset over the liberties we had taken with the historical facts of Mozart's life. I thought their objections pedantic and their passion complimentary. Our film had never purported to be a factual biography of an obscure relationship. It was clearly a historical fantasy, a dramatic construct, a meditation on possibilities past, a playful story.

Moviegoers responded to our film differently. *Amadeus* was and continues to be a money-maker.

In the spring of 1985, *Amadeus* was nominated for eleven Oscars, with Tom Hulce and F. Murray Abraham vying for the same prize in the

Best Actor category. It won eight of them, but my biggest reward came at the end of every screening I saw. All over the world, entire audiences sat glued to their seats right through the six minutes of end titles, listening to Mozart's divine music.

DEMON OF SELF-CONSCIOUSNESS

In the history of the cinema, only a few filmmakers have been able to direct themselves with success. To step in and out of a role while carrying the whole house of cards in your hands is to be both mother and midwife in a difficult birth. In this regard, the work of Charlie Chaplin and Orson Welles surely must rank among cinema's highest accomplishments.

In 1956, as an assistant to Radok on *Grandpa Automobile,* I had the responsibility of casting the extras and the very minor roles. One of these parts was that of an airline pilot who basically had to show up at Ruzyne Airport in Prague on the morning of the shoot and look good in a uniform. I hired a young actor who fit the bill. He didn't have any lines and didn't even need the script, so I considered my job done.

In those days in Czechoslovakia, actors were expected to hop on a streetcar or a bus and report to the set at the appointed time, which didn't always happen. I wasn't taking any chances; I called my pilot the night before his appearance to confirm that he was coming. He said not to worry, he'd not only be there, he'd be there early.

He didn't get there early, he didn't show up on time, and then it became clear that he was not coming at all. I later on found out that he had gotten drunk the night before and slept right through his movie career.

The set was tense to begin with that day because we had to fit our shots into the rhythms of a working airport. Radok was used to working in more controlled situations and I didn't want to unnerve him even more with the bad news about the pilot, so I put on his uniform myself. The thing fit perfectly, which was a huge relief. The part was so simple that I felt I could have done it in my sleep. All I had to do was stroll around the airport with a stewardess and point out a few things to her—child's play.

I reported to the set, put up with the inevitable jokes that the uniform provoked, took my place beside the stewardess, and waited for Radok's signal. As I started walking across the airport with the young woman, I discovered just how difficult acting is.

Suddenly, the demon of self-consciousness pounced on me and I was aware of how high I lifted my feet with each step. I felt how stiff and spasmodic my gait had suddenly become, and I couldn't think of anything else. The young woman by my side had become a ghost, the world beyond her a hallucination. I halted and pointed at something as I had been told to and the gesture felt totally unnatural, theatrical, stupid. I told myself to stop this nonsense, but by the time I finished the simple take, I was a nervous wreck.

Radok said nothing to us. He just had us repeat the take. We took another stroll and then Radok moved on to the next setup; evidently our performance had been serviceable.

I stood aside, still wearing the uniform, and waited to recover the normal balance of my senses. As the monstrous effect of the camera subsided, I found I expected someone to praise or criticize my perform-ance, or at least to acknowledge it somehow, but no one paid me the slightest attention.

The next day, as we watched the dailies, I learned that there was still more to this trauma: I barely recognized myself on the screen. I watched this guy in a pilot's uniform amble around the airport, and I knew that I could pass him on the street and never in a hundred years see myself in him—a very odd feeling.

It took me a couple of weeks to get over this experience, but it helped me realize several things that I've tried to keep in mind ever since. While it may look easy, acting before a camera is a very tough job. And it's even tougher for the actors with bit parts. Though they inhabit the edges of the cinematic world, they give it the scope and feel of life, yet they frequently don't get anything in return. They are always owed at least a word of praise or a friendly remark. I also understood that an actor gains nothing from watching dailies; they may even inhibit his performance. The power of the cinematic image is such that it over-whelms normal critical faculties.

In 1981, Mike Nichols asked me to appear in *Heartburn*. I tried to say no. I was still between movies, and Mike needed someone to play a Yugoslav cultural attaché. I had the accent and the uncouth Slavic vigor the role called for, but I still hadn't gotten over the low-grade trauma of pretending to be a pilot twenty years before, so I tried to say no. The problem was that I owed Mike a massive favor. He had loaned his children to us when we shot *Ragtime*, so I felt obligated to do it. I braced myself for embarrassment, for an implosion of self-consciousness, an urge to flee, massive regrets. As it turned out, I never wanted *Heartburn* to end.

Mike had Jack Nicholson and Meryl Streep as the leads in the film version of Nora Ephron's autobiographical novel. The production was a big deal—I had my own trailer and was picked up at the hotel every morning and driven to the set. As an uncouth Slav, I'd been cast perfectly, so all I had to do was memorize my lines. But I still didn't know how you delivered memorized lines while sounding as if you were saying them for the first time. Try to ignore the tape lines on the floor that indicate the range of the camera lens. Remember not to screen anyone. Just keep in mind the whole complex choreography that has been set up for the shot and tell the truth.

Mike watched the dailies with his cast, so I'd go to the screening room to confirm my old belief that there is no reason for actors to watch dailies. Watching myself, all I could think about was how fat I looked, how much hair I'd lost in the corners of my forehead, how gray the rest of it had gotten, how many wrinkles I had. I did hit the tape marks, though, and I didn't screen anybody.

Yet the main impression I took away from *Heartburn* was that it's a very good thing for a director periodically to step in front of a camera and, in James Cagney's memorable words, try to "tell the truth" to this supreme lie detector. The job of a movie director almost requires an innate arrogance, the arrogance that says, "I know best, and I'll tell you what to do," yet this arrogance is double-edged: it can make you less sensitive to human situations, stresses, and sorrows. And for me, acting was a healthy dose of humility.

LES LIAISONS DANGEREUSES

When I work, I am anxious and driven and can't wait until the job is done. When I don't work, I am miserable and envy those who have something to keep them busy. But by committing to a film, I am signing away roughly two years of my life, so I put a lot of thought into the decision.

Despite the serendipity of *One Flew Over the Cuckoo's Nest*, I do not believe that directors are fated to make particular movies. These decisions are often made by chance, by the opportunities that drift your way, by the state of your career. The rest, strangely, is a question of the calendar, a kind of psychological and emotional ripening not unlike the fertility cycle. When you happen to be ready, you just grab the nearest thing that excites you and fall in love with it.

It took me four years after *Amadeus* to find a story that would give me that sudden charge of feeling that comes when someone else expresses clearly something that you've been feeling only vaguely, or thinking about differently. But then, one evening in London, I went to see Christopher Hampton's adaptation of *Les Liaisons Dangereuses*, an eighteenth-century epistolary novel by Choderlos de Laclos. I'd read the book when I was a student in Milan Kundera's class at the Film Academy in Prague, and going to the theater, I recalled it very vividly. The story of two sexual overachievers tangling with each other had made a strong impression on a horny twenty-year-old.

As I sat in the theater and watched the play, I couldn't believe the liberties Hampton had taken in adapting the novel to the stage. I'd always believed in using original material as a springboard to new creation, but Hampton had completely distorted the story that I remembered.

I was intrigued enough to reread the book, but when I did so, I discovered a strange thing: Hampton had been as faithful to the original as you can be when you condense a long novel into a play. He had gotten all the facts right and had captured the spirit of the book. It was my memory that had been playing tricks on me. I wondered: was I bending reality in my other memories as well?

I needed to delve into the matter more deeply, so when the producer who controlled the film rights to the Hampton play called and asked if I'd care to see it when it opened in New York, I told him that I'd already seen *Les Liaisons Dangereuses*, but that I'd gladly see it again. I also told him of my "mis-recollection" of the book and how I was interested in using it for the film adaptation.

I saw the play again and arranged to meet with Hampton in order to explore the possibility of a film collaboration, and in June 1987 I went to London to see him. I checked into the Hyde Park on the appointed day, but Hampton didn't show up. I waited five days and called everyone I could think of to see if Hampton had had an accident, or had been misinformed, or whatever, but I wasn't able to get hold of anyone who could tell me anything.

Hampton would later send a letter to Robby, explaining that he'd been waiting for me at the Hyde Park a month earlier, exactly to the day, and that I had stood him up. Frankly, I'm not sure what really happened between us at that time—a misunderstanding of some sort, a missed connection, a mismatch, a subterfuge, who knows. Perhaps my intention to return to the book somehow turned Hampton off, though he didn't say so at the time. Perhaps he saw my personal quest, wrongly, as somehow being dismissive of his work in the theater. It certainly doesn't matter now.

As always, I'd done my homework before I arrived in London. I had prepared an outline of the film that was mostly a chase after my memories of the book. While I waited at the Hyde Park I went right on working on my version of the story. By the time I had given up on Hampton and checked out of the hotel, I knew how I wanted to shoot my adaptation of Laclos's novel.

My old friends Claude Berri and Paul Rassam offered to produce an independent adaptation of the novel, so I sat down with Jean-Claude Carrière again and we wrote our own script. We called it *Valmont,* after the main character in the story.

VALMONT

Before I can direct a scene, I have to tie it somehow to my own frame of reference. I need to test the authenticity of the characters and their behavior against something I myself have felt or experienced. Understanding the character of Valmont in *Les Liaisons Dangereuses* wasn't difficult. All my life, I've had relationships with women—some long, some brief. I have spent a lot of time in pursuit of the intoxication and grace that occurs when the whole world falls away from you and your lover. This state, by necessity, never lasts, but while it does, it is like nothing else.

In my version of the story, Valmont searches for this very feeling. He is a womanizer, a libertine with a long history of conquests, but only because he is seeking a deeper relationship. When he finds it, ironically with Madame de Tourvel, the prudish wife of a judge, it scares him so much that he drives her away and throws himself into a suicidal duel.

Valmont's longest-lasting relationship in the book, however, is with his female counterpart, Madame de Merteuil. She has wit, charm, and as much experience with the opposite sex as he. She is his equal in all things. He boasts, competes, and confides in her, but the real nature of their relationship in the book remains enigmatic: the relationship between Valmont and Merteuil is like the strange flirtation that often develops between a director and his leading lady. At least that's what has always happened to me.

I always project my most tender feelings and fantasies onto the women in my films. I show my leading lady my very real affection and encourage her to reveal her heart, her self, her innermost thoughts. As she does, I fall in love with her in a peculiar way—peculiar because we both know this odd emotional transaction helps the film.

I hold myself back and dare her to tempt me more, to reach out to me more, to charm me and show me that she will do anything I ask of her. At the same time, I am careful not to give in to the feeling between us; I am afraid to let her see me naked. I don't want to appear vulnerable before her. Our professional relationship requires a certain amount of mystery and authority on my part, but I always look forward to wrapping the production, when I'll be able to consummate the fantasies. But when we finish shooting, I discover that the actress is no longer interested in me, that her sentimental life has moved on, that she has begun a new flirtation with another director, that she has found someone else, someone who doesn't hold anything back from her.

I grounded my understanding of the enigmatic bond between Valmont and Merteuil in this strange push-pull of emotion, this unconsummated infatuation that I'd experienced on virtually all my films. Once I had this clear picture of the characters and their relationships, I could cast the film.

Michelle Pfeiffer had the beauty, charm, intelligence, and emotional reserve to make a memorable Madame de Merteuil, so I suppressed my reluctance to use Hollywood stars and offered her the role. To my surprise, she turned me down. A couple of days later, I learned that she had signed up to play the prude Tourvel in the film version of Hampton's play, which was casting at the same time with the young British director Stephen Frears in charge.

Shortly after that I met an actress who, immediately and with great authority, put her face on the character of Merteuil in my mind. Her name was Annette Bening, her background was theater, and she wasn't known to the general public, though it would only take her a year to change that completely. She showed me a razor-sharp intelligence, mental toughness, and a slow, confident manner that was perfect for a woman who had pulled herself up into the high society of monarchist France by her looks, her wit, and her unscrupulous daring.

I found it much harder to cast Valmont. I auditioned many American actors and several of them had the combination of raw virility, awareness, and quick-thinking charm that I associated with the role, but their accents just didn't go with the gold-embroidered waistcoats, the filigreed swords, Valmont's ingrained fine manners. I saw the man as an aristocrat who was absolutely secure in his bloodlines and class; American voices undermined that impression to my immigrant ear. I finally reconciled myself to the fact that I'd only accept an Englishman in the role and concentrated my casting efforts on the Eastern shores of the Atlantic, where I finally chose Colin Firth, a young Englishman who had played a variety of roles in British films.

Madame de Tourvel was easy to cast. I immediately saw Meg Tilly as the virtuous wife whom Valmont seduces on a dare and for whom he falls hard.

Our screenplay also told the stories of a pair of young lovers, Cécile and Danceny, who get caught up in the intrigues of Valmont and Merteuil. These two teenagers receive their sentimental education in the beds of our principals, and I was resolved to keep the age of the actors as low as it was in the novel because real innocence—the curiosity, the excitability, the bluffing and the sexual clumsiness—is very hard to recapture once it has gone. I cast fourteen-year-old Fairuza Balk as Cécile and gave the role of Danceny to sixteen-year-old Henry Thomas, who had played the little boy who befriends E.T.

In the summer of 1988, I had a cast I was happy with and I moved to Paris for preproduction. When I arrived, Frears's *Dangerous Liaisons* was just wrapping its shoot there. They had worked much more quickly and were going to release their movie first. Someone gave me the screenplay of *Dangerous Liaisons,* but I never opened it; there was no point in trying to measure our adaptation against theirs or in losing sleep over it. Both productions were a fact of life, so I simply put *Dangerous Liaisons* out of my mind.

I was joined by Mirek Ondříček and Dóda Pištěk in Paris. Paul Rassam and Claude Berri already had some of the best French talent under contract. They had also managed to procure a number of stunning and authentic locations in the country, even succeeding in renting the Royal Chapel at Versailles for our climactic scene. Everything was set for my fourth—or was it fifth—period film. The precise count depends on how you classify *One Flew Over the Cuckoo's Nest,* which looked contemporary when I made it, but which in fact bore the elements of a period film. The use of primitive electroshock therapy and heavy dosages of drugs belonged to the fifties, and, by the mid-seventies, no psychiatric establishments outside of the Soviet Union used them anymore.

Since *Cuckoo's Nest,* I've made nothing but historical films. I am content to live an unexamined life, and, for years on end, I figured that this orientation of my American films was purely accidental, that I was drawn to four strong stories that just happened to be period pieces.

But it was while preparing for *Valmont*—poring over the paintings of Watteau, Fragonard, Boucher, Huet, and Chardin—I finally had to admit to myself that, in America, I'd found my métier in period films. I started my career with a documentary, and it has always been the authenticity of a situation that excites me. Back in Czechoslovakia, I never let my performers read the script, so that my camera could watch them struggle with each dramatic situation for the first time. There is a certain vulnerability, a hesitancy, a dawning of emotion, a sense of discovery, that only purely spontaneous behavior has. Also, my imagination is extremely literal and earthbound, and I need to ground my films in plausible, naturalistic worlds. This is simply a given, a matter of taste, of artistic identity, of something deep and beyond reason. And it's precisely my yearning for authenticity that has drawn me to period films in America, where I can't easily achieve the standard of authenticity that I aspire to with contemporary material.

ROMY AND DAVID

While shooting *Valmont* in Paris I found that the city was now full of memories. The most vivid ones were five or six years old, and so tragic that they are never going to fade.

Back in the early eighties, I happened to be in Paris during the French Open tennis tournament and I went to see a lot of the matches. One Friday evening, Paul Rassam asked me if I'd mind taking Romy Schneider's son with me. Romy was shooting some film, the boy's governess had Saturdays off, and Paul, who would otherwise have taken the boy, couldn't make it. Of course, I agreed.

David was a bright and outgoing ten-year-old, and we spent a wonderful day at the courts. We played nonsensical word games, roamed the dressing rooms, where I introduced him to Martína Navrátilová and other players I knew, and had a great time. We didn't watch much tennis. I thought about my boys a lot that day and was sorry I'd never been able to do this with them.

I had to leave Paris the next morning; David was going to spend Sunday at his grandmother's house. When he got there in the morning, no one answered the doorbell, so he decided to climb into her house through a window. He was standing on top of the ornamental fence of iron spikes when he slipped. He speared himself on one of the iron rods. Some horrified passersby quickly dislodged him and set him down on the sidewalk. They were only trying to help, but they wound up killing David. The iron rod had entered his body cleanly and hadn't damaged any of the vital organs. As it was, waiting for an ambulance, David bled to death on the sidewalk. If the rod had stayed in the wound, David would not have hemorrhaged as massively as he did, so he and Romy might still be alive.

On the last evening of his life, David had been pumping with impressions from our afternoon at the tennis club. Apparently, he talked about me a great deal, so Romy's last memories of the boy got inextricably entangled with my name. At least this was what Paul Rassam reported to me, saying that Romy was very distraught and longed to meet me. David was Romy's only boy, and she took his death very badly.

My next trip to Paris was a layover. I was due to arrive late in the evening and leave early the next morning. There didn't seem to be any way to set aside enough time to meet Romy properly, so I intended to get together with her on my way back.

I checked into my room at the Lancaster at eleven o'clock at night. I hadn't even tipped the bellboy when the phone started to ring. It was Paul.

"Miloš, Romy knows you're in town. Can you see her?" he asked.

"Yes, sure."

"I'll come and wait for her with you." We waited till one o'clock. When Romy came, she looked absolutely stunning. She had probably called her hairdresser and made him do her hair at midnight. She had also clearly been drinking.

"Please, tell me all about David, Miloš," she said.

I told her everything David and I did on the wonderful Saturday that turned out to be the last day of his short life. Romy hung on my every word as if I could bring the boy back. It was very painful to watch her suffering. A year had gone by, but she hadn't been able to reconcile herself to the loss at all.

Somehow I'd become Romy's medium, her connection with the dead boy, but all I could communicate to her were the memories of four or five hours on one sunny afternoon. Ours was one of those helpless conversations deep in the night, full of stops and starts, uneven alcohol consumption, tears, paltry consolation, ghosts, despair.

"You should get some sleep, Romy," I gently suggested when it got to be four o'clock.

"No! I don't want to sleep, I never want to sleep." Romy was having nightmares about the boy, losing him over and over again in her dreams. We talked till dawn. I flew off again a few hours later.

When I returned several days later, Romy was dead. She had been drinking to forget and taking sleeping pills to chase away the dreams and her heart gave out from the strain.

Paul took me to her house. Her companion, Lauren Petain, was there, as were Alain Delon, Michel Piccoli, Claude Berri, and many people who'd been close to Romy. Her body was still lying in her bed as is the French custom, and friends were filing into the bedroom to say their last good-byes to her. Everyone said she was still one of the most beautiful women in the world, but I couldn't bear to see her.

A NOTION OF HOME

Valmont opened on November 17, 1989, and it was a commercial flop, which should have put me in bed for months. But on that very day an event happened on the far side of the planet that took all the pain away. In Prague a student march caused the jittery Communist government to panic and set its gorillas on the few thousand youths. The students took a vicious beating, but they started the democratic "Velvet Revolution," headed by my old schoolmate from Poděbrady.

Two weeks later, the Communist rule in Czechoslovakia was history. And in New York, instead of moping over reviews of *Valmont* and studying the gloomy statistics in *Variety*, I read the exhilarating news from Prague in all the major newspapers and scanned the cable channels for any scrap of information. My phone rang off the hook with the latest rumors of coups, countercoups, interventions, and assassinations. Among the Czechs and Slovaks, the most common response to the fast-forward crumbling of the Communist rule was the sensation that the whole thing was a dream. I had the same edgy feeling, but the Velvet Revolution also completely rearranged my perspective on my own life. The stinging collapse of Valmont, the hubris of my chase after old memories of the book, the rejection—suddenly it all seemed trivial.

At the end of December 1989, Havel was elected president of Czechoslovakia—by the old Communist legislature. They voted for him while gnashing their teeth, but they did so unanimously because they had never realized you could vote any other way.

I watched Vaclav's inauguration on TV from my farm in Connecticut. He promised the country a free election, the first in forty years, and a new constitution. He pledged to make Czechoslovakia a land of laws again and to oversee the transformation of the economy from the command system of the East to the free market.

I was very proud of the old country and President Vaclav, so proud that I caught myself thinking more and more about precisely what it was that had made my old Connecticut barn a home for me. For many years, I had a very practical definition of home. Home lay under the roof that sheltered my suitcase. Home was also the place where I could work most comfortably, and it was much easier to make movies on the western shores of the Atlantic than in Central Europe or anywhere else. But now, after the Velvet Revolution, I realized that when my energy starts to wind down, when I begin to move beyond my work the way I'd seen James Cagney do, then the centrifugal force of my life may push me back to the place of my youth, back to my childhood, back to where the memories have the clearest outlines.

It may, but then again, who knows?

HELL CAMP

The failure of *Valmont* put me right back to work, which meant reading, reading, reading. I wore a path in the carpet from my easy chair to the refrigerator, but I found nothing that seemed worth a couple of years of my life.

The good scripts I was offered required only a competent executor. I suppose I was looking for some half-baked idea I could make my own. The only thing stirring in me, however, was the remembrance of a story I'd seen on "60 Minutes" sometime before. It was about a school for Japanese managers, which was unofficially called Hell Camp. The place lay under Mount Fuji, and in spite of its nickname, it inspired boundless enthusiasm in its graduates. It seemed a natural setting for a fascinating film.

At the time, I was also drawn back to a story idea I'd had years before, about a husband's paranoia and a young marriage in trouble. One sleepless night, I figured out a way to connect the two notions, which led to a rather scary idea: what if I went back to the way I'd worked once, back in Czechoslovakia? What if I simply sat down with someone and tried to write an original screenplay again? Hadn't I learned enough about America in the last twenty-two years to make a film from scratch here? But did I dare to drop all the costumes, sets, and choreographers and try to see the world clearly through a camera again?

It took me a while to get used to the notion of going back to simple filmmaking, but in the end I mustered up the courage. I read and saw everything I could about Japan and soon discovered sumo wrestling, a tough and picturesque sport, that seemed to have been invented for the camera. Slowly, a rough outline of a script about two Americans in Japan—outsiders, of course—formed in my head. I was excited by the story. The Japanese were becoming a big presence in the movie industry, so the screen play idea also seemed quite practical. I met with Peter Guber, who ran Sony Pictures Entertainment, the parent company of Columbia Pictures and Tri-Star. I told him I wanted to make a gentle comedy about a couple of transcultural love affairs, one of which involved sumo wrestling.

"Don't talk to anyone else about this! I love this!" said Guber, and he steered me to Mike Medavoy of Tri-Star. I'd known Medavoy for twenty years and was very comfortable with him. We decided to launch project *Hell Camp* with a screenplay that I'd write on spec, with Tri-Star underwriting my research.

I found a talented young filmmaker, Adam Davidson, and, in the spring of 1990, we flew to Japan together. Sony provided us with the best translators, guides, and connections. All doors sprung open. Davidson enrolled in Hell Camp and finished its two-week course while I ate a lot of celestial sushi and watched a lot of sumo. I went to a Kabuki show in which one of the characters entered holding a severed hand, an unexplained image, strange and powerful, of which the country was full.

Davidson and I returned to America and wrote a screenplay about a young American whose marriage is falling apart just as his corporation transfers him from New York to Tokyo. On the plane, he meets Joe, an obese kid who dreams that he will redeem his huge body in sumo.

In Tokyo, it turns out that the kid doesn't have a penny to his name and the young corporate man gets fired. Drowning their sorrows in liquor, they meet a couple of young Japanese women. The story goes on from there.

Medavoy liked the script, and I signed a contract to make the movie for Tri-Star with Michael Hausman as producer. Davidson and I sat down with Japanese writer Shigeko Sato to make sure that the behavior of our Japanese characters looked authentic to Japanese eyes. She suggested a few revisions and pronounced the script realistic, so I sent it to our Japanese contacts, who then moved forward to secure some critical shooting locations in Japan. It was at this point that our problems began, and they didn't stop.

When the actual administration of Hell Camp in Fujiyama read the screenplay, they were shocked to see that it wasn't primarily about their school, as they had hoped—as often happens in writing, the original inspiration for the screenplay ended up being just a backdrop to our story. But the change of focus so disappointed the Hell Camp people that they refused to let us shoot on their premises.

I took the news calmly. There are many ways to misread a screenplay, and the list of institutions that had misunderstood my scripts is long and distinguished. It includes the U.S. army, the Morgan Library, the Mozart archive, numerous mental hospitals, and the highest levels of the old Czech government. I flew to Japan and took the administrators of Hell Camp to several lavish dinners. I told jokes, drank beer, slipped gentle arguments between sake toasts, agreed to a few changes in the script. A million words and a few hangovers later, the Hell Camp leadership agreed to rent us their school.

Our script contained two brief scenes outside a Tokyo airport. They could have been night scenes, so filming them wouldn't have tied up any traffic, but none of the Tokyo airports would allow us to shoot. Not for a day, not for a night, not for a river of sake.

I decided to forget about the aiports. The scenes were minor, so I could work around this problem. I could not, however, make the film if I didn't get the collaboration of the "Rikishi," the sumo wrestlers, and access to the traditional sumo arena in Tokyo, a stadium of great and austere visual beauty, that was absolutely essential in the story of our obese kid. The Japanese regard sumo as their national sport, a revered expression of their national character, and we were not sure how the Sumo Association would react to the idea of Americans making a movie on its hallowed mats, so we looked for someone who was influential in the world of sumo to make overtures on our behalf. Through a complicated web of contacts, we were introduced to Mr. Dewaunomi, the second-highest man in the Sumo Association. He read our script and right away started to help us. He called the Japanese television executives who broadcasted all the tournaments to match us up.

But now one Noboru Kojima stepped in. He was an elegant, stern gentleman in his fifties, a historian of Japan's imperial wars and a member of the sumo's all-important Yokozuma Committee. I didn't realize at first how powerful Kojima was, but it would later turn out that his opinions swayed the sumo establishment completely.

When Kojima read the script, he declared that the story reminded him of American propaganda films of the Second World War. He thought that Sayuri, the young Japanese woman who falls in love with an American, was "an easy lay." He was even more offended by the juxtaposition of Hell Camp, a "lowly" institution in his opinion, with the exalted art of sumo. The two phenomena, he proclaimed, simply could not be set side by side in the same narrative.

These objections were as bizarre to me as if an American maintained that a movie would soil baseball by including roller derby in the same fictional framework.

"You know, Mr. Kojima," I told him, "just last night, I saw a commercial right here on television that featured the top sumo wrestlers dancing in *Swan Lake*. They wore tutus. They hopped around. They didn't look dignified at all. And that didn't bother you?"

"This is their hobby," said Kojima, smiling.

"Yes, but Mr. Kojima, making movies is *my* hobby." I pleaded with the historian for a little tolerance, but he just smiled again and proceeded to talk about his son who lived in Los Angeles with his wife. Junior had been inviting the historian to come and visit him in California.

"I told him I'd come as soon as my daughter-in-law conceives . . ." Kojima told me.

I never managed to sway Kojima, never was able to convince him that he had our script all wrong, so we were forbidden access to the sumo arena. The Sumo Association wouldn't even let us work with their wrestlers. There was no taking the sumo out of the film, however. Our fragile screenplay needed both strands of the story, needed the fat kid and his pathetic dream, needed the visual power of the sumo ceremony. It wouldn't survive without these elements.

In a flurry of frantic meetings, strategy sessions, transpacific flights, false hopes, and futile last-ditch negotiations, *Hell Camp* collapsed just four days before the principal photography was to begin. Two hundred people lost their jobs, and several young, unknown actors forfeited a chance to make a big-time debut. As for me, I lost a year of my time. And time, at my age, ticks faster and faster.

Though I didn't get to make the film, Sony honored my contract. I was paid my money, so I can only say that what happened to *Hell Camp* reminded me of a strange Ping-Pong match I had gotten myself into some thirty years before. Back when Jana and I were still a pretty glamorous couple around Prague, we were invited to a screening at the Chinese Embassy. The film dealt with, of all things, the composition of the Chinese national anthem, and it was interminable. Its poker-faced composer sauntered through postcards of China and listened to the sounds of the land that slowly, very, very slowly, coagulated into musical motifs.

Groping for something to say to the likable cultural attaché after the screening, I asked him if he played Ping-Pong.

"All Chinese play Ping-Pong," he said with a big laugh.

"We should play sometime," I jokingly suggested, because I'd once been on the table tennis team in Poděbrady. As soon as I said it, a crowd of Chinese gathered in front of me and broke into impassioned chatter. After a long, animated conversation, the attaché turned back to me, grinning from ear to ear.

"Yes, yes, we play, you and I."

Ten minutes later, I was handed a typed sheet of paper. It bore an address, a time late in the afternoon, and a date three months away to the day.

"Could this be right?" I asked, pointing to the month.

"Yes, yes," said the attaché.

"Okay, I'll be there."

Three months went by, and I borrowed a table tennis paddle and found myself in a furious match before a cheering crowd of Chinese. It took place at another reception, so I was wearing my dress shoes and a suit while the Chinese cultural attaché wore shorts and sneakers, but that didn't matter. The attaché was a much better Ping-Pong player than I. His counterdrives had so much top spin on them that they slid right off my paddle. Perhaps he had been training for this event during those three months, or maybe he didn't have to prepare for me at all; in any case he easily beat me in the first set, twenty-one to eight.

The Chinese cheered the attaché on. The noise from the crowd rattled the windows. I lost the second set twenty-one to twelve, so I put the paddle down and walked around the table to shake hands with the winner. A commotion broke out everywhere around me.

"Not finished, not finished!" yelled the onlookers.

"We play three set! Always three set," said the attaché in his broken Czech.

"Yes, but I've already lost two, so the third one would be meaningless."

"Three set, three set," insisted the attaché, and everyone seconded him.

"Okay, fine," I said, and picked up my paddle again just to make them happy.

The crowd now switched sides and applauded my every ball, building up to a rousing ovation at the end of the set, which I took twenty-one to twelve. The attaché clearly let me win—but only after I'd lost everything first.

"THAT I CAN IMAGINE"

With *Hell Camp*, I hadn't lost everything: I'd only wasted a year of my life. I don't think that I quite reached the peace that passeth understanding, but something burned out in me, something to do with my old drive to win, and oddly enough, I don't miss it. I had to force myself to read all the scripts that had been collecting in piles on my desk while I was pursuing *Hell Camp*.

A strange thing started to creep into my life: I'd stroll down a crowded street in New York and every face I saw was someone I had once known, every random phrase I overheard sounded familiar, every perfume brought back a woman I'd once been with. I'd read a new screenplay, and ten, fifteen pages into it, I'd remember the rest of the story.

Was my memory slowly overwhelming my imagination? Perhaps imagination is only a faculty of youth anyway, perhaps it only makes up for a lack of experience. If so, I don't want to hear about it—I take heart in a story I once heard about Otakar Březina.

This Czech poet of massive cosmic visions was an old man at the turn of the century when he took one of his daily strolls through Prague. His young secretary was walking with him. Suddenly, there was a crush of people in the street. A big crowd quickly collected to stare up at the sky. They were witnessing a miracle. The first airplane was buzzing over Prague.

"Sir!" yelled the excited secretary. "Look! The first flying machine!"

The old poet never bothered to lift his eyes from the pavement. "That I can imagine!" he muttered, and kept on walking as if his heart was the only place where anything could still surprise him.

But maybe he was just having a bad day. What do I know?